Book 'n Record Shops

556 Talbot Street St. Thomas, Ontario

BUY SELL TRADE

TAKE A VOYAGE TO THE UNKNOWN THAT LIES BETWEEN TWO WORLDS

In these exciting pages you will find amazing case histories from the private files of the world's foremost psychic "detective," Nandor Fodor.

Dr. Fodor personally investigated these cases. His expeditions took him to the strangest and most dangerous places on Earth. He saw things which cannot be explained by modern science—invisible bells, modern vampires, reincarnations, magic spells, telepathy, dreams that reveal the future, hauntings and healings.

Now, you, too, can share these incredible psychic experiences.

**START READING—IF YOU DARE!
YOU WON'T BE ABLE TO STOP!**

D1249094

Book 'n' Record Shop

388 ... St. Thomas, Ontario

BUY SELL TRADE

BETWEEN TWO WORLDS

Nandor Fodor

PAPERBACK LIBRARY
New York

PAPERBACK LIBRARY EDITION

First Printing: *January, 1967*
Second Printing: *April, 1969*

Copyright © *1964 by Nandor Fodor*

All rights reserved, including the right to reproduce this book, or any portions thereof, in any form, except for the inclusion of brief quotations in a review.

Library of Congress Catalog Card No.: 64-21753

This Paperback Library edition is published
by arrangement with Prentice-Hall, Inc.

Covers Printed in U.S.A.
Body Text Printed in Canada.

Paperback Library is a division of Coronet Communications, Inc. Its trade-mark, consisting of the words "Paperback Library" accompanied by an open book, is registered in the United States Patent Office. Coronet Communications, Inc., 315 Park Avenue South, New York, N.Y. 10010.

CONTENTS

It is not a simple task to write an introduction to this volume of fantastic adventures in the little-explored regions of the human mind; the reader is apt to be taken aback by, even to turn away from the vistas that suddenly emerge before his eyes.

No matter how many of the famous and the great have shared similar super-normal adventures—and kept them a secret from the outside world; no matter how much testimony bears out the existence of strange byways of the mind, or appears to indicate interaction with terrifying states of existence (perhaps the abode of ghosts, nonhuman shades)—we are apt to shy away from the thought of how *little* we know of the world.

We should, instead, express concern or wonder over the blind spots that orthodox science still contains regarding phenomena that have been with us throughout the ages of man —phenomena that should, perhaps, have transformed our life in this universe. For, it appears, that the age-old claims of religion, metaphysics, certain Eastern teachings and modern parapsychology cannot be ignored with impunity.

We must remember Alfred Lord Tennyson's words: *"The ghost in man and the ghost that once was man are calling to each other in a dawn stranger than earth has ever seen."*

We are witnessing today the growth of a new mysticism, no longer based on faith and belief but on new scientific discoveries. Materialism has been dealt a deadly blow. Strange as it may seem, matter has no substance. It is an illusion of our senses. Atomic research has revealed it to be a state of incredible energies bound and interlocked, and now it also tells us of antimatter, a collision with which would totally annihilate even the energies themselves.

Almost daily new horizons open up before science; gradually the conclusion is being forced on us that mind, life, logos, spirit, or God is the only reality in this mysterious universe. Ignorance is the only limitation that reins us back. The battle against the unknown is gradually being lost or rather won by the new generation of scientists who are finding themselves more and more in Alice's Wonderland where nothing is impossible.

This book represents a lifetime of adventure and research. I would feel hard put to answer the question as to what has enthralled me most. It appears to me that in the wonders of the human mind no scale of comparison exists. Time, place and mental disposition are the decisive factors in fascination. In this volume there is enough to choose from for the most delicate taste. The reach is open from Heaven to Hell. Ample room exists for every kind of approach: the psychological, the philosophical, the psychoanalytical, the occult and the religious. I have no drums to beat, no isms to serve. Like Lewis Carroll's child "with a pure, unclouded brow and gleaming eyes of wonder" I sat before the unknown, and sailed into it, for the best years of my life. I can truly say that my three score and ten years have been marvellously lit up by the excitement and unceasing wonder of this quest.

I have worked my way through orthodox religions, Spiritualism and psychical research to psychoanalysis, mainly in the hope of finding the missing answers. Some I have found, many more I have missed. A new ism may be necessary. Parapsychology, as psychical research is called today, has made a significant inroad but hardly covered more than the initial part of a long journey. But, every journey begins with the first step, and the outlines of a new ultra-science are perhaps already discernible along the path, I do not know what it will be like. All I know is that human destiny will be profoundly affected by it and that eventually, and hopefully, we shall understand the meaning of human life.

Then, perhaps, all dissensions will cease; the golden age of dreams will be at hand.

New York, 1964

NANDOR FODOR

PART I.

THE FAMOUS AND THE GREAT

Introduction. Parapsychology, as psychical research is called in our day, is not the happy—or unhappy—hunting ground of a scientist with a mystic bent, of adventure seekers in the realm of the occult, or of escapists from drab materialism. That it is a very important field of human interest is best illustrated by secrets in the lives of the famous and the great.

Why was MacKenzie King, late Prime Minister of Canada, accused of being a spiritualist? How did it happen that President Lincoln consulted mediums before he emancipated the slaves, and how could he dream of his own death the day before he was murdered? Who was the *real* Francis Grierson hidden under the literary mask of the noted author? What was the nature of the strange spell that the characters created by Charles Dickens cast upon their creator's mind? By what manner or means did Vaslav Nijinsky, the world's greatest ballet dancer, defy the law of gravity? How did Sandor Ferenczi, a chief disciple of Freud, become deeply committed to psychic phenomena? How could it remain a deep secret that Dr. Carl G. Jung was endowed with stupendous mediumistic gifts?

These are questions that will be answered in Part I of this book.

It is difficult to believe that a man who was Prime Minister of a country for 22 years, and made his nation great and prosperous, could have had a secret life of sensational nature and have kept it totally guarded from millions of voters and followers. Yet such was the case of William Lyon MacKenzie, the great Canadian statesman whose interest in, and exploration of, the supernatural has remained strictly private until after his death in 1950.

It was a Canadian parliamentary reporter, Blair Fraser, who made the first public revelation of MacKenzie King's secret life in *MacLean's Magazine* on December 15, 1951, calling the late Prime Minister a convinced and practising Spiritualist. The revelation was followed by a pictorial article in *Life* magazine under the double title:

STATESMAN'S OTHER SIDE

CANADA'S LATE MACKENZIE KING IS REVEALED NOW AS SPIRITUALIST

The designation sounds like an indictment, and is completely nonsensical. Spiritualism is not "practised." He who comes to accept its central belief of human survival after death does not become a sectarian nor is he called upon to subscribe to any doctrines and practices. In fact, in all probability, he will have nothing to do with Spiritualism as a religious movement or philosophy. While MacKenzie King, as a result of years of careful personal inquiries, came to accept human survival after death as a demonstrable fact as early as 1920, he never ceased to be critical in appraising the evidence. He did not act on spiritualistic faith, and his conviction did not make him an ardent Spiritualist or propagandist for the psychic "cause." The insinuation was not only uncalled for but was based on a misconception of the issues involved. Had they called him a psychical researcher or parapsychologist, the magazines in question would have paid greater respect to the memory of this truly great man.

The reason why I express myself strongly is that for some years in the past I was in personal correspondence with MacKenzie King and knew where he stood on this issue. The letters that he exchanged with me have not been published until now, because they were marked private and confidential. Over 12 years have passed since his death and there appears to be no reason now for continued silence.

I was in charge of research at the International Institute for Psychical Research in London when, early in 1938, I received a request from him: would I send him a copy of Baron Palmstierna's recent book, *Horizons of Immortality*, and have it autographed by the author.

It was an unexpected request and it revealed more than ordinary interest. There was a Bulletin published by my institute on a lecture of Baron Palmstierna about his book and a copy of this Bulletin must have reached him, I do not know how. The letter reminded me of the rumors that were current in psychic circles in London that MacKenzie King had paid visits to some well-known mediums during his visits to England, notably to Helen Hughes, Mrs. Hester Dowden, and Geraldine Cummins. The visits were arranged by my friend, Mercy Phillimore, who was then secretary to the London Spiritualist Alliance, and the mediums had no idea of their visitor's identity for many years. When they found it out, they kept the secret so well that no indiscretion was committed until a few days after his death when *Psychic News* of London, through an interview with the Duchess of Hamilton, came out with the fatuous sensation that MacKenzie King was in the habit of relying on spirit guidance in conducting affairs of state!

I knew MacKenzie King as far back as 1929. As a journalist, I was on the special train that carried him from Le Havre to Paris in that year for the signing of the Kellogg Pact which, optimistically, was expected to end all aggression among its signatories. At that time I was at the beginning of my psychic investigations and had no idea that MacKenzie King not only shared my interest but was far advanced in his personal research.

On hearing from him in 1938, I hastened to comply with his request. Baron Palmstierna felt complimented by MacKenzie King's interest, and the publishers promptly mailed the book. To my surprise, I received no acknowledgement until almost six months later. It came in a double letter, the first being mislaid and turning up belatedly. This first letter was dated April 19, 1938 and reads:

I have just received from the publishers a copy of *Horizons of Immortality*, which you have been kind enough to have autographed for me by Baron Palmstierna. I am making my acknowledgement to the publishers by current mail, and will be more grateful still if, when you next see him, you would express to Baron Palmstierna my warmest appreciation of his courtesy in autographing the book.

I am indeed grateful to you for your good offices. I much appreciate your kindness in suggesting that I might become a member of the International Institute for Psychical Research. At some later time, I would much welcome this opportunity. For reasons which you will appreciate, it has seemed to me inadvisable to become too actively identified with Psychical Research work, pending the time that I may continue to hold my present position.

The phrase, "pending the time," is a clear hint at possible retirement from public life. Helen Hughes declared to Blair Fraser: "He was warned. At least three years before he died, his mother told him he was doing too much, his heart would not stand it. He took her advice in the end, but not soon enough."

The advice of his mother came from the other side of life and was renewed in a message from Miss Cummins. But MacKenzie King made it a rule to ignore all such advice and rely on his own judgement. (Which again is contrary to what a "practising" Spiritualist would do.)

The second letter, in which the first was enclosed, is dated August 8, 1938 and reads:

You will think it strange—and hard to explain—that I never acknowledged the receipt of Baron Palmstierna's *Horizons of Immortality,* nor the receipt of your kind letter of April the 7th. You will see from the enclosed that I have all along been under the impression that both were duly acknowledged.

Since my letter of April 19th was written, I have read

with quite an expression of interest Baron Palmstierna's book. Reincarnation is still a good deal of a mystery to me, and the part of Baron Palmstierna's book which had to do with reincarnation seems to relate to a subject in which I have still to come to believe. The parts of the book which had to do with evidences of personal survival, also of teachings, appealed very strongly to me, and were in the nature of confirmation of experiences of my own concern, of which there can be no doubt whatever.

I notice, in the letter of April 19th I say, and for reason which you will appreciate, it has seemed to me inadvisable to become too actively identified with psychical research work. What I really meant to say was too actively identified in the public mind.

                          With kind regards, etc.

The firm belief in human survival that this letter reveals rests on highly interesting grounds.

It appears that the first suggestion to take an interest in psychism came to MacKenzie King through the Marchioness of Aberdeen in London. She suggested that MacKenzie King contact Mrs. Etta Wriedt, a direct-voice medium in Detroit of whose mediumship Admiral Moore published startling reports in two books. Voices spoke through a trumpet that floated in the air in the dark and also in daylight, and in many languages. Luminous forms, so-called *etherealisations* were seen in the dark, dogs materialized and barked, and the sitters witnessed almost all kinds of mediumistic phenomena in abundance. These stories were not quite tales that grew by the distance in space, because Mrs. Wriedt—on the invitation of W. T. Stead, the famous editor of the *Review of Reviews* of London—was invited to London and records were kept of nearly 200 séances in Julia's Bureau—so named after Miss Julia Ames, editor of the *Women's Union Signal* of Chicago. Mrs. Wriedt, after her death, was sending messages to Stead through automatic writing in his own hand.

The story of the materialization of dogs was to be of special significance for MacKenzie King in his later years. He was very fond of dogs and he used to tell a weird story of a premonitory experience the night before Pat (his first dog by that name—there were two more so named afterwards) died. His watch fell off his bedside table "for no apparent reason" and was found in the morning face down on the floor, the hands stopping at 4:20. As quoted by Blair Fraser from Helen Hughes, MacKenzie King continued the incident:

"I am not psychic, but I knew then, as if a voice were speaking to me, that Pat would die before another 24 hours went by."

The premonition was fulfilled. That night Pat climbed out of his basket with a last effort and died on his master's bed. The time was exactly 4:20.

In order to understand this incident, one should know of the depth of emotional feeling that MacKenzie King, a lonely and sorely bereaved man, had for his pet. Pat's picture was framed over the mantlepiece with a lyric prose statement entitled, *Tribute to a Dog*.

It was through Mrs. Wriedt that MacKenzie King was first impressed with the possibility of contacting the dead. She was the medium in a famous estate case. A Liberal senator had lost his father-in-law, and his wife, unable to find the will, consulted Mrs. Wriedt. The medium told her that the lost will was in a chest of drawers in a house in France. There it was found —and no one but the dead father could have known its whereabouts.

In the rooms of the College of Psychic Science at 16 Queensberry Place in London a gold watch is seen[1] on display, mounted on a blue velvet cushion. It was presented to the College by MacKenzie King on behalf of Mrs. Wriedt. It was the watch that Queen Victoria bequeathed to John Brown, her brawny Highland manservant and favorite medium through whom she used to contact Prince Albert after his death. In the annals of Spiritualism I could find no records of this medium. Possibly it was a pseudonym. At any rate, after his death the watch came—through W. T. Stead—into the possession of Mrs. Wriedt in acknowledgement of the communications that came through her from Queen Victoria. Before her own death, Mrs. Wriedt decided that the watch should go back to London and had asked MacKenzie King to present it to the London Spiritualist Alliance, which was the name of the College of Psychic Science at the time.

In view of his widespread involvement in psychic matters, I made it a habit to send MacKenzie King whatever reprints and books I had on such related matters. Here is a letter I received from him on September 21st, 1942:

[1] The watch referred to was stolen recently.—*Author's note.*

It is most kind of you to have presented me with a copy of a reprint of your article on "Telepathic Dreams"; also a copy of a reprint on "Masonic Dreams." I was much interested on glancing at the latter to see reference to the trip we had together from Le Havre to Paris in 1929. I am looking forward with great interest to reading both articles which, I think, I will find of exceptional interest.

Psychic study affords me considerable relaxation. It is a field of research to which I would devote much time, had I the time to spare.

The study of Telepathic Dreams was published in the *American Image*. It announced the finding that telepathic contact between two unconscious minds can only occur if the psychological background is similar. Whatever relaxation I might have been able to afford with these and later presentations to MacKenzie King, is a matter of considerable satisfaction to me.

* * *

Another Prime Minister, well before the days of MacKenzie King, who took considerable interest in psychical research was W. E. Gladstone (1809-1898), the Grand Old Man of the Victorian age, four times Prime Minister of England. He is still quoted for his memorable statement that psychical research is "the most important work which is being done in the world today—by far the most important." Unlike MacKenzie King, he had no fear of joining the Society for Psychical Research as a member after a seance with William Eglinton on October 29th, 1884. The story of this seance went around the world—not without causing him inconvenience, as letters poured in, mainly from pious people who were horrified at seeing him engaged in "sorcery" and who were anxious to save him from becoming the victim of imposture. Eglinton failed Gladstone in discretion. The daily press got the story from the interview he gave to *Light*, the leading London spiritualist weekly, in which Gladstone was quoted as saying:

I have always thought that scientific men run too much in a groove. They do noble work in their special line of research, but they are too often indisposed to give any attention to matters which seem to conflict with their

15

established modes of thought. Indeed, they not infrequently attempt to deny that into which they have never inquired, not sufficiently realising the fact that there may possibly be forces in nature of which they know nothing.

Looking back on the account given by the naturally biased medium, one wonders what really happened at the slate-writing séance to move Gladstone so deeply. Today, slate writing is in such disrepute that mediums who have unusual psychic gifts no longer resort to it. Too many ways are known in which these ordinary school slates can be witched and substituted by another slate on the inside of which there is an answer previously prepared. The marvel of hearing a crumb of slate pencil write between the locked slates is the most brazen form of the demonstration. The sound is usually produced by the medium's thumbnail scratching on the outside of the slate that is held away from the sitter. The illusion that the writing occurs within the slates is astonishing. As Eglinton's mediumistic record was known, at least occasionally, to be more than shady, there must have been something of a telepathic nature in the slate writing to make an impression on Gladstone.

It appears that Gladstone wrote a very trite question, by way of first test, on the slate. It was: "Which year do you remember to have been more dry than the present one?" Whoever the "spirit" to whom the question was addressed, his answer was correct: "In the year 1857." Eglinton, on reading the question through a bit of sleight-of-hand, may have been able to answer this one. It is more difficult to know how he did it the second time when Gladstone, retiring into a corner, wrote another question on the inside of the slate, taking care to double-lock it and keeping it in sight. The question was: "Is the Pope ill or well?" The answer came in red pencil: "He is ill in mind, not in body."

These were trivial, introductory questions. They were followed by more purposive ones and Eglinton claims that the answers were written between slates fully exposed to view or held over the table of a brilliantly lighted drawing room. Gladstone is said to have made a careful record of all the questions and of all the answers.

The trouble is that this is Eglinton's own version. Gladstone, on being challenged by the *Daily News,* only answered through Horace Seymour:

16

Sir, I am directed by Mr. Gladstone to acknowledge the receipt of your letter of yesterday, and to say that while he cannot undertake to enter into details, he has expressed no conclusion upon the subject to which you refer.

But Gladstone did join the Society for Psychical Research, so we must assume that the Eglinton séance, cheap as it may seem today, must have had some features that have not been revealed.

* * *

Another British Prime Minister who committed himself even further than Gladstone was the first Earl of Balfour (Arthur James, 1848-1930). He proved himself to be one of the most brilliant and eminent students of psychic matters. He became interested in them through his sister, who was the wife of Professor Henry Sidgwick, first President of the Society for Psychical Research, and in 1894 Balfour accepted the presidency of this learned society. This post was also held later by his brother, the Right Honorable Gerald W. Balfour, who became Earl after Arthur James's death. The latter is still quoted in psychical research for his paper on the Ear of Dionysius, read before the S.P.R. in November 1916, dealing with cross correspondences attributed to the discarnate minds of Professor Butcher and Professor Verrall. It is a very constructive presentation of some impressive evidence of human survival.

Lincoln and the Unseen

Of no single President of the United States has so much been written as of Lincoln.

In view of the unique role he played in American history and in the struggle for the freedom of the human spirit, no tribute to his memory could be called overdone. As a liberator of the slaves he will live for humanity ages after other presidents will have been forgotten.

Immediately after his first election, rumors were rife that

in his spiritual quest Lincoln took a lively interest in psychic matters. An American medium called J. B. Conklin claimed to have recognized him as the anonymous sitter in several séances in New York. In fact, the Cleveland *Plain Dealer* seized upon this to charge that Lincoln was a Spiritualist. The charge was given substance by Colonel S. P. Kase in the *Spiritual Scientist* as follows:

> For four succeeding Sundays, Mr. Conklin, the test medium, was a guest at the Presidential Mansion. The result of these interviews was the President's proposition to his cabinet to issue the proclamation [of the freeing of the slaves].

Apparently, other mediums joined in this effort of persuasion.

According to Colonel Kase, there was a Mrs. Laurie, his own daughter Mrs. Miller, and Nettie Colburn, who became very well known as an inspirational speaker when she was scarcely out of her teens. She approached the President with closed eyes and addressed him for a full hour and a half. The sum total of her address was:

This civil war will never cease, the shout of victory will never ring through the North, till you issue a proclamation that shall set free the enslaved millions of your unhappy country.

In the same séance at Mrs. Laurie's house, the President is said to have witnessed some startling phenomena: the piano on which a medium was playing rose four inches from the floor in spite of the efforts of Colonel Kase, Judge Wattles and two of the soldiers who accompanied the President, to hold it down.

In 1891 Nettie Colburn, by marriage Mrs. Maynard, published a book on her psychic contact with Lincoln under the title: *Was Abraham Lincoln a Spiritualist?*

We are facing here again the same situation which we considered in relation to MacKenzie King. What does it mean to be a Spiritualist? In the days of Lincoln, Spiritualism enjoyed its first boom. It was not yet exploited by fraudulent seekers of fame and fortune to the same extent as in later years. The appellation was not as ambiguous as in subsequent years when in the press and in the public a growing prejudice began to develop. Again, the answer is that Lincoln may well have accepted the central teaching of Spiritualism (which is a belief in survival after death) and may well have conducted his own inquiries in a spirit of seeking the truth; but that did not identify him with the movement as such. Hence describing him as a Spiritualist is a misnomer, to say the least.

This construction of Lincoln's spiritual beliefs in no way denies his psychic sensitivity. Convincing evidence is on record that Lincoln had strange presentiments of his coming end. In his Dickens biography, J. Forster quotes from a letter of the novelist dated February 4, 1868, in which he says that on the day of his assassination an extraordinary change was noticeable in Lincoln. According to Senator Charles Sumner, he said:

"Gentlemen, something extraordinary will happen, and that very soon."

The statement was made because of a dream of the night before, occurring the third time. It was:

"I am on a deep, broad, rolling river: I am a boat, and I am falling in! I am falling in!"

Six weeks before his assassination, he had a clearly prophetic dream that made a deep impression. He told it to a few friends, commenting: "Somehow the thing has got possession of me, and like Banquo's ghost, it will not down." This was the dream:

There seemed to be a deathlike stillness about me. Then I heard subdued sobs, as if a number of people were weeping. I thought I left my bed and wandered downstairs. There the silence was broken by the same pitiful sobbing, but the mourners were invisible. I went from room to room; no living person was in sight but the same mournful sounds of distress met me as I passed along.

It was light in all the rooms; every object was familiar to me; but where were all the people who were grieving as if their hearts would break? I was puzzled and alarmed. What could be the meaning of all this? Determined to find the cause of things so mysterious and so shocking, I kept on until I arrived at the East Room, which I entered. There I met with a sickening surprise. Before me was a catafalque, on which lay a corpse wrapped in funeral vestments. Around it were stationed soldiers who were acting as guards; and there was a throng of people,

19

some gazing upon the corpse, whose face was covered, others weeping pitifully.

"Who is dead in the White House?" I demanded of one of the soldiers.

"The President," was his answer. "He was killed by an assassin."

Then came a loud burst of grief from the crowd, which awoke me from my dream. I slept no more that night, and although it was only a dream, I have been strangely annoyed by it ever since.

The premonitory dream may have had its origin in a vision of Lincoln on the night of his first election as President. As he was resting, tired but awake, in a mirror opposite he saw two images of himself, one in perfect health, the other pale as a ghost.

Ever since, Lincoln was haunted by this vision. When it recurred the second time, he had the feeling that a catastrophe would befall him in a second term of office. According to Harriet Beecher Stowe, the author of *Uncle Tom's Cabin*, the President said: "Whichever way the war ends, I have the impression I shall not last long after it is over."

Five days after the surrender at Appomatox, he was killed at the Ford Theatre by the bullet of an assassin.

It is probably due to the violent nature of his death that stories of Lincoln's appearance as a ghost in the White House found their way into gossip columns of the press. According to an article in the New York *Journal-American* (March 22, 1961):

Any number of persons in the White House believe in the ghost of Lincoln. It was rumored backstairs that Queen Wilhelmina had seen the ghost of Lincoln when she opened the door to a strange knock. The next morning she is supposed to have told FDR, who was not too surprised, because his wife had felt something strange also.

There is no reason why the presence of Lincoln should not be felt at the White House. A great man's memory may well impregnate the place where he had to make momentous decisions at the cost of the anguish of his soul. But that does not make Lincoln a ghost. It is not he who haunts, but the living who remember. Clothing the memory in visual or auditory garb is dependent on the sensitivity of the living. Speaking of the inspiration of his life, we express the same thing in more mundane terms.

Who Was the Real Francis Grierson?

Men of literature are so frank about themselves in their writings that they hardly deserve the epithet mysterious. Yet, on reading the appreciation of their life and work in biographical dictionaries, occasionally one discovers glaring lacunae, the omission of facts so vital that the glamor that made them scintillate in their own time is totally lost.

Such is the case of Francis Grierson (1848–1927), of Scottish-Irish descent (his full name was Benjamin Henry Jesse Francis Grierson Shepard), who was brought to this country by his parents at the age of one and who, in his mature years, was acknowledged as an American literary genius. Of his *Modern Mysticism* and *the Celtic Temperament* (adopted as a textbook by Japanese universities), Maeterlinck wrote that he knew nothing more admirable and profound. His *Valley of Shadows* was hailed for its poetic freedom and delicacy of reminiscence of the Civil War as the work of a literary giant. He proved himself superior in vision to H. G. Wells, George Bernard Shaw, and Hilaire Belloc, his fellow-contributors to the *New Age*. He shook the literary world by his *Illusions and Realities of the War* and he revealed unknown personality traits of the great liberator in *Abraham Lincoln, the Practical Mystic*.

He shared the company of the great from early childhood. At the age of 13 he was a page boy to General John C. Fremont. Later, in Europe he became the darling of royal courts and enjoyed, long before his literary reputation was founded, fame and fortune equalled by very few men of peace in human history.

Webster's Biographical Dictionary glosses over the mystery phase of Francis Grierson's life with the short sentence: "He gave successful piano recitals in foreign capitals." This was, perhaps, the understatement of the century. *Twentieth Century Authors*[1] tells us a little more:

> With only two years of formal musical training, Shepard exhibited an extraordinary talent at the piano. At barely 21, he set out for Paris, with scarcely enough money to buy his own passage, and almost overnight became a sensation.

How can an unknown man from the United States, with only two years of formal training in music, not even recognized as a musician on the American continent, rise like a comet in the sky, conduct fabulous music tours and become the darling of royalty all over Europe?

The mystery deepens yet comes within reach of relative understanding with the discovery I was fortunate in making of a self-advertisement of Shepard's. One year after his arrival in Europe, in 1870, the following advertisement appeared in the *Medium,* a London spiritualistic publication:

JESSE B. H. SHEPARD

The celebrated American Medium
(late from Paris)
Gives Sittings, Clairvoyant, Prophetic, Writing
Impression, Psychometric
Also gives diagnosis of disease, and discovers
mediumistic faculties.
Charges are made according to the amount of time and
labour undertaken.

*N.B. The music manifestations are not given at
the same sitting.*

There is no question about the identity. The B. H. stands for Benjamin Henry and the reference to Paris and musical demonstrations clinch the case. Further, the advertisement was supported, in the May 6, 1870, issue of the *Medium,* by a biographical article under the title: "How I became a Musical Medium!"

In this article, Jesse Shepard does not admit two years of

---

[1] W. H. Wilson Company, New York, 1942.

formal training as claimed in the *Twentieth Century Authors*. He says he was not taught music in the usual way. His psychic faculties were first manifested in 1867 in the form of clairvoyant seeing, hearing and the power of healing. Later he heard raps around the room, the physical source of which could not be traced and discovered himself in possession of the gift called psychometry: sensing the story of an object or of the people connected with it by simply holding it in his hand. The turning point of his career came in January 1868. He wrote:

> While I was in the theatre, the spirit of Rachel came to me and asked if I would like to be developed in singing. She advised me to go next day and have the quality of my voice examined, by a competent professor. I did so; called on a celebrated musician and told him my business.
>
> He was astonished at the power of my voice and facility of execution, facts of which I was ignorant myself, and of which I was no judge. The professor gave it as his opinion that the voice would not last long; it was too wonderful to be permanent. However, I was only two weeks in being developed, but when the important result had been accomplished, I was too sceptical to believe that I really can sing, and was in great doubt as to the propriety of making the attempt in public, all of which I expressed to the music professor, asking his opinion on the matter.
>
> He replied that he would be very proud to have me sing the *Ave Maria* in St. Xavier's Church, where he was organist. This is one of the most fashionable churches in the city, and the choir is composed of superior singers. On taking my place in the service, I was influenced to sing the pieces allotted to me to the astonishment of all who heard me.

Note that the only supernatural element in this account is the reference to the spirit of Rachel (whose identity is not indicated) and that no mention is made of piano playing. Yet, two years later, by 1870, he was a musician—and a professional medium until his musical gifts, and still later his literary talent, blossomed out to such phenomenal heights that he no longer had to rely on taking money for a demonstration of his psychic powers.

The reasons why he is not known as the greatest musician the world has ever known is his bald and startling claim that he did not play by inspiration, but that actually the spirits of Mozart, Beethoven, Meyerbeer, Rossini, Sontag, Persiani, Malibran, Lablache, Liszt, Berlioz, and Chopin played through his hands.

The claim, even at the height of the wave of Spiritualism that had swept over Europe, was too impossible for general acceptance. But let us bear with it and see the length to which it had gone, by quoting Prince Adam Wisniewski's account in the Italian *Vessillo Spiritista* of a musical séance he attended on September 3, 1894:

After having secured the most complete obscurity, we placed ourselves in a circle around the medium, seated before the piano. Hardly were the first chords struck when we saw lights appearing in every corner of the room. The great pianists and composers of all epochs arrived, some to perform, others to hear the music.

The first piece played through Shepard was a fantasia of Thalberg on the air from *Semiramide*. This is unpublished, as is all the music which is played by the spirits through Shepard. The second was a rhapsody for four hands, played by Liszt and Thalberg with astounding fire, a sonority truly grand, and a masterly interpretation. Notwithstanding this extraordinary complex technique, the harmony was admirable, such as no one present had ever known paralleled even by Liszt himself, whom I personally knew and in whom passion and delicacy were united. In the circle were musicians who, like myself, had heard the greatest pianists in Europe; but we can say that we never heard such truly supernatural execution.

A globe of light which appeared on the hand of Mme. D, announced the arrival of Chopin. He always manifests his presence in this fashion. He executed a fantasia which recalled the *Duet Adalgisa* and *Norma,* with mysterious arpeggios of crystalline and expressive tones which distinguish Chopin. On this occasion his spirit vouchsafed most exquisite melodies with a pianissimo of diminishing tones and notes full of despair—a prayer to God for Poland.

After him came Georges Sand. As I expressed my pleasure to find this genial soul in our midst, she gave three powerful raps on my knee. Mme. D. having said that she was jealous of this friendly sign, Georges Sand granted her the same favour.

Then Mozart came and played with the agility and lightness of a sylph, with a variety of touch and a melodious style which were the invariable marks of his genius.

But the most marvellous incident of the evening was the presentation of the spirit of Berlioz by his two chaperones, Liszt and Thalberg. That was the first time that Berlioz had played through Shepard. He began by saying that the piano was toned too low for his music (Shepard is also clairvoyant and clairaudient) and he tuned it a tone higher himself. For ten minutes we heard the spirits working with the piano, which was closed. Then Berlioz played sweet, ideal music. It seemed as if we heard the little bells of a country church; as if we saw and heard a marriage procession descending the mountain side, and entering the edifice; then a music which imitated to perfection the sound of the organ and continued piano, pianissimo and morendo, as if indicating that the marriage was celebrated, and the procession returning to the mountains. This piece finished, Berlioz, with the aid of several other spirits, restored the instrument to its first tuning and began playing on its ordinary tone while the lid was still shut.

Several spirits came afterwards, speaking each his own language. Now Shepard is English, and, in addition to French, knows no other tongue. Once in trance, however, he speaks—or rather the spirits speak through him—in every living language. Thus Goethe has recited passages in German; a spirit calling itself Isaiah has spoken in Hebrew; Mahomet in Arabic. Spirits have come and translated these speeches, and promised to help us in our psycho-researches, and indicate to us the persons with whom we shall put ourselves in communication.

After the séance, Mr. Shepard was much exhausted and had to retire to rest.

No musical party by the Mad Hatter could sound more preposterous than this account. It leaves breathless the most ardent spiritualists. They no longer prefer the return of the great ones and accord them a skeptical reception. Was Prince

Wisniewski a gibbering idiot? Was it an exuberant enthusiasm of this type that had ruined Jesse Shepard's chances for universal acclaim?

Whatever the facts are, he was received in the highest circles—and left them dumbfounded. He played at the Imperial Palace at Gatchina for the Czar of Russia and before a reunion of three royal houses at Cumberland Palace in Gmunden, Austria. His hostess was the Duchess of Cumberland, sister of the Empress of Russia, of the Princess of Wales, and of the Queen of Greece. This is the account given of this musical event by Lauritz Waldemar Tonner, of The Hague, in *Light,* March 17, 1894:

I had also the good fortune to be present at Mr. Shepard's reception at the Cumberland Palace; I shall not soon forget the impression made on the royal assemblage by his music. The music room was so brilliantly lighted by lamps and candles; H.R.H. the Duchess of Cumberland asked me if Mr. Shepard would not prefer less light; indeed, the Duchess seemed to realise, as if by intuition, that so much light would not add to the beauty of the music. Accordingly, some of the lamps were extinguished and the concert was given with only the candles burning. I feel certain that the darkness would not have been objected to on this memorable occasion as Mr. Shepard has never been heard by a more cultured and intelligent audience. The Queen of Hanover, who was sitting beside H.R.H. the Reigning Duke of Saxe-Altenburg, rose from her seat during the singing and exclaimed: "I have never heard anything like it." And the Queen of Denmark, who sat immediately behind Shepard, complimenting him at the close, said that the piano playing had the effect of four hands instead of two.

Why not? If someone can play the piano closed, he might as well be credited with a ghostly duet. Apparently Shepard accompanied his playing with singing—in bass and soprano. Here is how this feat is described by the editor of *Dagblad,* the leading orthodox and aristocratic newspaper of the day in The Hague, on March 14, 1894:

All of a sudden, in a moment of ecstasy, the bass voice turned into a soprano—not one of the falsettos one some-

26

times hears in theatres, but full, large and of extraordinary volume, from the lowest to the highest register. It was as if the room had suddenly been filled from all sides with splendid and ringing tones, melting together in a mighty harmony. It surpassed the piano music in power, although the tone of the piano became more and more fortissimo, and seemed like waves of tone swelling up from the instrument. It was as if one heard the word "Excelsior!" Although we do not believe in the supernatural, the soul was taken hold of and carried to higher spheres. The inspiration which is awakened through Mr. Shepard's power is already quite wonderful enough. Why try to find an explanation in the supernatural?

Indeed, why? The penalty may be considerable. Mr. Henry Kiddle, Superintendent of Schools of New York, was forced to resign because he publicly stated his belief in Shepard's "spirits." At one time Shepard stayed in his house for twelve months. Mr. Kiddle was careless enough to say that he had heard him playing, under the control of Mozart, a magnificent impromptu symphony and deliver, at the same time, under the influence of Aristotle, learned philosophical dissertations; also that he had heard him speak, while in trance, German, Latin, Greek, Hebrew, Chaldaic, and Arabic.

No one in his sane mind could be expected to subscribe to such stupendous claims. And it appears that Shepard himself began to realize their enormity. As the years passed, he only sat for his friends and in the strictest confidence. More and more he drifted away from Spiritualism. Finally, he sacrificed his name and became Francis Grierson. The editor of *Twentieth Century Authors* believes he did this "lest his literary efforts be regarded as mere diversions." But, for that matter, he still could have gone on with his mysterious concerts. He did not, and no one heard of Francis Grierson's past spiritualistic ties until 1921 when he published a pamphlet on "Psychophone Messages." It is only at this point that *Twentieth Century Authors* discovers his "serious interest in psychic phenomena, although the extent of his own ability as a kind of medium appears somewhat undefined."

It is rather unreasonable that a man of his gifts both as an author and a musician should end his last years in utter poverty. But Jesse Shepard (or Francis Grierson) never believed in reason. "Intuition and emotion were the sources of his artistic energy." Money-making was not within the range.

The mystery of his life has never been rationally explained. The notes we find about him in Guy Endore's *King of Paris*[2] only add to wonderment. Apparently, Jesse Shepard had visited Dumas for advice on how to get along. He had just arrived, "a handsome young giant who didn't know one note of music from another, and who nevertheless, with those huge hands of his able to span an octave and a half, improvised such enchanting music and accompanied himself with a voice equally untrained, but of such strangely haunting power, that the artistic circles of Europe stood in amazement. Crowned heads became his admirers. Countesses, one after another, fell madly in love with this man who had the beauty of a Wild West colt."

Guy Endore makes no mention of mediumship or spirits. Dumas told Shepard that he knew very little of music. Shepard allegedly answered: "I know even less. The first time I saw a piano, I just sat down and played. I don't know why. I don't know how. And I'm afraid to find out."

This must have happened in 1869. In 1927 "he was old and penniless in Los Angeles. His great novel, the *Valley of Shadows*, which he had written under the name of Francis Grierson, lay forgotten. His improvisations, never recorded, were to become a vanished art. The case worker from the Los Angeles Assistance League was just knocking at his door as he expired. She had refused to believe that this old man (78) had toured the world as a pianist and singer. She had refused to believe that he was a well-known writer. She had refused to believe that he had just pawned his last piece of jewelry, a watch given to him by the King of England. It was her duty to investigate first. And meanwhile, he died of hunger." [3]

[2] Pocket Books, Cardinal Giant, 1958, pp. 93-95.

[3] *Ibid.*

The Unknown Dickens[1]

On July 14th in the year of 1870, Charles Dickens was laid to rest in Poets' Corner, Westminster Abbey, in London. In his Will he had insisted that no monument be erected in his honor.

"I rest my claim to the remembrance of my country on my published works."

It is not always that an artist can so confidently count on the verdict of posterity.

In view of the popularity of his works, to talk of an "unknown Dickens" sounds eccentric. Yet there was a side to Dickens' genius of which his biographers give but vague intimations.

In his editorial capacity the great novelist could rarely resist a really good ghost story. In *All the Year Round* one could always find stories of supernatural experiences. Its editor was never certain where fiction ended and reality began.

It was his habit during the summer months to rise very early, and to put in a good day's work in his study before breakfast time. The stillness and the solitude affected him profoundly. It was in just such an hour, in daylight and while he was still in bed, that he once saw the apparition of his father. He made it into a Christmas contribution to *All the Year Round* in 1859. The story is:

> My father was alive and well, and nothing ever came of it; but I saw him . . . sitting with his back to me, on a seat that stood beside my bed. His head was resting on his hand, and whether he was slumbering or grieving, I could not discern. Amazed to see him there, I sat up, moved my position, leaned out of bed, and watched him. As he did not move, I spoke to him more than once. As he did not move then, I became alarmed and laid my hand upon his shoulders—as I thought; and there was no such thing . . . For all these reasons and for others less

[1] *Darshana International*, Moradabad, India, April 1962. Reprinted by permission.

easily and briefly stateable, I find the early morning to be my ghostly time.

This then was an apparition of the living, a transition from hypnopompic hallucination to reality. In the psyche of a novelist a dream-image may persevere sufficiently long after awakening to assume the shape of an apparition. The very wording of Dickens suggests that the father image was "slumbering" in his mind. It was not his father who was "grieving" but it was, in all likelihood, he himself who had guilt feelings toward him.

Some further very interesting testimony regarding Dickens' twilight experiences is contained in the pages of the old *Fortnightly Review* when George Henry Lewes, the devoted comrade of "George Eliot," was its editor. (Dickens, incidentally, was the first to guess the feminine identity—Marian Evans—concealed in the masculine pseudonym of the author of *Adam Bede*.) Lewes tells how Dickens once declared to him that every word uttered by his characters was distinctly heard by him.

To his friend, Jack Fields, Dickens confessed that when he was writing *The Old Curiosity Shop*, the creatures of his imagination so haunted him that they would neither allow him to sleep nor eat in peace. No matter where he might have happened to be, *Little Nell* was constantly at his elbow calling for his attention and demanding his sympathy as if jealous when he spoke to anyone else. And when he was writing *Martin Chuzzlewit*, Mrs. Gamp kept him in such paroxysms of laughter by whispering to him in the most inopportune places—sometimes even in church—that he was compelled to fight her off by main force, as it were, when he did not want her company and to threaten to have nothing more to do with her unless she behaved better and came only when she was called.

Only the creative aspect of the experience saves Charles Dickens from being put into the schizophrenic category. That he had an idetic mind, or supernormal awareness—if you like—was evident during his visits abroad. In describing a scene he witnessed on his first sight of Ferrara, Italy, he said:

If I had been murdered there in some former life, I could not have seemed to remember the place more thoroughly, or with more emphatic chilling of the blood;

and the real remembrance of it acquired in that minute is so strengthened by the imaginary recollection that I hardly think I could forget it.

This is an excellent illustration of "déjà vû," of the feeling that one has been in a place before when such familiarity could not have been acquired.

Dickens was accustomed to mingling with crowds in populous thoroughfares, and liked it. From Lausanne, he wrote plaintively:

> The absence of any accessible streets continues to worry me, now that I have so much to do, in a singular manner. It is quite a little mental phenomenon. I should not walk in them in the daytime, I dare say; but at night I want them beyond description. I don't seem to get rid of my spectres unless I can lose them in crowds.

This clearly hints that preoccupation with other sights and sounds was necessary to free Dickens from the phantoms of his own mind.

Not long before his death Dickens confided that one night in Washington, after one of his famous public readings, he dreamed that he was in a room where everyone was dressed in scarlet. He stumbled against a lady who had her back towards him. As he apologized she turned her head and said, quite unprovoked: "My name is Napier." The face was perfectly unknown to him; nor did he know anyone named Napier. Two days later he gave another reading in Washington; and before it began, a lady friend came into his waiting room accompanied by an unknown woman in a scarlet opera cloak who, said his friend, was "very desirous of being introduced." Jokingly Dickens inquired: "Not Miss Napier?" "Yes," came the answer, "Miss Napier."

This was a prophetic dream in the technical language of parapsychology, a premonition of approach. It is fairly frequent in the waking state in the form of a hallucination. There is no better word to describe it. One sees a long lost friend coming towards him and is about to greet him in joyous surprise—to discover that he made a curious mistake. The man does not look like him. The next moment, however, the real friend heaves into view.

In Dickens' dream, however, everybody in the room was

dressed in scarlet. The term "scarlet woman" needs no explanation. Possibly there was a scarlet character in the text of Dickens' reading. Possibly there was another explanation. We shall never know.

So much we can say, however, that one need not be particularly psychic to have an experience of this sort. Yet to fight shy of the word "psychic" is quite unnecessary. All great artists of all nationalities and at all times belonged to this category. They saw with more than the mortal eye and heard with more than the mortal ear. They saw and heard "adown titanic glooms of chasmed fears" the spiritual pattern of life, woven and interwoven upon the Eternal Loom.

* * *

This essay would fall short of certain legitimate anticipations if it failed to give a post-mortem summary of another riddle of Dickens—that of the story of his last unfinished book. *The Mystery of Edwin Drood.* I shall quote it from my *Encyclopedia of Psychic Science:*

Dickens' last novel, *The Mystery of Edwin Drood,* was interrupted in its monthly publication by the death of Dickens on July 8, 1870. T. P. James, an uneducated American mechanic of Brattleboro, Vermont, obtained messages in automatic writing which purported to emanate from the author. Between Christmas 1872 and July 1873 scripts came from under his hand which contained the continuation of Dickens' unfinished novel. The posthumous section was longer than the other and presented a surprising continuity of thought, style and peculiarities of orthography of Dickens. The two sections were published together: *The Mystery of Edwin Drood, Complete,* by Charles Dickens, Brattleboro, Vt., published by T. P. James, 1874.

Spiritualists the world over hailed the book as a most convincing proof of spirit return. Prof. Flournoy, in *Spiritism and Psychology,* undertook to demonstrate that Dickens himself had nothing to do with the affair and that everything is easily explained by processes of latent incubation and subconscious imagination in the medium himself. He quotes the conclusions of Mme. R. Fairbanks, a distinguished member of the Geneva University, from

32

her *Le Cas Soirite de Dickens*[2] according to which "there are certainly very successful passages, such as the scenes between the two women. Billicken and Twinkleton. But there are others which are just the contrary." Further, J. Forster, author of *The Life of Charles Dickens*, discovered among the papers of the deceased author a whole scene in Edwin Drood, written in advance and destined to figure later in the novel. Flournoy finds it incredible that the author who remembered so clearly the part of the volume already published that no more than three new persons are introduced in any part of the second section should have completely forgotten the chapter written and left in manuscript. He avers that as a striking proof of identity Dickens would have made an allusion to it.

In the book itself and in the advertisement quotations on the cover, T. P. James does not pretend that he has not read Dickens and his last novel. "Now it is evident," said Flournoy, "that if he had not read Dickens he would most probably have boasted of his accomplishment, because that would have rendered his performance much more extraordinary. Let us not forget," he finally remarks, "that the medium had two and a half years to imbibe the original work of the author, and letting this 'simmer'—without counting the six months afterwards employed in automatic writing—three years in all were completed. We must confess that this greatly reduces its marvellous character."

A. Conan Doyle (in *The Edge of the Unknown*) concluded that "the actual inspiration of Dickens is far from being absolutely established. . . . It reads like Dickens gone flat." In the same book he records some personally obtained automatic contributions to the solution of the mystery of Edwin Drood.

Only one addition is necessary to this summary. The lack of reference to the chapter found posthumously among the papers of Dickens is a specious objection. Writers are carried away by their inspiration. It is most of the time impossible to include fragments in a later continuity, and they may not even remember that such a fragment had been written.

[2] Archives de Psychologists, T. I., June 1892, p. 411.

The Riddle of
Vaslav Nijinsky

Vaslav Nijinsky, perhaps the greatest ballet dancer the world has ever known, had the doubtful distinction of having died twice. Once when he entered a mental hospital where he lived in strange and happy dreams for 20 years, the second time when he died, sane but unhappy, in April 1950. He was counted among the dead for so many years that the news of his passing was a shock to all who had seen him on the stage and had treasured the memory of the exquisite beauty of his art. With so much having been written about it one may find it strange that he should still be a riddle and that so little should be known of the mystic element in his extraordinary career.

Theatre Street is a book of the reminiscences of Thamar Karsavina. She tells in it how in one of the rehearsal rooms of the Imperial Theatre School of Warsaw she saw one of the boys rise in the air so far above his fellows, and with such ease, that she asked Nicolai Legat, the master, the name of the pupil.

"It is Nijinsky," he replied. "That little devil never comes down in time with the music."

Other dancers have also been noted for delaying in the air. Vestris Père, the "Dioux de la Dance," said of his famous son Augustus: *"Il resterait toujours en l'air, s'il ne craignait pas d'humilier ses camarades."* (He would stay up for good in the air if he were not afraid to humiliate his comrades.) It was said of Maria Taglioni: "She seems to be able to walk on a cornfield without bending the ears." Nicolai Legat observed N. P. Damaschoff stay "for some time in the air." It was said of Nijinsky that he definitely possessed "the ability to remain in the air at the highest point of elevation before descending."

Is this gift of famous dancers a rudimentary form of the levitation of the human body, familiar to those who are interested in parapsychology, or is it only an illusion? Let us quote Cyril W. Beaumont from his biography of Nijinsky:

He had a wonderful *ballon*, so that he leaped in the

air and came to the ground with the elasticity and ease of a bounding India rubber ball. His *élévation* was really extraordinary. That wonderful leap by which, as the sprite in *The Spectre de la Rose,* he entered from the rose garden, through the open French windows, to alight beside the young girl asleep in her chair, must still linger in the memories of all those who saw it. There was a rose-coloured flash, and he was seen to describe a graceful parabola with the ease of a grasshopper leaping from one blade of grass to another. There was no flurry, no strained features, no thud as the feet came to the ground; it was just as though a rose petal had been caught up by a night breeze and wafted through the open window.

In *Les Sylphides* he used to make his exit with another unusual leap. There was no suggestion of an athlete attempting the high jump; it appeared as though the dancer had decided to fly, instead of walk, off the stage; for as he made his exit, he suddenly rose in the air and disappeared behind the wings.

Beaumont remembers that even when Nijinsky "lifted Pavlova in the air with one arm, they both seemed to me to be rising from the floor and ready to disappear in the stage 'flies'." But Pavlova, he admits, could never stop in the air, "as we hear Taglioni did, and as we saw Nijinsky do."

We may rule out illusion, as it would have operated equally in Pavlova's case. Remaining in the air appears to be due to a special technique. Diaghilev gives us a hint. Speaking of Nijinsky, he said:

> I am positive that not since Vestris has such a vigorous dancer been seen. This young man . . . springs to an incredible height. His *élévation* is nearly three feet . . . Nature has endowed him with tendons of steel and tensile muscles so strong that they resemble those of the great cats. A real lion of the dance, he could cross the diagonal of the stage in two bounds.

This explanation only covers the height of Nijinsky's *élévation.* The greater mystery of remaining up and coming down slower than the law of gravitation would demand is passed over in silence by most of the writers. Nicolai Legat, however, writing of Damaschoff, revealed the technique as follows:

35

Tightening his leg muscles, especially those of the thighs, in the air, he made all his moderate jumps fairly high. During the leap he held his breath, *i.e.*, he breathed in shortly before the spring and breathed out as soon as he was down again.

The enquiries I made disclose this as a standard technique. I found one further point of importance: the relaxation of the trunk on the stiffened thighs in the air: I was also told that lung power has nothing to do with the feat; the key to the mystery, so far as it is known, is in breath and muscle control.

Breath control is an important feature in Indian mystical training. It is claimed to be the esoteric means of rendering the human body buoyant. But dancers do not go through any occult training. Somehow, they seem to acquire the technique unconsciously. They cannot explain it. It is the teacher who traces the *modus operandi* from observations. Nijinsky certainly did not know how he achieved his momentary suspension. I had long discussions on the matter with his widow, whose friendship I enjoy. Romola Nijinsky was herself a dancer. She knows all there is to know about her husband. This is what she told me:

I often asked him how he managed to stay up in the air. He never could understand why we could not do it. He just took a leap, held his breath, and stayed up. He felt supported in the air. Moreover, he could control his descent, and could come down slower or quicker as he wished. I know he had extraordinary thigh muscles, and I know that in the matter of filling his lungs with air he has, in a friendly contest, easily beaten Caruso and Erich Schmedes.

For Nijinsky, dancing was religion. He believed that he had a mission to perform, and that his gifts were given to him in order to convey ideas to the world through dancing. Nobody was allowed to enter his dressing room before the performance. No one could speak to him after he came out. He never answered. He looked, and acted, like a stranger. When once, in admiration, I told him what a pity it was that he could not see himself, he answered in all seriousness: "But I do. I always see myself. I am detached. I am outside. I make myself dance from the outside."

I was extremely interested in the last statement. It seemed to indicate a trance-like state, a curious dissociation which might go some way towards explaining his later mental collapse. Moreover, he did dabble in psychic matters. As Romola remembered:

In St. Moritz we had a governess for my children, who had spent a long time in India. She spoke to us about *Hatha Yoga,* a school of esoteric training, and my husband became very interested. He began to read it up, and corresponded on the subject with Maeterlinck.

Eighteen years ago, on the day of my father's death, we tried an experiment with the ouija board. It moved under our hands, running to the letters of the alphabet spread out under it; it answered various questions. It told us that the war would end on June 29th, 1919, that Hungary would become a kingdom without a king, and that Premier Tisza would be murdered. We did not take the messages seriously, but, as they provided amusement and interest, we continued to hold sittings throughout June and July.

My husband found these experiments more fascinating than we did. He was advised to try automatic drawing, by letting his hand go free and forgetting all about it; he did this with remarkable success. He composed a dance, and asked me to dance it in Yoga fashion: by disconnecting my personality and abandoning myself entirely to the spirit of the dance. I did so, and danced for hours in a state of trance. When I recovered consciousness and heard congratulations I thought that I had made a fool of myself. I continued with the experiments for a few months, but the drain on my vitality was too much, and I had to give it up.

Regarding my husband's mental breakdown, I don't think that his dabbling in occultism was the immediate cause of it. He inherited a very delicately balanced brain. He had to be guarded and shielded from emotional storms. During the war we were stranded in Hungary. I had great difficulty in saving him from being interned. The excitements of these years preyed on his mind. He would have won through but for the brutality of others. They did not understand his strange ways and, unknown to me, reported him to the authorities as insane. When the keepers came to remove him, the shock of his arrest drove him out of his mind.

To understand more about the riddle of Nijinsky's famous elevations we have to return to Hindu practices of generating a force that apparently counteracts gravitation. They say that he who awakens the *Anahata Chakra,* which is situated in the heart and is the seat of *Prana* (cosmic energy), "can walk in the air." This is the essence of the practice of the Tibetan *lung-gom-pa* adepts who can take extraordinary long tramps with amazing rapidity. Alexandra David-Neel, the French anthropologist, claims to have met one in Northern Tibet and this is what she observed:

> The man did not run. He seemed to lift himself from the ground, proceeding by leaps. It looked as if he had been endowed with the elasticity of a ball and rebounded each time his feet touched the ground. His steps had the regularity of a pendulum.

We are told that the breathing exercises of the *lung-gom-pa* have to be practiced for three years and three months in complete darkness and in strict seclusion. It is claimed that the body of those who subject themselves to this harsh discipline becomes exceedingly light, nearly without weight:

> These men, they say, are able to sit on an ear of barley without bending its stalk or to stand on the top of a heap of grain without displacing any of it.

Shades of Maria Taglioni! Was she an unconscious *lung-gom-pa?*

Badinage aside, there is a similarity between the psychic state of Nijinsky on the stage and the *lung-gom-pa.* Mme. David-Neel says that during their walk they are in a state of trance. They concentrate on the cadenced mental recitation of a mystic formula with which, during the walk, the in-and-out breathing must be in rhythm, the steps keeping time with the breath and the syllables of the formula. The walker must neither speak, nor look from side to side. He must keep his eyes fixed on a single distant object and never allow his attention to be attracted by anything else.

Others assert that after a certain distance, "the feet of the *lung-gom-pa* no longer touch the ground and that he glides in the air with extreme rapidity." Some are even said to wear iron chains around their body for "they are always in danger of floating in the air."

This is by a long shot beyond the range of Nijinsky's elevation. It places considerable strain on Western imagination. Yet, we know of a mystery connected with breathing in the so-called lifting game to which the late Dr. Hereward Carrington's scientific experiments lend a startling reality.

Four persons lift a fifth, seated in a chair, by placing their fingers under the arms and knees of the seated person. At the start of the game they bend forward several times in unison, inhaling and exhaling deeply together. The person seated in the chair also inhales and exhales at the same time. On the fifth count all five persons hold their breath; the fingers of the four lifters are rapidly inserted under the arms and legs of the seated subject and the lift is easily made. The lifters' feeling is that the person in the chair has suddenly lost considerable weight.

Carrington tried the experiment upon the platform of a large self-registering scale. This is what he reported:

> On the first lift . . . the needle of the dial had fallen to 660 pounds (the combined weight was found previously to be 712 pounds), a loss of 52 pounds. On the second lift there was an apparent loss of 52 pounds; on the third lift of 60 pounds; and on the fourth lift of 60 pounds, and on the fifth lift of 60 pounds. No gain of weight was any time recorded (owning to muscular exertion); invariably there was a loss which, however, slowly returned to normal as the subject was held for some considerable time in the air.

Carrington could not explain these findings. They are reported fully in his book, *The Story of Psychic Science*. I do not know if others checked up on these claims. But it does seem that we are in the presence of a mystery and that Nijinsky's famous elevations are somehow tied up with it.

In Jones' *Biography of Freud*, Sandor Ferenczi, the favorite disciple of the founder of psychoanalysis, emerges as an enigmatic personality. In particular, Jones regards Ferenczi's strong leaning toward psychic phenomena as a description of Freud's sober scientific spirit. Visibly pained, Jones gives a summary of the correspondence between Ferenczi and Freud on these recondite matters, but he makes no attempt to explain how Ferenczi had been drawn into this strange field of phenomenology beyond the statement that Ferenczi's interest in the subject goes back as far as 1899, the year in which Ferenczi's first scientific paper was published.

Following this clue, and consulting Dr. Michael Bálint's bibliography of Ferenczi's writings, I found that the title of Ferenczi's early paper was "Spiritism." But what it contained, nobody seemed to know. I wonder if it contained an account of Ferenczi's personal experiences.

It happened that in my correspondence with Dr. Lila Vészy-Wagner, a London psychoanalyst and research assistant to Jones until the latter's death, a record came to light that was startling enough to be the beginning of a psychic quest. The record was confidential, and I was referred to Dr. Istvan Varró, an old friend of Ferenczi, now living in Chicago. Dr. Varró, now in his eighties, was formerly engaged in public administration in Hungary. He taught economics and published a sociological monthly, *Our Century*, with Dr. Rustem Vambery. Dr. Varró received my inquiry with sympathy and, in a letter dated November 18, 1960, gave me permission to quote him as follows:

> With Dr. Ferenczi we used to talk of everything *à propos* of something, as the French say. In one of our rambling conversations we dealt with all sorts of curiosa,

[1] From the *International Journal of Parapsychology*, Vol 3., No. 3, Summer 1961. Reprinted by permission of the Parapsychology Foundation, Inc., New York.

among others with the so-called spiritists we had come across. Ferenczi had had a personal experience with them and told me of it in great detail, however, without adding any commentary—clinical or otherwise—to his story. After all those years, I still remember it very vividly, unlike other similar ones I had heard but have half forgotten.

What he told me had happened when he was a young M.D., at the very beginning of his career. At that time he held a poorly paid minor position with free room and board at the Rókus Hospital at Budapest. To bolster his income he occasionally took on some outside professional work. Just then, a senior colleague had recommended him to the family of a very sick old man who needed medical supervision round the clock. Ferenczi was on the night shift from 6 P.M. on, relieving another young doctor who was on duty during the day.

His story, Ferenczi said, needed the following introduction:

Shortly after he had taken on this job, Ferenczi ran into a former acquaintance of his, a certain *Privat Dozent,* Dr. Emil Felletár, whose classes at the university he had visited years back. After having dropped by mere chance into one of the professor's lectures, he attended them regularly, although the subject (forensic medical chemistry or the like) was not a required one and carried no credits. He did so partly because he was intrigued by the subject, and partly because the somewhat queer, kindly personality of the lecturer appealed to him. Since there were only two other students in the class besides him, the young student and the elderly professor became very friendly. Once out of school, however, Ferenczi did not keep up this relationship. When they met once in a long while, the professor would mildly upbraid him for neglecting his old friend, inviting him nonetheless to come and visit. The young man would always promise to look him up very soon, but never could get around to it. Then, one day when they happened to meet again in the street, the professor asked him to come to his home at a certain date for a special occasion.

Now Ferenczi vaguely remembered having heard that the dear, queer old man was a dedicated spiritist. He himself was not specifically interested in spiritism, but as he

41

was already headed for a practice in psychiatry anyway, he thought "if there is going to be a séance—let's see what it is all about." So he accepted the invitation and presented himself in the late afternoon of the appointed day at the fairly distant home in Buda (the "rive gauche" of Budapest) where the professor lived with his sister and her young granddaughter.

Dr. Ferenczi was welcomed to an intimate little gathering and his host proposed to hold a séance in his honor. As a guest, he was invited to address the first question to the spirit with whom the medium was in rapport. The medium was none other than Dr. Felletár's grand-niece.

The question which Ferenczi wrote down on a piece of paper was (in exact quotation): "What is the person of whom I think doing at this moment?" And the answer (also quoted verbatim by Ferenczi) was: "The person of whom you think sits up in bed—asks for a drink of water—slumps back and—dies."

Ferenczi, startled, looked at his watch, suddenly realizing that it was a few minutes past the time he should have been at his patient's bedside. Without taking leave, he hurriedly left the house and jumped into a cab. On arriving at his destination, he learned that everything had happened exactly as the medium had told, and at precisely at the same time: the patient sat up in bed, asked for a drink of water, and died.

This story is very interesting and was not difficult to date. Ferenczi was born in 1873 and if he was a first- or second-year intern at the hospital, he could not have been more than 24 or 25 years old. That would give the year as 1897 or 1898. His essay in 1899 may well have been, so I thought, based on the Felletár séance.

I turned for further information to Dr. Michael Bálint, who is Ferenczi's literary executor. He told me that my chronology was wrong. Ferenczi took a long time to qualify and his internship at the Rókus Hospital started in 1898 or 1899, therefore his paper on Spiritism must have been written almost immediately on his arrival in Budapest. Further, Dr. Bálint stated:

Ferenczi's interest in telepathy and predictions is very old indeed. I think it went back to his early youth. There

42

are many references to this in his correspondence with Freud which, however, for the time being must remain unpublished. The interesting thing is that both men were deeply impressed by their experiences, but each reacted in his own characteristic way: Ferenczi with great enthusiasm and ready acceptance of the experiences, while Freud, although sincerely believing in the ultimate truth of it, remained highly critical and cautious.

In a subsequent letter, Dr. Bálint added:

I remember that Ferenczi talked on several occasions about his friendship with Felletár and his experiences at his house, but unfortunately I do not recall any of the details.

After considerable trouble, through friends in Budapest I was able to get a full transcript of Ferenczi's article on "Spiritism." Dr. Bálint was right. The article must have been written before Ferenczi visited Felletár's house. It reveals an interest in psychic phenomena that—contrary to Dr. Varró's supposition —was manifested in many years of reading and, possibly, investigating; but it does not deal with personal adventures. The paper is a plea to science to accept psychic phenomena as a legitimate field of inquiry. Ferenczi explicitly mentions Aksakof's *Animismus und Spiritismus*, the original title under which this well-known book was first published in Leipzig, Germany, in 1890, and uses it as his chief source of reference.

This book, written by an Imperial Counsellor of the Czar of Russia and a pioneer of Spiritualism in that country, organizes psychic phenomena, and the testimony of scientists to their reality, in a very creditable manner. Apparently, Ferenczi used the Aksakof work as his spiritualistic Bible. His attitude seems to have been that even if the reported phenomena did not turn out to be based on objective reality, they might reveal a subjective reality, and offer a rich harvest to students of psychology.

At the time when Ferenczi wrote his plea, psychology was in its infancy. The relationship of the unconscious to the conscious was just being explored and Ferenczi revealed deep insight in suspecting that the mediums of Spiritualism have a split personality and that the confusion between two levels of mental activity might be responsible for fraud, but also enrich psychology with new and important knowledge.

At this stage of our knowledge, the Felletár séance seems to be the first clinical record—through Dr. Varró's recollection—of Ferenczi's personal adventures. Jones dates the exchange of occult information between Ferenczi and Freud from the year of 1907, six or seven years subsequent to the startling clairvoyant message of Felletár's grand-niece. Dr. Bálint confirms this dating. According to him, Ferenczi did not make contact with Freud until 1906 or 1907.

As it happens, the message was not the end of the Felletár story.

I shall now continue Dr. Varró's account of what happened in the year of 1917, at the funeral services of Dr. Felletár:

Feeling embarrassed because of his abrupt departure from the séance, Ferenczi thought that he owed an apology to the good doctor Felletár. Nonetheless, he put off the planned visit from week to week, until it was too late. For one day he read in the morning papers of Dr. Felletár's death.

Since he saw in the obituary notice that the funeral was to take place at Dr. Felletár's home on the afternoon of the same day, he decided to atone somehow for his omission by paying a last visit to his late friend and by offering his condolences to the ladies of the family.

In the tree-shaded courtyard of the family home in Buda, he found a small group of people surrounding the bier: some elderly university professors, Felletár's old sister and a few other relatives. Yet, to Ferenczi's surprise, the young girl who had served as a medium was not present.

After a brief valedictory speech, the men sent out by the undertaker proceeded to lift the coffin onto the funeral wagon. But try and strain as they might, it would not budge. The tremendous weight of the simple wooden coffin defeated all their efforts.

The coachman of the horse-drawn black funeral carriage was waiting, and so were the dumbfounded bystanders. At long last the old lady went into the house, returning—after a little while—with the girl. Led and supported by the old person, the deadly pale girl approached the bier with faltering steps, her eyes closed, as

44

in a trance. Reaching the coffin, she just touched it with her hand, and the men could lift it at once, with no difficulty at all.

This then is the whole story told to me by Dr. Ferenczi, and as I remember it. Impressed though I was, I did not ask any questions, nor did he volunteer any interpretation or explanation of the event.

This is the type of phenomena witnessed in table turning experiments. It is rather unusual to see telekinetic power applied to a coffin that was not even within immediate reach. Interpreting it psychologically, the grand-niece did not want to let go of Dr. Felletár; and this resistance to accepting the fact of his death had to be responsible for the remarkable demonstration of physical mediumship, added to her ability of message-giving in trance. Who was she? Was there any record extant of her during the seventeen years between Ferenczi's first and last visit?

Dr. Varró thought there was a chance of finding out her name. He wrote to the National Széchenyi Library of the Hungarian National Museum in Budapest for information, suggesting that the funeral notice must have listed her name as one of the mourners. Unfortunately, the Library did not have a copy of the funeral notice. From the information they were able to give, it appears that Dr. Emil Felletár (1834-1917) was a Doctor of Pharmacology, had the rank of a Court Councillor, and taught forensic chemistry as "Privat Dozent" at the University of Budapest. But, according to Dr. George Pajkossy, Chief-in-Charge of the Library, "our catalogues and bibliographies show no evidence that he was interested in parapsychology or spiritism."

Another unknown incident should be mentioned. It comes from Dr. Bálint:

Once, I think it must have been before 1914, a clairvoyant pestered Ferenczi to make some experiments with him. After some resistance, Ferenczi agreed that at a given time immediately after lunch, he would think concentratedly of something and the thought reader would read his thoughts.

On arriving at his consulting room at the given time, Ferenczi picked up a statue of an elephant, lay on his couch for ten or fifteen minutes, holding the elephant in his hands.

A few minutes later he was rung up by his friend, Robert Bárány, telling him that he had just had a terrifying dream in which he saw Ferenczi in a jungle, fighting with all sorts of wild animals, among them an elephant.

In due course, the letter of the thought reader appeared, containing utter rubbish.

I think Dr. Varró may have further details of this incident.

But Dr. Varró could only add a correction. The name of the dreamer was Robert Berény and not Bárány.

Ferenczi's psychic adventures between the two Felletár incidents and later are recorded by Jones.

On studying Jones's record of the correspondence between Ferenczi and Freud, one cannot help feeling that Ferenczi served as a scapegoat on whom Jones could vent his resentment against Freud for the many strange and uncanny experiences with which the father of psychoanalysis liked to regale him.

Jones would not admit that a telepathic or precognitive experience could be due to anything more than coincidence. He accused Freud of "an unexpected fund of credulity," noting that—under the influence of his friend Wilhelm Fliess—he was ready, as far back as the nineties, to believe even in numerology! He was also perturbed by Freud's unconscious magical actions to ward off evil, traced back as far as 1905, by his belief in omens (seeing a man who uncannily resembled him, Freud thought it portended his death), and his unconscious leaning to a belief in spirits. "So, after all, it is true that the dead return"—was Freud's first impression (as described in his Gradiva book in 1907) on meeting the sister of a deceased patient who resembled the dead woman.

It was soon after this that, to Jones's profound regret, Freud came under the influence of Ferenczi and Jung, his two chief friends who were very favorably inclined to occult beliefs.

The use of the word "occult" is significant. Jones never knew how to draw the line between occultism and psychic phenomena (a vagueness of orientation that he seemed to share with Freud). He merged superstition, numerology, astrology, telepathy, poltergeists, soothsayers and mediums into one grisly lump and hated them all—for fear of the harm the lump might do to the young science of psychoanalysis.

Jones is probably wrong in stating that Jung was the first to win Freud's interest in the "supernatural" by giving him a demonstration of knockings on the furniture in Freud's own room. Jones calls this "playing the Poltergeist," and practically makes a medium out of Jung because of the startling aftermath: Freud trying to imitate Jung after the latter's departure, but finding obvious physical reasons for any faint noises he observed, warned Jung to keep a cool head on the matter.

It is an odd coincidence that Jung began his mediumistic investigations in the same year (1899) that Ferenczi attended the Felletár séance. No doubt he and Ferenczi had a lot in common in this field but the break between Jung and Freud closed this channel of mutual experimentation and exchange of ideas too soon.

To evaluate all the psychic adventures about which Ferenczi and Freud exchanged ideas and the attempts that Ferenczi made to bring this new knowledge within the realm of psychoanalysis would require a special study. When some of the people concerned who are still living have passed away, Dr. Bálint promises to attend to this fascinating task. I understand that the whole correspondence has been transcribed and a microfilm of the originals has been deposited in the Freud Archives in Washington.

In the meantime it is possible to list a number of the psychic adventures which Freud and Ferenczi jointly discussed. Jones tells us that in 1909 on the homeward journey from America, Freud and Ferenczi visited a "soothsayer" in Berlin, a Frau Seidler of whom Ferenczi had heard from a brother who lived in Berlin. The clairvoyant, blindfolded, read letters, but Freud, according to Jones, saw through the trick. However, both Freud and Ferenczi were inclined to think that Frau Seidler did have telepathic powers and had read Ferenczi's thought concerning Freud. They decided to put the matter to another test. Finally, Freud concluded that Frau Seidler did possess a "physiological gift" that enabled her to perceive someone else's thoughts, though often with distortions. He swore Ferenczi to absolute silence on the matter.

Ferenczi then sent several letters to his brother in Berlin who took them to Frau Seidler, but nothing much seems to have come of this. Nor did much come, according to Jones, of Ferenczi's visits to a "soothsayer in Budapest named Frau Jelinek."

Some months later Ferenczi sent Freud notes of what a

47

homosexual masochistic patient had said at the beginning of an analytical hour. It had happened on several occasions that the patient's words reminded Ferenczi of thoughts he himself had had in the previous twenty-four hours. The data deeply impressed Freud, Jones admits, and Freud said that henceforth there could be no possible doubt about the reality of thought-transference.

Freud then communicated to Ferenczi data about a patient of his who had consulted Frau Arnold, known in Munich as the "Court Astrologist." He gave Ferenczi the address of Frau Arnold so that he could consult her, and he himself published the case some 20 years later.

Ferenczi continued to send Freud examples of telepathy from his homosexual masochistic patient and finally declared that he himself was "an excellent soothsayer or thought reader." Jestingly, Ferenczi said that he intended to present himself as the "Court Astrologist of Psychoanalysts." More seriously, he proposed to publish his data and conclusions, but Freud suggested that he wait two years, until 1913.

The next narrative of the Freud-Ferenczi relationship adventures into the best example of telepathy he had so far encountered: the case of the woman who was to bear twins at the age of 32. And Ferenczi told about the soldier in a tramcar whose name he had correctly guessed. Freud at first could not attribute this to telepathy, but later conceded something to Ferenczi's argument that a man's name was a sensitive area that could be communicated to a stranger.

The next narrative of the Freud–Ferenczi adventures into psychic phenomena appears in 1912—the wonderful horse in Elberfield, Germany, "the clever Hans," who could add, subtract, draw circles, and perform other feats that showed, it was argued, that telepathy was a primitive endowment in animals. Ferenczi was excited about the horse, but Freud did not think the feats of the clever animal indicated the operation of telepathy. He thought that the native intelligence of animals accorded well enough with his ideas of the unconscious.

Soon afterward, Freud who had not heard from Ferenczi for several days resolved that he would write Ferenczi and ask the reason. Then he inferred from his resolution that Ferenczi was in fact writing him a letter from Budapest—"a telepathic message to this effect presumably reaching him," Jones interjects—and he delayed writing so that their letters should not cross. And soon a letter from Ferenczi did arrive.

In the fall of 1913 Ferenczi addressed the Vienna Society meeting and brought with him a soothsayer called "Professor" Alexander Roth who proved a dismal failure, according to Jones. Four days later Freud arranged a séance for Roth at his own home, after which he refused to give him a testimonial. Ferenczi, however, had already given Roth a testimonial which Freud wanted him to recover. Ferenczi could not see his way to do this, but he gave up for the time being any intention to publish on the subject of telepathy.

In November 1914, Freud's half-brother Emmanuel died, and Ferenczi gave the opinion that his death was a confirmation of a prediction Jung had made, namely, that a great misfortune would happen to Freud in 1914. Nonsense, said Freud, or words to that effect.

This almost ends the list Jones has drawn up of Freud–Ferenczi discussions. In 1924 Ferenczi told Freud that he would like to give an account of his telepathic experiments at the Homburg Congress scheduled for 1925, and Freud wrote back: *"Don't do it."*

A full treatment of all the material listed by Jones necessarily awaits the publication of Dr. Bálint's special study.

Jones's deep-seated prejudice is best illustrated by his concluding statement about Ferenczi's "evil genius," an ex-patient who made Ferenczi believe that "he was being successfully psychoanalyzed by messages transmitted telepathically across the Atlantic."

Jones says it was Freud who called this woman Ferenczi's "evil genius." I thought for a time that the woman might have been my good friend, Elizabeth Severn, the New York psychoanalyst who was analyzed and trained by Ferenczi. However, shortly before her death Elizabeth Severn assured me that the woman was somebody else and that she knew her identity. Unfortunately, I failed to make a further investigation. The woman was then still living and could have answered Jones's charge. I must add that I find it quite possible that the "evil" existed only in Jones's fervid imagination.

The Incredible Psychic Life
of Dr. Carl G. Jung

My entrance as a researcher into the incredible psychic life of
Dr. Carl G. Jung grew out of unsuspected, highly personal
and dramatic circumstances through my first contact with Dr.
Sigmund Freud in London, during the latter's exile, in the year
1939.[1]

The motives that had led Freud to take an interest in the
manuscript of my Poltergeist investigation (subsequently published as *On the Trail of the Poltergeist*)[2] were, at the time,
unknown to me, and only emerged after the publication of
Ernest Jones's third volume of *The Life and Work of Sigmund
Freud*, in 1957.

In this volume, in the chapter on Occultism, Jones makes
brief mention of Jung's first visit to Freud on March 25,
1909, on which occasion he (Jung) "displayed his powers as
a Poltergeist by making various articles in the room rattle on
the furniture." [3]

Jones sensed the connection between this early experience of
Freud—to which he applied the wrong terminology—and his
letter on my manuscript, and he reprinted the letter (in his
own translation) *in extenso* in the same volume.[4] However, he
only rendered a desultory account of Jung's demonstration,
and made a cursory mention only of Freud's letter to Jung,
three weeks later, and not immediately, as he said. Apparently,
Freud needed the intervening time to recover from the shock
of Jung's demonstration.

Only with the publication in May 1963 of Jung's posthumous
Memories, Adventures and Reflections (Pantheon Books, N.Y.)
and partly through an advance account in *The Atlantic* magazine (Nov. 1962) has the full story of the momentous meeting
between the two giants of psychology come to light.[5]

---

[1] "Freud and the Poltergeist," Nandor Fodor, *Psychoanalysis*, Vol. IV,
No. 2, Winter 1955-56.
[2] Citadel Press, New York, 1958.
[3] Vol. III, p. 383.
[4] *Ibid.*, p. 396.
[5] *Memories, Adventures and Reflections*, pp. 155, 361-363.

To understand Jung's astounding self-revelation of this feat of modern sorcery we must review the hereditary background of the great psychologist as first revealed by his secretary, Aniela Jaffé: *C. G. Jung und die Parapsychologie, Zeitschrift fur Parapsychologie und Grenzgebiete der Psychologie* (Munchen, Vol. IV, No. 1, 1960); published in translation as: "The Psychic World of C. G. Jung." [6]

Jungian psychologists must have been grievously affected by being told that Jung's grandfather and grandmother were ghost seers, and that Jung's mother had kept a diary in which she recorded ghostly phenomena, presentiments and other unusual occurrences in his parents' house.

One of the psychic gifts that Jung inherited from his parents is called *telekinesis:* the ability to move objects at a distance without contact or to produce explosive sounds in them.[7] Jung had no doubt about the supernormal character of such phenomena. In his present reminiscences he gives an account of the somatic sensations he had at the time of his demonstration to Freud. When, in his early years, a bread knife split with a loud sound in the kitchen drawer and fell into four pieces— apparently due to his mother's agency in the psychic sense— he had the pieces photographed and sent a copy of the picture to Dr. Rhine at Duke University.[8]

Apparently, Jung had used his inherited witch-like power in an unconscious aggression against Freud in the two incidents of Freud's fainting in his presence in 1909 and in 1912.[9] Freud promptly accused Jung of death wishes against him, though he did not dwell on the problem how such wishes could have knocked him out. Jung denied the charge, but he began to wonder when, in a dream,[10] he made Freud into an old-fashioned, decrepit ghost.

After his break with Freud, Jung seemed to have developed a Judas complex, the first signs of which appeared in print in his *Psychology of the Unconscious.*[11] Before Christmas of 1912, he actually killed Freud in a dream. Of course, his victim

[6] *Tomorrow* magazine, New York, Spring 1961.

[7] *Op. cit., Memories,* pp. 104-106.

[8] *Reach of the Mind,* by J. B. Rhine, William Sloan's, 1947, pp. 89-90.

[9] *Op. cit.,* Jones: *Sigmund Freud,* Vol. II, p. 146, Vol. I, p. 317; *op. cit.,* Jung: *Memories,* pp. 151-156; Fodor: "Jung, Freud, and a Newly-Discovered Letter on the Poltergeist Theme," *The Psychoanalytic Review,* Summer 1963.

[10] *Op. cit., Memories,* p. 163.

[11] Dodd, Mead and Company, 1916, pp. 37-40.

was disguised, from "Sig" Freud he became Siegfried, of the Wagnerian saga, whose father was Sigmond like the father of psychoanalysis. In the very dream, his conscience threatened him with terrible retribution. A voice said, on waking, that he would have to kill himself if he failed to understand the dream. He grew frightened because he kept a loaded revolver in his desk. Then, in a flash, understanding came. Siegfried stood for a ruthless drive for power in himself, and he had to free himself from this megalomanic trait. However, it never occurred to him how close Siegfried was to "Sig" Freud and that it was from Freud and his ideas that he wished to liberate himself by an act of violence. He did not want to be Freud's Crown Prince and successor, to which role Freud had already appointed him; he wanted to be the whole works, a Caesar by divine right—and he supported this feeling of destiny by another dream, shortly following, in which the Holy Ghost descended on him in the shape of a dove.[12]

Presently, Elijah appeared to Jung, but instead of Moses he was accompanied by a blind Salome and a big black snake. In a subsequent dream or vision (by this time the line of demarcation between the two began to fade out) Philemon came flying through the sky, horned like the sacred bull of Mithraic worship and his wings shining with the color of a kingfisher—a hint for later Redeemer fantasies of becoming a Fisher of men. Philemon (a servant of the gods in Greek mythology) became Jung's spirit-guide. Walking up and down in the garden in full waking consciousness, Jung carried on conversations with him, as Cromwell used to consult his Devil or Socrates his Daimon.

By this time Jung was aware that he was in a state of psychotic breakdown.[13] He states that but for his professional work and love of family the last shreds of sanity might have snapped. The risk of going insane was the penalty he had to pay for the stupendous uprush from his unconscious. It lasted for five to six years and the revelations kept him supplied with material for his psychological researches for the next 45 years.[14]

The guilt feeling concerning Freud does not sufficiently explain this psychotic phase of Jung's life. Heredity was the chief dominant. His classical doctoral thesis of 1899 on *The*

[12] *Op. cit., Memories,* pp. 171-172.
[13] *Ibid.,* pp. 170-199.
[14] *Ibid.,* pp. 189-192.

Psychology and Pathology of So-Called Occult Phenomena[15] was based on his studies of a young spiritualist girl-medium in whose séances Jung's grandfather appeared to be one of the spirit-guides. Jung kept it as a dark secret that the 16-year-old girl was his own cousin. Her initials were S. W. and her grandfather and Jung's grandfather, acting hand in glove in the séance room, may have supplied a strong incentive for Jung's later obsession with ancestral life.

Jung's father was a Protestant minister. So was his grandfather who could only write his sermons in peace when his daughter (Jung's mother) stood guard over him and kept at bay the spirits that disturbed him. Jung's grandfather was also Grandmaster of Masons and—according to gossip—a natural son of Goethe. The gossip was never substantiated, but Jung showed its spell by a fascination for Goethe and Faust all his life. He said:

> Goethe had virtually written the basic outline of my own conflicts and solutions. The dichotomy of Faust and Mephistopheles came together within myself into a single person, and I was that person.[16]

To this fantastic statement should be added that Jung fancied he was living, simultaneously, in two ages (a kind of Bridey Murphy story with self-hypnosis), and that—in his fascination for the 18th century—he actually accepted the image of an old man as his real self.[17]

The descent of the Holy Ghost and the arrival of Philemon produced a fantastic development in Jung's life. Under the influence of several dreams he became obsessed with the idea that the dead live but can only gain knowledge through the consciousness of the living. Hence, he accepted it as his duty to instruct the dead.[18] Under the influence of Philemon this conviction culminated in writing his bewildering *Septem Sermones Ad Mortuos.*[19]

This writing of the *Seven Sermons to the Dead* was preceded by a pandemonium of pentecostal proportions in Jung's own

---

[15] *Psychiatric Studies, Collected Works,* Vol. I, pp. 3-88, published by Pantheon Books, 1957.

[16] *Op. cit., Memories,* p. 35.

[17] *Ibid.,* pp. 34-35, 235, 291, 319.

[18] *Ibid.,* pp. 305-306, 309, 315.

[19] Privately printed by Neill and Company, Ltd., Edinburgh, 1925, p. 103.

house. He dreamed that he had lost his soul,[20] then he became a haunted man. There was an outbreak of Poltergeist phenomena and other supernormal manifestations. Spirits of the dead came crowding in and demanded in a loud voice to be instructed. His son dreamed of a fisherman whose head was a chimney with smoke shooting heavenward. The following day Jung found a dead kingfisher in his garden. As Philemon's wings, when he first appeared, reflected the colors of a kingfisher, Jung could not fail to associate these events with the Fisher of men and the Holy Ghost which, to him, was "a manifestation of the inconceivable God." [21] So he worked uninterruptedly for three days on the *Seven Sermons,* and when he finished them, Philemon was satisfied and the dead left the house.

Jung writes of his mother that "by day she was a loving mother, at night she seemed uncanny. Then she was like one of those seers who is at the same time a strange animal, like a priestess in a bear cave. Archaic and ruthless." [22]

He was not far from falling in with this description himself by now. It should occasion no surprise that, after his initiation into Spiritualism by his cousin, Jung began to experiment with some mediums of the day, notably with Rudi Schneider and Oscar Schlag, two strange people in whose powers Baron Schrenck-Notzing, the famous German sexologist, was deeply interested. In a letter to Prof. Fritz Blanke,[23] Jung declared himself convinced that he had seen genuine parapsychological phenomena (including telekinesis and materialization). An article by Dr. Bernoulli, in whose house the séances took place, bears out this statement.[24] Further, in Dr. Fanny Moser's book, *Spook,* we have a sensational story told by Jung himself of his experience in a haunted house in England in 1920.

At the age of 3 Jung had a dream that he kept to himself for 65 years, though it had a profound influence on his life.[25] It was a birth dream with an element of phallic worship. As Jung had accused Freud of making a god out of sex, it is odd that all his life he had concealed a personal apotheosis of the same divinity.

---

[20] *Op. cit., Memories,* pp. 189-192.
[21] *Ibid.,* p. 98.
[22] *Ibid.,* pp. 50-51.
[23] Published in *Neue Wissenschaft,* Vol. VII, 1951, p. 14.
[24] Published in *Zeitschrift fur Parapsychologie,* 1931, p. 315.
[25] *Op. cit., Memories,* pp. 11-13.

Only a very short summary can adequately show how far reaching Jung's interest was in psychical, mythological and parapsychological matters.

One of the many contributions for which Jung will long be remembered is his theory of *synchronicity:* an explanation of meaningful coincidences beyond the law of cause and effect.[26] He saw a mythological revelation in flying saucers,[27] and dreamed about them.[28] He had premonitions of approach,[29] déjà vû experiences,[30] prophetic dreams (death of his mother, torn by the Wolf of the Wild Huntsman),[31] he traveled with the dead,[32] had clairvoyant experiences,[33] received telepathic messages,[34] and had personal experiences with God.[35] Next to this, the hearing of voices [36] is of small account. But all this is crowned by an enthralling revelation of being out of the body: he "died" in a heart attack,[37] but was called back and told an incredible story of the Beyond. For three weeks after his "death" he was in a state of delirium and in a state of ecstasy. He was in the *Pardes Rimmonim,* the cabalistic Garden of Pomegranates, and witnessed the wedding of Tifereth and Malchuth (two of the ten spheres of divine manifestations in which God emerges from his hidden place; they represent the male and female principles within the Godhead). Then he was Rabbi Simon ben-Jochai, whose wedding in the after-life was being celebrated. It was a mystic marriage that faded into the Marriage of the Lamb in Jerusalem at which angels were in attendance. That, too, vanished and in a last vision he saw the celebration of the Hierosgamos: in which All-Father Zeus and Mother Hera consummated in public the divine marriage as described in the *Iliad.*[38].

[26] Cf. The Story of the Golden Scarab in *The Structure and Dynamics of the Psyche,* Jung, pp. 438, 526; fish coincidences (in the same volume), pp. 423-427.
[27] Cf. *Flying Saucers,* Harcourt, Brace and Company, New York, 1959.
[28] *Op. cit., Memories,* p. 323.
[29] *Op. cit., Structure and Dynamics,* pp. 521-522.
[30] *Ibid.,* pp. 522-523, and *op. cit., Memories,* pp. 254-255.
[31] *Ibid.,* p. 313.
[32] *Ibid.,* p. 312.
[33] *Ibid.,* pp. 50-51.
[34] *Op. cit., Structure and Dynamics,* pp. 317, 413-415, 520-531.
[35] *Op. cit., Memories,* pp. 10-11, 48.
[36] *Ibid.,* p. 313; Hans Bender: *Wunderheilung,* 1963.
[37] *Op. cit., Memories,* p. 291.
[38] *Ibid.,* pp. 293-294.

All this is a revelation of how, after his fight with Freud, Jung cast back his sexual emotions into the mythological age. We read nothing about Jung's romantic life, his courtship of his wife and the birth of his children, in a biography of nearly 400 pages. Not a word is said about the love of women in Jung's early life, but there is a hint at a tremendous disappointment that must have jaundiced his attitude to the female sex. Apparently, Jung was in love with his young cousin, the spiritualist medium, and her exposure in fraud must have hit him and wounded him to the core. He could neither forgive nor forget her deception, but we can guess the depth of his emotions from a dream he had about his wife after her death.[39]

> She was in her prime, perhaps about thirty, and wearing the dress which had been made for her many years before by my cousin, the medium. It was perhaps the most beautiful thing she had ever worn. Her expression was neither joyful nor sad, but rather objectively wise and understanding, without the slightest emotional reaction, as though she were beyond the mist of affects [sic].

The message that Jung failed to understand was the knowledge that throughout her marriage his wife stood for the never-forgotten young girl, the medium in whose footsteps she followed, and that she is no longer upset by this emotional substitution.

S. W., the cousin who was responsible for Jung's wonderful fantasies of a previous life and for his unforgettable dreams in the present, died at the age of 26. This was a blow from which Jung never recovered.

[39] Ibid., p. 296.

PART II.

HIGHWAYS AND BYWAYS
OF THE MIND

Introduction. The most enigmatic thing in this universe is the human mind. Telepathy and foretelling of the future is an openly discussed problem of our day, but the human mind operates in many other mysterious ways that are comparatively little known. We can hear voices without being insane, we can act like ghosts without being haunted or haunting, mind can affect mind in a variety of ways, dreams have yet-undisclosed secrets, memory may not be a mental monopoly but belong to an ocean of life from which strange adventures may beset you, under a dominating idea your personality may change into another one and you may fall victim to a curse because your mental defences are down.

All this, and more, will be discussed in the chapters that follow.

In the romantic period of his early life, Freud had auditory hallucinations. As told by himself:

> When as a young man I lived alone in a strange city, I frequently heard my name being pronounced by an unmistakable, dear voice, and I then made note of the exact moment of the hallucination in order to inquire carefully of those at home what had occurred at that time. There was nothing to it.[1]

Ernest Jones, Freud's biographer, commented:

> He was specially lonely at the time and also finding it hard to understand the foreign speech. As is well known, this belongs to the banal type of hallucination that lonely tourists so often experience when abroad, the incomprehensible words of the natives being "assimilated" through the mechanism of wish fulfilment into more familiar and welcome expressions. But Freud had to make note of the exact time of each of these occurrences and then to inquire what was happening to his beloved at that precise moment, actions which clearly postulate a belief in the possibility of messages being transmitted in space through hundreds of miles.[2]

Loneliness is a good clue but does not go deep enough. In search of companionship the mind may wander into the future or into the past. The need of love that made Freud's mind seek his fianceé has its foundation in the deeper desire to re-experience the mother's love and support. The fascination by the Beloved is an echo of this early spell, so beautifully described by Byron:

[1] *Psychopathology of Everyday Life*, Fisher Unwin, Ltd., London, 1920, p. 313.

[2] *Op. cit., Sigmund Freud*, Basic Books ed., Vol. III, p. 380.

I have a passion for the name of Mary,
For once it was a magic sound to me;
And still it half-recalls the realm of fairy
Where I beheld what never was to be:
All feelings change, but this was least to vary,
A spell from which even yet I am not free.

(*Don Juan*, Canto Fifth, IV.)

It is the voice of Mother that calls to us from the dim past
when we hear our name. The hallucination satisfies an emotional need because the sound of our name is the strongest
auditory association with our childhood. For an adult, the
name is a point of contact with the rest of humanity; for the
child it meant that identity was bestowed upon him. It dis-
tinquished him from another child, it stood for the self, it
was the foundationstone of this being. No wonder then that
there is magic in the name and that Mother should be the
first person its sound evokes.[3]

I will not go into clinical evidence to prove this. People
who do not like to face life, wake up in the morning with
great difficulty and in a very disagreeable mood. An epileptic
patient of mine was a particular victim of this morning
madness. I suggested that her husband should awaken her
by softly calling her name. The advice worked and the morning
rage was completely cured because the tone of the voice
assured her of love instead of discord. It is a common practice
to awaken a hypnotic subject who refuses to return to consciousness by calling his name. Practitioners of magic used
to evoke principalities and powers by their name. The Tetra-
grammaton is a cypher for the ineffable name of God by the
knowledge of which miracles could be worked. The masonic
quest for the Secret Word of Master Masons centers on this
ancient mystery. The name of God is evoked against evil, and
malefactors are still being arrested in the name of the law.

Those who remember the delightful motion picture "The
Ghost Goes West," will find in it an excellent illustration of
the association with a parental figure of the sound of our
name. Whenever the romantic young hero tries to flirt, he
hears the imperious voice of his father warning him off by

---

[3] "Nomen est Omen," by Nandor Fodor, *Samiksa*, Calcutta, Vol. X,
No. 1, 1956.

calling: *DONALD!* He looks up toward heaven, says meekly: "Yes, Father," and turns away from the girl.

Authorities that played an important role in our early life may step into the parental role. I recall a curious personal experience from my high school days. When the head teacher was turning the pages of his class book (in which he put marks of evaluation of his students after each recital), I used to feel a sudden stab of pain, an icy feeling running down my spine just before he reached my name in the alphabetical list, and I rose automatically and gathered my papers before he called it out. The stab of pain was not due to an overall anxiety. It was specific and it never failed. It was a phenomenon of *déjà entendu.*

The element of interaction was entirely missing in an earlier auditory experience that I had around 7 years of age. My grandfather was being buried. There was a ladder leaning against the wall of the cemetery near the grave. I was doing gymnastics on it and felt happy and unconcerned. I think I was profiting from his death. He was accustomed to cover his head with a long muslin sheet to protect himself from the flies. The muslin was promised to me for a butterfly net. I was looking forward to the happy chase when suddenly I spun around as if I had been shot in the back and gaped at the group around the coffin. I saw them opening it for a last blessing and I heard, as clearly as I ever heard anything, my grandfather answering back. No one found it unusual, so—after a while—I assumed that the dead have the last word, and said nothing. A year or two later I discovered that I was wrong, but by then it was too late to speak of the experience.

Perhaps, it was my conscience—the still small voice that tried to lodge a protest against my behavior. Grandfathers enter into a chain of ancestral associations, as I learned much later in pondering the ancient cry of the prophets: *Speak, O Lord, thy servant heareth.* I did not know what my grandfather was saying because the voice spoke Hebrew. It shook me a little; my guilt feeling manifested itself in subsequent years by a constant doodle of the initial of his name.

The voice that the prophets heard was followed by wonders. When Elijah hid himself in a cave from his would-be murderers and cried out to the Lord, he heard the command:

Go forth, and stand upon the mount before the Lord!
And, behold, the Lord passed by

And a great and strong wind rent the mountains,
And broke in pieces the rocks before the Lord;
But the Lord was not in the wind;
And after the wind an earthquake;
But the Lord was not in the earthquake;
And after the earthquake a fire;
But the Lord was not in the fire;
And after the fire a still small voice.

(1 Kings 19:9-12)

When Habakkuk heard a voice ordering him to take pottage to Daniel, he was lifted by the Spirit of the Lord and transported over the lions' den. When John baptised Jesus, the Heavens opened up, the Holy Ghost descended in the shape of a dove and "a voice from Heaven" uttered the undying words: "This is my Beloved Son in whom I am well pleased!"

This is a far cry from the voice of conscience that is usually associated with the still small voice. The phenomenal reactions cover a very wide range. I am still deeply puzzled by the effect that Hitler's rabble-rousing voice had on me long after the World War Two. I listened to his speech on two occasions in a broadcasting studio. His German, due to his raucous and harsh inflection, was totally incomprehensible, but slowly, ever so slowly, my blood began to boil, and I wanted to shout and scream. It was not a rage against him. It was *with him*, like a flow of lava is with the volcano. Then the realization hit me: some quality in his voice reduced me to a member of the mob. It was a lesson in the psychology of the crowd—and I shivered from the reaction.

Some people create voices that endure. W. M. Thackeray confessed: [4]

I have been surprised at the observations made by some of my characters. It seems as if an occult power was moving my pen. The personage does or says something and I ask: "How did he come to think of that?"

More surprising than this is the confession of Dickens to his old friend, James Field about how he was haunted by the

[4] "Roundabout Papers," *Cornhill Magazine*, Aug. 1862.

creatures of his imagination while writing of them in *The Old Curiosity Shop* and *Martin Chuzzlewit*.

The story is close to sorcery and spirit communication. I want to parallel it by a statement made by T. Herbert Noyes, B.A., before the London Dialectical Society during an investigation of the claims of Spiritualism:

> I know that I should excite the derision of the skeptics if I were to say that I have conversed with spirits after a fashion which was asserted to be that in which spirits communicate with each other—by an "inner voice," which I could only compare to the sensation which would be caused by a telegraphic apparatus being hooked on to one of the nerve ganglia—a distinctly audible click accompanying every syllable of the communication, which one could not say one heard, but of which one was made conscious by a new sense, and which was clearly distinguishable from thoughts originated in one's own mind.

Lest we should be carried away too far and too soon, let us give consideration to the voice of the "Maggid" which Joseph Caro, a famous figure in Judaism, the author of *Shulhan Aruk* or *The Prepared Table* (a book and code for religious Jews), had heard for 52 years of his life, accepting it as an invisible messenger from Heaven, a familiar spirit, a divine mentor.

Quoting from H. L. Gordon's analysis in *The Maggid of Caro*,[5] Dr. Sylvano Ariety writes:[6]

> While Caro was bent over his sacred tomes in search of deeper meanings, grave fears and daring ambitions would rise in his soul. The spirit would then enter Caro's mouth, articulate his tongue, and reveal his destiny, unveil the coming events of his life.
>
> Caro described all these experiences in a book called *Maggid Mesharim*. It is uncertain whether, from a technical point of view, we should call Caro's experiences hallucinations or delusions. Thus, if Caro was hearing his own voice, used by the Maggid, the phenomenon would be more delusional than hallucinatory. In some

---

[5] Pardes, New York, 1949.
[6] "The Loss of Reality," *Psychoanalysis*, 1961, pp. 21-22.

passages, however, Caro refers to the voice of the Maggid as the "Voice of my Beloved" which "began to resound again in my mouth." At any rate, whether these experiences are predominantly delusional and only occasionally hallucinatory or not, it does not matter very much. The important point is that no matter how we classify them, these phenomena usually are found in psychotics.

In his book, Dr. Gordon, who is both a rabbi and a psychiatrist, asks the questions whether Caro was mentally ill, and if so what psychiatric syndrome did he have.

We know many things about the life and work of Caro, up to the time of his death. Gordon, reviewing them, rightly concludes that Caro was not mentally ill. It is thus obvious that Caro's abnormal experiences of 52 years' duration occurred while he was in religious ecstasies or in a state of autohypnosis and have to be included in the category of religious loss of reality. These experiences, however, had not a regressive, but on the contrary a very constructive effect, inasmuch as it was during these experiences that Caro could conceive and write the *Shulhan Aruk,* a book highly honored for centuries.

We meet with the same phenomenon in some unusual products of automatic writing. The first book of Marjorie Livingston, *The New Nuctameron,* was dictated by a voice. When it was finished, the voice—with some degree of reluctance—stated itself to be Apollonius of Tyana, giving back to the world a copy of his book that was lost in the burning of the Alexandrian Library. The book was good, but the claim is staggering. However, the literature of parapsychology abounds with similar wonders. The study has its dangers and delusions.

The late Violet Tweedale, a grand old Victorian lady and author of many books, told me of her bewilderment when, after a visit to Katherine Bates, a fellow writer, she received a letter from her profuse with thanks for her wonderful Derby tip.

"But I gave you no tip," she answered back.

"Oh yes, you did. You were sitting in your carriage and when I said good-bye, you told me that Good Fortune will win the Derby."

In talking to me about it, Violet Tweedale said: "I did not even know that there was such a horse. Nothing was further from my mind than giving Katherine Bates Derby tips."

The probability is that Katherine Bates' mind was too occupied with horses. Violet Tweedale may have used the words "good fortune" in wishing her farewell, and Miss Bates fell victim to a lucky trick of her own mind.

The voice of wish fulfilment pays to be watched. The story of the gambler at Las Vegas is a good illustration. After he lost steadily and left the tables in disgust, he heard a voice saying: "Go back, bet on 12." He went back and played, with the remnants of his funds, the number suggested. It won. As he wanted to withdraw the money, the voice spoke again: "Leave it." He did and he won. Again he wanted to withdraw the money, but the voice would not let him. So he left it the third time—and lost. Whereupon, the voice said: "Oh, hell!"

The story is fictitious, but it could be true. A voice that shouts a warning may preserve your life but it may also lead to disaster. All depends on the health of the psyche. A disordered mind may embark on murder or on a religious mission and ascribe it to the Voice of God. It is surprising how often the voice heard on radio becomes a means of schizophrenic evocation. Psychotics hear themselves discussed or complain of radio waves being used against them.

Another mystery emerges from the power that sound and voice have over the animal kingdom. Reporting for *The New York Times* from Harrar, Ethiopia, on January 1, 1962, special correspondent Jay Walz stated:

> One old Harrarite, inhabiting a hut near the wall (of the city), sleeps in the daytime. At night, he practices the art for which he is celebrated even as far away as Addis Ababa, 220 miles to the West. This is summoning wild hyenas from their hillside lairs to eat out of his hand. . . .
>
> The Hyena Man, as this ancient is known, sits outside his hut as night falls and gives out a startling hyena laugh. Presently, hyenas show up by ones and twos, to take from the fingers of the Hyena Man an old bone, or better, a scrap of meat.

Does the story indicate a definite affinity between man and hyena, near enough to a psychological disposition to lycanthropy? I am inclined to doubt it. The hyena call is imitable. It is quite possible that it would be obeyed and strengthened by the reward of tidbits the old man threw to the beasts. Yet moderate manifestation of a similar affinity occurs in the life of human beings with less exotic animals. At haunted Aldborough Manor in Yorkshire England I met a 16-year-old maid from whom mice did not run but nestled in her hand and on whose shoulders birds would descend and follow her into the house with an apparent feeling of complete confidence and security. However, the story rests on the creditable statement of Lady Lawson-Tancred, the owner of the Manor House where Joan, the maid, was the center of mysterious bell-ringing phenomena. I do not know whether she had to speak to the birds and mice before she got close to them, but I know of the legend centering around Irish horsetamers. It tells of a mysterious word they would whisper into the ear of a wild horse, which thereupon becomes completely docile. It is not the word that does it. They blow hot air into the ear of the horse and the horse happens to like it.

The same response is the explanation of the sudden return of milk in the udder of "dry" cows when the wise woman of the village manipulates them in secret. I have a friend who is the son of a wise woman. He knows the secret from his mother. It is not in a word but in a weasel skin. His mother learned it from her own mother that by gently rubbing the udders with the smooth skin, the cows will gratefully respond.

Another secret of this kind is the possession of a word that, when pronounced over a wound, immediately stops it from bleeding. This is an Irish secret, handed down from father to son. The power in it undoubtedly is due to hereditary suggestion.

It does bring us to a consideration of words of power which we find abundant in fairy lore, magical and religious literature. According to Aubrey,[7] the fairies utter *HORSE AND HATTOCK* (Scottish for hat) when they wish to carry away somebody. Witches improved upon it by adding: Horse and Hattock in the Devil's name, or

> Horse and Hattock, horse and go
> Horse and Pellatis, ho, ho!

In France the Devil spoke Latin. The magic word was *CITO, CITO*, which means quick.[8]

---

[7] *Miscellanies*, 1721, p. 158.
[8] *Mind Over Space*, 1962, pp. 43-44.

In religious literature the magic word varies with individuals. St. Peter of Alcantara was unable to hear the lofty words of St. John: *Verbum caro factum est,* without falling into ecstasy and being raised above the earth. The Franciscan Biagie of Caltanisetta went into ecstasy by hearing *JESUS AND MARY.* Enraptured with the beauty of the words, he sprang into the air!

In an earlier age one heard of a primitive or nature language. It began with the famous Elizabethan astrologer, Dr. John Dee (1527–1608). It was supposed to be the tongue of man before the Fall, and Hebrew was alleged to be its corrupted form. This "angelic" language was revealed to Dr. Lee by his assistant, Edward Kelly, a rogue of many hues who acted for him as a trance medium. Each name expressed the properties of the thing spoken of and the utterance of that name had a compelling power over that creature. Several later mystics adopted the notion and as late as the times of Dr. Julius Kerner (1786–1862), a patient of his called Frau Frederica Hauffe, better known as the Seeress of Prevorst, spoke and wrote in it. In the latter half of the 19th Century this odd belief vanished. But the idea of the compelling power of a name over animals here and there still persists. Paul Brunton in *A Search in Secret Egypt* explained the snake charmers' ability of calling out a snake from its hiding place on the utterence of the *real* name of the snake. The belief in this type of magic may originate from Genesis. God gave dominion to Man "over the fish of the sea, over the fowl of the air, and over every living thing that moves upon Earth." A racial wish fulfilment had to be expected, if not *de facto,* at least by pretense.

The only nature language that we know of today as the fundamentals of communication is the call and the cry in the animal world. There is a call for food, for mating, for distress and for cooperative functioning. Porpoises whistle for help if attacked by sharks, and by concerted, torpedo-like action of their snouts, disembowel the enemy.[9] There is a good deal of evidence that porpoises and whales have a language of their own. Crows are said to hold a court and pass a judgment of excommunication on a guilty crow that dejectedly awaits the verdict in the middle of the circle. Bees communicate by

[9] The *Reader's Digest*, Feb. 1962, p. 108.

dancing, ants seem to use their antennas for sending out messages, other animals may use gestures.

I vividly remember an instance in Central Park. I was feeding the pigeons with bread crumbs. Suddenly, I felt a tug at the end of my trousers in the back. I turned around. There was a squirrel standing on two legs, looking at me as if to say: What about me?

The chatter of monkeys may express a lot more than we know. The point at which the babble of animals ceases to be a play with sounds and approaches communication is not easy to determine. But there is a similar stage of transition in human development from the babble of children to speaking in tongues. This is an age-old phenomenon, well known since Biblical days. Judgment on it always depended on the point of view: It was either a sign of the presence of a demon or of celestial inspiration. The latter view still prevails in religious revivals. The coming of the tongues is a seizure. That words break forth with a frenzy that cannot be resisted by the sense is very questionable. The Martian "language" of Helen Smith, as investigated by Professor Theodor Flournoy,[10] was clearly proven of terrestrial and French origin. The same ingenious drawing on unconscious verbal residue applies to other languages from the stars. Even Theresa Neumann's Aramaic is a debatable question because the phrases she uttered exist in print with translation into modern languages. The most puzzling of such linguistic feats is perhaps the archaic Chinese that Dr. Neville Whymant, an Oriental scholar, claims to have heard in trance messages from the medium, George Valiantine. He claimed, in *Psychic Adventures in New York*, that the voice ascribed to Confucius gave him "a complete new reading of the Analects of Confucius over which learned scholars differed for centuries." However, not one of the later experiments supported Dr. Whymant's sensational claims.[11]

My personal experiences with speaking in tongues were negative. I have made gramophone records of several American Indian languages spoken by Red Indian spirit-guides of English mediums. I sent them on to the Smithsonian Institution in Washington for analysis. The answer was: there is no such

---

[10] *From India to the Planet Mars*, reprinted in University Books, 1963.
[11] *Encyclopaedia of Psychic Science*, by Nandor Fodor, 1934, pp. 410-414.

Red Indian dialect; the words spoken are European gibberish.

I did hear, though, my native Hungarian spoken in my very first séance with William Cartheuser in 1928. The messages were excellent, but the diction was strange. It took me 20 years to discover that Cartheuser had his schooling in Hungary and that his Hungarian was the emergence of forgotten linguistic memories.[12]

Do then the tongues arise from childish babbling? I could support that conclusion by a dream adventure. I spoke a "foreign" language and when I woke up I could continue the utterances with a remarkable speed and fluency. But the syllabic frequency of the strange words that poured out of my mouth was repetitive and restricted, and I did not have the slightest doubt that they were utterly meaningless.

"About these voices you hear," a psychoanalyst was supposed to say to his patient, "have you ever considered an answering service?"

I am sure that I did not need one.

Ghosts Within and Without

Many years ago Andrew Lang made a memorable statement: Since the days of ancient Egypt ghosts have learned and forgotten nothing. This no longer holds true. Fortunately, we have learned a few things since then. Increasing knowledge of the unconscious mind of man has furnished us with some keys to this ancient mystery. In the least admission, the ghost is a vision or illusion; whether in dream, hypnotic sleep, trance, drug-induced state or religious ecstasy, it is actually perceived. It may be an image of the imagination, an hallucination, projection of repressed mental contents, wish- or fear-fulfilment, evidence of bad conscience or disorder of the mind; but it may well be something beyond all this: an apparition of the living asleep or of the dead, a telepathic perception, a vision of something in the past or in the future and it may be a happening beyond present understanding.

To take it in easy steps, let us approach the subject by

[12] *The Haunted Mind*, by Nandor Fodor, Helix Press, New York, 1960, pp. 23-36.

saying that the ghost is a product of the mind, conscious or unconscious (and, perhaps, even of the impersonal unconscious—on the line of Jung's archetypes). Appropriate headings on the road to understanding might be as follows.

The Ghost Is the It

The concept of the It has been introduced into psychoanalysis by Dr. Georg Groddeck, a brilliant Viennese physician. He considered the It the total mind (embracing the conscious and the unconscious) and said that we are lived by the It which kills us when we lose our usefulness.

A man had a recurrent dream of walking in a jungle, constantly dreading that a tiger may pounce upon him. One morning he was found dead. The conclusion was: the tiger jumped—and his heart killed him.

Plainly, the tiger was a ghost of the dreamer's mind. So was the other tiger that kept clawing Poltergeist-ridden Mrs. Forbes.[1] Whether the claw marks on her arms and back appeared through the conscious act of scratching or were hysterically produced, the tiger was a dangerous image in her mind.

The Ghost Is the Id

The Id is the name coined by Freud for the lumber room of the unconscious in which our worst instincts are kept in a state of repression. When the repression fails—as a result of excessive cruelty or other mental and physical shocks—the result is dissociation: an increasing encroachment on consciousness by the Id. "Why didn't you kill your father when you had the chance?" demanded an inner voice from a psychotic patient who had just returned from a visit to his father's farm. It is under the impulse of the Id that paranoid patients sometimes kill their psychiatrist or psychoanalyst. One persecution maniac whom I shall call Mr. Z. was driven away from me by the voices he heard and eventually found his way to Dr. John Rosen's office. Dr. Rosen succeeded in helping him but not before—on one particular occasion—Z. had seized him by his tie, and brandishing a jackknife shouted: "The voices told me to cut your throat!"

[1] See *On the Trail of the Poltergeist*, 1958.

The Ghost Is the Super-Ego

The super-ego is Freud's term for conscience deep down in the unconscious. In haunted Ash Manor House, after a spectacular attempt to lay the ghost through an interview with the entranced Eileen Garrett, whose body the ghost seemed to possess, a strange aftermath developed. The owner of the haunted house rang me up in despair: "The ghost is no longer in that house alone, but it is in me, too!" The ghost-laying broke up the mechanism of projection and the ghost returned home to roost.

The Ghost Is the Family Pattern

Hereditary suggestion, compulsive conformation to family traditions, sharing in the shame and guilt of ancestors and the psychological entity I call the *Family Gestalt*—an independent mental mechanism built up through generations of family pride and worship—can create a ghost specific to ancient feudal families, such as witnessed in British ancestral hauntings.

The Ghost Is a Tyrant

This is a case of rebellion against the *Pater Familias*. A well-known British parapsychologist finds himelf incapable of accepting his own, sometimes rather remarkable experiences because he had a tyrannical father and—as I found out from his dream life—he had identified the supernormal with the father authority. Hence, every ghost was his father, and he had to defend himself against each to the last breath with continual denial.

The Ghost Is Fictional or a Hoax

No explanation is required. This type of ghost obviously only exists in the conscious mind of its creator. One may recall a terrifying story by Arthur Conan Doyle of a materialization séance in which—due to the intense concentration of one of the sitters—a unicorn appeared, and threatened them with death and destruction. Fortunately, the séance and the unicorn were the products of the author's imagination.

My attempted investigation of a victim of the vampire foxes of Hungary rested also on fictional ground, instigated by the spirit of mischief. Nor did the horror story of Mrs. Forbes' vampire visitation rest on other facts than she consciously or unconsciously dreamed up.

So far so good. The sceptic has not yet been forced into the open. But he probably will be when the psychic element enters into this analysis in increasing measure.

The Ghost Is a Werewolf
or a Familiar

These creatures are kith and kin to the vampire. They serve destructive instincts of the unconscious and may also furnish a mechanism of escape from the human level by means of an evolutionary regression.[2] Recently, I appeared as a werewolf in the dream of a male patient because I was a threat to his Id that wanted him to be a girl. This was a similar motivation to the vampire case of Mrs. Forbes. There, in a sense, the vampire was also the psychoanalyst: I happened to discover her in a gross fraud that threatened her promising psychic career with total ruination.

The familiar of the witches seems to have died out. The nearest case I know of is that of the Talking Mongoose. (See Part III.) Geff, the mongoose, acted like a familiar in killing the geese and turkeys of a neighbor who spoke ill of the family of his host.

The Ghost Is a Legend,
Myth or Folklore

The Wandering Jew is an undying ghost. He is also Elijah, the prophet for whom the Jews still open the door at the Passover festival. For the Mormons it is the Three Nephtites who wander on the face of the Earth to do good. Fairies and the Little People fulfill—occasionally—the same function. I have known many people who have seen fairies in their child-

---

[2] "Lycanthropy as a Psychic Mechanism," *New Approaches to Dream Interpretation*, by Nandor Fodor, Citadel Press, New York, 1951, pp, 146-159; see also *The Haunted Mind*, op. cit., pp. 200-212.

hood, but I only had one firsthand story of the possession of a leprachaun by a beautiful Irish woman.[3] It fulfilled a very important need in her life: that of belonging to an old lineage which—for an orphan—was the fulfillment of a dream.

The Ghost Is a Paranoid, Sado-Masochistic and Self-Protective Projection

The fear of one's own desire often leads to persecutory delusions. Ghostly disturbances sidetrack attention from one's own problems. In Ash Manor House the haunting covered up a drama of homosexuality and kept a family together. The ghostly victim of murder could be a warning for the presence of homicidal tendencies.

The Poltergeist is unquestionably sadistic. It indicates projection aggression through unknown biological factors against authoritarian persons. It is the only way a youngster of pubertal age can discharge hostility with conscious innocence. The result can well be considerable destruction of household effects, but rarely is serious harm worked through this agency. One type of Poltergeist, however, can be exceedingly dangerous —it is the incendiary one. It produces spontaneous outbreaks of fire, occasionally burning down the house.

Masochism is manifested in stigmatic attacks, self-strangulation, blowing up of the body (aerophagia), writing appearing on the skin, or in the ghostly threats directed against the victim (and unconscious agent) of the ghost. "Esther Cox, you are mine to kill" was the terrible message that the Amherst ghost had etched into the plaster wall (before burning down the house). Obsession by a ghost can be no less frightening, nor does the smell of decomposition and a charnel house atmosphere present acceptable projections.

The spirit-guide is the best self-protective mechanism. It may originate from the depth of the unconscious to counteract the destructive instinct. I found this instance well demonstrated in the mediumship of Lajos Pap, the Hungarian carpenter who had two controls: an evil and a benevolent one. The sudden acquisition of the leprachaun by my beautiful Irish patient was another outstanding example.

---

[3] *The Haunted Mind, op. cit.,* pp. 209-212.

The Ghost Is a
Dramatic Memory

The so-called psychometric visions that reveal to sensitive persons the history of objects they held, or spread out historical visions of the past before their eyes, strongly suggest that we do not know everything about memory. It appears as if memory could slip away like the proverbial fish, and that it can exist beyond the mind that was its original host or that it belongs to the impersonal unconscious of Jung, to the *Anima Mundi* which is equivalent to the mediaeval concept of the Planetary Mind. In the East they call it Akashic Records. For the West, the Great Memory is a more commendable term. If there is such a memory and if it can spring into visual existence at certain times (particularly on anniversaries of fatal events), and at certain places where an emotional drama has been acted out, we could understand the blind automatism, the cinematic presentation that characterizes many psychic manifestations.

The Ghost Is a
Telepathic Perception

I have presented an excellent illustration in my *New Approaches to Dream Interpretation.*[4] It concerns the same Mr. Z. who had tried to kill Dr. John Rosen. Through his homosexual drives he became party, in a dream, to so-called astral projection experiment, which an analyst friend tried with me without advising me in advance. As far as I was concerned, the experiment failed, but my psychotic patient—who was sent to me by this analyst friend—latched on to it and dreamed of crawling out of his own body like a ghost. He thought that my friend was trying to do something to him and decided to kill him. Luckily, I was able to check his murderous impulse by explaining to him the incident as a case of telepathy *á trois*.

The Ghost is the Double or
Astral Body

The case of Mr. Z. is a good illustration. For another—and rather gruesome one—I would quote the confession of G. R. S.

[4] *Op. cit.*, pp. 184-187.

Mead, the great gnostic scholar, who felt attacked on the astral plane by his living enemies and had a terrible battle with them.[5] One need not, however, resort to sensational chronicles. The vision of the double—one's own or other living men's—is fairly frequent. It is an excellent illustration of the ghost within.

The Ghost Is the Devil

This is another illustration of the ghost within, and a rather frightening one. People who are certain that they will go to Hell because of their sins are the likeliest victims. A landscape painter used to torture himself as a child by looking—clandestinely—at Doré's illustration of Dante's Inferno. Then she would dash into the sunshine to get rid of the horror. She knew she was doing penance. She was brought up in the knowledge that if you commit a sin you would literally burn, and had an insatiable curiosity to know what Hell was like. The penance was both for herself (having been conceived before marriage) and for her mother who was called a "scarlet woman" and had contracted syphilis.

But the Devil may be more real than that. In a haunted house at Leeds in the Catskills I found the image of the Devil drawn with soap on a mirror, with the words: *Beware, We are Here!* Only I did not believe that the Devil was the one that tried to scare me. However, I know of a genuine scare that a strange woman experienced. She was a Devil-worshipper and, by hynotising her young secretary, she commanded him to bring up the Devil. After the sixth session—I was told— there was an earthy smell in the room, an icy cold and a dreadful breathing sound. Two eyes as big as eggs appeared and looked at her with an awful, penetrating expression. She heard the words: "The Evil that you conjured up speaks to you!" She shrieked, turned on the light and ran out of the room. She never dared to dabble with the Devil again.[6]

In Rumania, the Devil is called *Dracu*. It manifested itself as an obsessive entity in the case of Eleanor Zügun, investigated by Harry Price. In plain sight, teeth marks appeared on the back of her hand, which was a rather rare type of stigmatic phenomenon.

[5] See *The Haunted Mind*, op. cit., pp. 177-180.
[6] *Ibid.*, pp. 123-127.

Terrifying, yet patently psychological in motivation was the confession of a beautiful girl patient who believed that her first lover was the Devil. She felt locked in a closet, waves of emotion or desire came over her—and she said: "I did not know then what was happening, but now I know that I was having intercourse with my father in the shape of the devil." [7]

The Ghost Is an Incubus

But for the identification of the Devil with her father, the previous case would properly fall under the heading of demon lovers. There were two kinds: the incubus that made love to women and the succubus that made love to men. None of them were really demons. Spirits of the dead obsessed with earthly desires (earth-bound) would describe them better. For examples I would again refer to the *Haunted Mind*,[8] but would point out as an outstanding example a later case in this book under the title, "Lo, the Incubus!" It is a faithful record of a new and totally unbelievable experience.

However, it was not to be the ultimate story. A 40-year-old woman from Texas solved the problem of her love-starvation by succubus fantasies. Her beloved was a preacher and she found a strange way of getting rid of her guilt of culmination. God himself took the place of the preacher and gave her sexual instruction.

The Ghost Is a Witch

This is on a par with the incubus but not on a sexual level. The Bell Witch of Tennessee is the weirdest example.[9] The story precedes the Spiritualistic age. The witch did not call herself a spirit of the dead, did not believe in communication with the dead, and her only mission seemed to be to persecute Betsy Bell's father—and finally murder him.

Similar stories are found in voodoo literature. The reader should consult the "Goblin of the Loaf." (*See* Part III.)

---

[7] *Ibid.*, pp. 270-273.
[8] *Ibid.*, pp. 270-276.
[9] *Haunted People*, by the author, together with Hereward Carrington; E. P. Dutton & Co., 1951, pp. 142-172.

With this we have reached the *pièce de résistance* of this essay. Are there any real ghosts?

The question cannot be answered until we draw a line of distinction between apparitions and ghosts. Apparitions, unless the word is used in a literal sense, are not associated with haunted houses. They are not tied to any locality. Because they are frequently purposive and bring news of death, give warnings or help in a crisis of life, they are associated with the spirits of the dead more than with ghosts. They have a human touch and are seldom frightening. The ghost is *sui generis*. The cold shiver you get from a ghost is due to the feeling that you are facing something alien, something that hovers between two worlds and belongs to neither. An apparition, in some way, is felt to be close to the living. The ghost is more like a shell, a disembodied menace that bodes no good. Self-opening doors, footsteps that can be heard but not seen, disappearing objects, light phenomena or sudden changes of temperature are more upsetting than the appearance of an actual phantom in human shape. If they acted always like automatons, they would not scare us so much. But sometimes they appear to be animated by a purpose, and they seem to be dominated by a fixed idea.

In at least one instance I know of, the ghost was set at rest by the pure divination of his restless quest. The story was told by Lady Harris in England. It happened to her in her own house. She saw the ghost. It seemed to be searching and searching. On making inquiries she found out that the previous owner of the house had had a tremendous beard and when he retired for the night, he used to tie it up with an elastic. The crazy idea occurred to her that the ghost was searching for an elastic. She put one on the tallboy. The ghost pounced upon it. The elastic disappeared and the ghost was no longer seen.

This is not an invented story, however strange it sounds. I knew Lady Harris. She was a very earnest old lady with a perpetual trumpet at her ear, a very eager listener. I have no doubt she told the truth. But how odd that truth is. Do some human habits survive the change of death to the exent of demanding compulsive satisfaction? The affirmative still would not explain what a ghost really is and how it appears. But then the only thing that we really know about ghosts is that they do appear and seem to have very odd motives. When murder has been committed in a house ages before, it is not the murderer but the victim that becomes a ghost. Why? Is the victim, though dead, still dreaming of this tragic end? How can such a dream last for centuries?

Spiritualists have developed a technique for ghost-laying. A rescue circle is formed with a medium and several sitters. The medium goes into trance and surrenders her body to possession by the ghost. The appearance is that the ghost avails itself of this opportunity for adventure, and those present have an argument with him and try to convince him that he is dead and has no business to stay bound to the house of his sorrows. It is reported that after such interviews the ghost is persuaded to leave the haunted house in which it "lived." Something happens by way of an emotional discharge and thus the house is cleared.

I have tried the technique in Ash Manor House with Eileen Garrett as the medium. The experience was exceedingly dramatic, but only of partial immediate success.

Ghosts do not necessarily "live" in a house. They seem to haunt woods, lakes, trees, caves and even the seas (phantom ships). Moreover, they are not exclusively human. There are animal ghosts and—for living animals—they are exceedingly frightening. If we are to believe the theosophists, there are nonhuman creatures, called elementals that are said to be very dangerous. Nor should we forget the records according to which some guides of mediums are "pure" spirits; *i.e.*, they claim never to have been incarnated. Such was Mlle. Tomczyk's Little Stasia and Mrs. Linczegh-Ignath's Nona. The phenomena they produced were far more astounding than those of spirit-guides. Furthermore, we should not forget the angels of religion. They do appear in visions of the devout. They are not ghosts, but they are certainly nonhuman. Believing in them or not does not alter the appearance that we may share existence—in body of in spirit—with denizens that are truly out of this world.

The Dark Side of Telepathy[1]

Instances of telepathic communication are usually accepted with wonderment. Owing to the accidental nature of telepathic

[1] From the *Indian Journal of Parapsychology*, Sri Ganganagar, Sept. 1951. Reprinted by permission.

reception, the cause is rarely questioned and the facts are shrugged off with "what can you do about it?" Still less consideration is given to the effect of reception. The purpose of this section is to show that in this direction lies an important field for research.

Inhibitive Telepathy

After a very pleasant lunch with a publisher and her editor, I wanted to cite as an example of automatic poetry *The Lyric of the Morning Land,* by Thomas Lake Harris. For some reason, I was unable to recall "Harris." All I could say was Lake, Lake, somebody Lake. To get around the inhibited name I wanted to call attention to a biography of Thomas Lake Harris by Lawrence Olyphant. Again, for the life of me, I could not recall "Olyphant."

Puzzled, I gave up the effort. Some time after we had parted, the memory returned and with that came the startling query: could the inhibition have originated in negative telepathy? Could the name Harris have meant something unpleasant to my lunch hosts? Unknown to their conscious thinking, could they have stopped me from uttering the name?

The only way to solve the problem was by direct questioning. To my surprise, the publisher answered:

> On that very day there was a letter on my desk from a certain Harris with whom I have been good friends abroad. For certain reasons I did not want to see him in New York. He was very insistent and I felt disturbed.

As to the editor:

> Harris is the name of a girl way back in the past, a girl I would rather not talk about.

Was the mental content of the mind of these two people powerful enough to dominate my own?

Cathartic Telepathy

Could a telepathic message have a cathartic effect on the recipient? May it help him to discharge repressed emotions that are a threat to mental health? This is another very important question. Here is a dream of a patient of mine, dated October 28, 1957:

I was alone in a hospital in a very wide bed, and knew I was dying. I felt extremely peaceful, but I was expecting you and was anxious whether you would make it before I died. The door opened and you came in, sat down by my bedside and asked: "How is it, Maria, tell me?" Obviously you knew I was dying. You took my hand and I told you: "Nandor, it is so very simple. It is only another door." You said: "And behind it is a corridor, then another door." It was typical of you. I said: "No, there are no more doors, no more corridors, it is just one opening, a last door. Too bad, I never knew it was so simple."

At the time of the dream I was busying myself with the problem of death for my new book, *The Haunted Mind*. I assumed that the dream of my patient was of telepathic origin; it clearly reflected my ideas in contradistinction to hers. But there was more to it. The doors and corridors recalled to the patient torturing nightmares under anaesthesia. Therefore, her complacency and acceptance of an "only door" indicated a discharge of anxiety. The mental content of my own mind was used as a blessed feeling of assurance.

I thought that the dream was a splendid example of a positive and universal beneficial function of telepathy. Only now, on re-reading my notes of the dream for the purpose of this book, am I struck by the precognitive element in it that at the time was beyond me to suspect. The patient had no reason to dream of dying. She did not believe in psychic perception. Yet, by what seems to be precognitive transference, she was acting out my own future hospital condition. During the spring and summer of the year that followed, I was at the door of death for 11 days. As a result, she was in a state of tremendous distress. Two of her previous analysts had died. If I would also die, it would be proof positive that she was doomed. She had been cursed by her mother before she had committed suicide and the family made her responsible for it. How could she continue living if I, too, died because of the curse laid on her?

I did not know at the time that I was dying. I had no experience in it. But strangely enough I did tell her afterwards: "It would have been so simple; any damn fool can die."

Seeing now the same thought reflected in my patient's dream ten months before the event, I am filled with wonder. Was she trying to reassure herself with my own words and feelings that were as yet in the womb of time?

She had paid me several visits in the hospital. I had told her that because I lived, the anguish she had experienced would be the best catharsis for her curse complex. Having forgotten her dream it is only now apparent to me that she had anticipated not only my words, but also my conclusion.

For another example of catharsis, I shall now quote a simultaneous telepathic dream between a patient and her one-time partner in business. He lived in the same house and both of them were invited to a Bar Mitzvah party in that house. The night before she dreamed:

> I went to the Bar Mitzvah, and congratulated the mother. But she turned away from me. I was about to leave but one of my neighbors said: "Don't be foolish, you have to eat first."

The patient was conscious of the presence at the party of her ex-partner. When, on the following afternoon she actually attended the party, she was invited by the wife of her ex-partner to go to the Temple with her. She excused herself by saying that she was much disturbed by a dream. Being pressed for the dream, she told her. Whereupon the woman answered:

> You are not going to believe this, but my husband had the same dream the same night. He went to the party and congratulated the father. The father turned his head away. So he picked himself up and walked out.

The difference between the content of the two dreams is that in one it is the mother, in the other it is the father who turns away and shows indifference or veiled hostility. The question that appeared important to me was whether the dreamers used the telepathic dream as mutual encouragement for separation from a parental figure holding them in emotional bondage. In her case it was the mother, in his case, presumably, the father. Bar Mitzvah is the strongest possible declaration that a young boy, until then dependent on his parents, has now reached manhood and can leave his childhood behind.

As I was collecting my thoughts on this two-year old dream, I wondered whether I should ring up the dreamer and ask her for association about the food that she could not leave uneaten. Suddenly, the telephone rang, and there she was on the line. She explained that she felt impelled to inquire after my health. The timing of her call could not have been more perfect. If it was coincidental, the coincidence is more amazing than the telepathic reaction.

Malignant Telepathy and
Paranoid Reactions

Another class of telepathic reports revives the ghost of Mary Baker Eddy's malicious animal magnetism. The question has been forced upon me: Could telepathy produce malignant effects?

I have personally known several people who claimed the possession of a demonic power that made people drop dead if, in a sudden flare of temper they hurled venom at them. To mention one example, my friend cursed a Great Dane that suddenly reared up in a friendly greeting when she entered the house of a friend. For some mysterious reason, the dog died the following day. Her friend never forgave her because she had heard stories of her power of wishing people to death.

While this story is more or less of an anecdotal character, I can illustrate the same power of sudden rage or intense mental ill-wishing by recalling a rather unsavory character with whom I have observed psychokinetic phenomena in London. He was a drunkard and a criminal. During the First World War he became involved in German espionage in Canada. He got away with a loot of $50,000. But there was an accomplice who could have given him away. He did not like the prospect of a long term in prison, so he wished, with a fierce concentration, that his partner-in-crime would commit suicide.

He did commit suicide, following which my medium was arrested on suspicion of murder. For the accomplice went to *his* house and shot himself with *his* gun, carrying out the telepathic suggestion with a vengeance. He succeeded in clearing himself of the murder charge but to me he admitted: if ever there was a psychic murder, this was it.

Whether the telepathic suggestion is only a threat or an actual malignant command, defensive reactions may set in. Aggression is a form of defense. "If I get pregnant I will kill you," a woman patient threatened her analyst when, unknown to the analyst, she was listening on the telephone to my discoveries regarding her psychological sterility. Paul Federn, the great Viennese psychoanalyst, felt himself under attack by my views on the trauma of birth and on the night that I was writing a letter to him, he identified me with an "Untier" that was attacking him.[2] The case of the homicidal patient who was intent on killing Dr. John Rosen raises the problem of whether the voices that demented patients hear may not, at least at times, be ascribable to telepathic perception.

The paranoid background appeared clearly from the story of a patient who had practiced malignant telepathy. He failed in a theatrical line and wished to revenge himself on his enemies by concentrating on their destruction. He came for treatment because he became badly frightened of this success. The daughter of a producer fell off a horse and fractured her skull. A play from which he had been left out suddenly fell off in box office returns. His malignant concentration, in which his wife participated, began after a barrage of telephone calls from a director who tried to get out of his obligations.

The patient always felt that the telephone was an invasion of privacy. "A person can break in on me. It is a sort of a door. Anybody can open it." I had to warn him that malignant telepathy may rebound on him and his wife, and due to the pressure of guilt it may be the cause of future failures.

Forerunner of the
Collective Man

The basic question regarding telepathy has been worded in twofold manner: Is it a survival of an archaic, pre-lingual communication or is it developmental, a faculty that may be shared in the future by the majority of the race, and may even take the place of, or occasionally substitute for, normal communication?

This question is bound up with the over-all problem of human evolution. In "Doomsday Deferred," a science fiction story by Will F. Jenkins, originally published in the *Saturday*

[2] "Paul Federn's Untier," *Psychoanalysis*, Vol. II, 1954.

Evening Post, the plot involves a colony of army ants that developed into a single organism of which the individual ants were only mobile cells. The intelligence of this ant-organism was far superior to that of the single ant, and became an actual menace to humanity.

This story raised disquieting thoughts. Ever since the days of the herd fathers, we have developed a variety of social organizations. Many of them had failed in the course of history, but many are still practical forms of binding together groups and communities. What if all these social efforts represent a grouping towards the evolution of a Collective Man, of something that corresponds, on the physical plane, to the Group Soul of which Geraldine Cummins wrote in *The Road to Immortality?* It is by telepathy that the ant-organism communicated with its cells. Would not the Collective Man, the Group Man also, rule by some form of E.S.P.? Is parapsychology a study of rudimentary manifestations of things to come?

Whether the gregarious instinct in men will lead to some such development, the thought should not be ignored that telepathy may yet turn out to be the cohesive force that will hold humanity together in a far distant future.

Through the Gate of Horn[1]

"Listen then to a dream that I have had, and interpret it for me if you can. I have twenty geese about the house that eat mash out of a trough, and of which I am exceedly fond. I dreamed that a great eagle came swooping down from a mountain, and dug his curved beak into the neck of each of them till he had killed them all. Presently he soared off into the sky, and left them lying dead about the yard; whereon I wept in my dream, till all my maids gathered round me, so piteously was I grieving that the eagle had killed my geese. Then he came back again, and perching on a projecting rafter spoke to me with human voice, and told me to leave off crying. 'Be of good

[1] Reprinted from the *American Journal of Psychotherapy,* Vol. IX, No. pp. 283-294.

courage,' he said, 'Daughter of Icarus; this is no dream, but a vision of good omen that surely shall come to pass. The geese are the suitors, and I am no longer an eagle, but your own husband, who am come back to you, and who will bring these suitors to a disgraceful end.' On this I woke, and when I looked out, I saw my geese at the trough eating their mash as usual.

"This dream, madam," replied Odysseus, "can admit but of one interpretation, for has not Odysseus himself told you how it shall be fulfilled? The death of the suitors is portended, and not one single one of them will escape." And Penelope answered: "Stranger, dreams are very curious and unaccountable things, and they do not by any means invariably come true. There are two gates through which these unsubstantial fantasies proceed; the one is of horn, and the other ivory. Those that come through the gate of ivory are fatuous, but those from the gate of horn mean something to those that see them. I do not think, however, that my own dream came through the gate of horn, though I and my son should be most thankful if it proves to have done so."

Disguised in rags as a beggar, Odysseus had already resolved to kill the suitors of his wife at the tournament of axes which was to be held on the following day. Hence Penelope's dream could have been of telepathic and not of prophetic origin. The remarkable ease with which the manifest content is translated into the latent thought by the speaking eagle justifies Penelope's assumption that the dream was but a wish, whether her own or that of Odysseus, telepathically received, hence indeed coming through the pure and shining gate of ivory;[2] but in the vision of Odysseus the suitors were already dead, consequently to him in the face of the time element that had yet to be overcome, his reflected mental accomplishment through Penelope's dream must have appeared as coming through the gate of horn. Did not the eagle, with which he immediately identified himself, clearly state that this was no dream, "but a vision of good omen that shall surely come to pass?"

An omen, for archaic man, was more than a shadow fore-

---

[2] Paul Federn claims that "the patient's intuitive understanding and translation of symbols indicates hidden schizophrenia" but he makes no allowance for a telepathic determinant. (*Ego Psychology and the Psychoses*, p. 131.)

cast by future events. It was a sign of the participation of the gods in human affairs, the epitome of a divine reality against which humans could only shadowbox. The best a man could do was to interpret the symbolic content of the omen and bow his head to the accomplished design of the gods, revealed by grace. Many superhuman deeds of the heroes of antiquity must have sprung from the psychological strength thus derived. It is the absence of this psychological shaping power in our age that makes comparative weaklings of fanatics of today.

But have we really lost contact with the source from which the dragon-slayers had derived their strength? Is the gate of horn closed to modern man? To put it more plainly: Is there a reality transcending our time-bound mind of which we get an intimation in precognitive dreams?

Telepathic dreams no longer meet with the same fierce opposition in psychoanalysis as they used to. The time is at hand to take the next step and investigate the possibility of precognition in dreams, waking fantasies or in association processes.

The first thing we have to guard against is coincidence. A wish dream followed by coincidental fulfilment would create a strong bias in favor of precognition. An anticipation based on telepathic or extrasensory perception, as in Penelope's dream, is the next pitfall.

The third is a confusion between telepathy and precognition. Telepathy is a message from mind to mind without the recognized channels of sense. Precognition or premonition is an extrasensory awareness of events still in the future. It is easy to define the difference between the two, but in practical dream interpretation we may find them considerably interlocked. Therefore, we should value all cases of apparent precognition, whether they permit objection on one ground or another. A case without loopholes may prove too baffling for acceptance. The loopholes permit an analytic approach and help us to greater understanding.

I shall present as my first case a dream of my own dated December 3, 1944:

Case 1. I heard two youngsters recite *Jisgadal Jisgadash*, the Jewish prayer for the dead. (On awakening, one of the youngsters seemed to have been my nephew, Ali. It struck me that the pronunciation was not as it should be. It should have been, I thought, *Jiskadal Jiskadash*. I know now that *Jisgadal* was right, but *Jisgadash* is still wrong.)

Then I was dressing from a steel filing cabinet which had No. 60 over it. (I had seen a cabinet like that the night before at a place where I was lecturing. There were air slits on top which had given me the idea that one could be locked up and be buried alive in a cabinet like that.)

Then I was taking leave from the boys, and told them that I was sailing for Europe that day, or in a few days, dependent on the availability of passage. (In writing the dream down I replaced the word passage with berth.)

I also remember trying to put on a shirt, but the hole left after it was fully opened was not wide enough to put my head through. (The description is contradictory—there is no hole in a fully-opened shirt.)

As I was about to sail the boys were taking my place at the *Hungarian Daily* (where I had my first job on emigrating to the United States), and I told them that the paper would do well with young blood. There was a melancholy touch to my farewell. It seemed vaguely as if I were going back to "Az Est" (*The Evening,* on the staff of which I was in Budapest before I was "born" into America).

The associations in brackets indicate that they occurred simultaneously with noting down the dream. The dream itself had a chilling effect on me. It seemed to speak of approaching death. I felt that the prayer for the dead was being said for me. Because in my previous writings I had identified birth with death, the multiple references to birth only added to my uneasiness. "Gadal" in *Jisgadal* suggested Guadalcanal, a place of violent death and the birth canal. The filing cabinet associated with the womb and with being buried alive, the hole in the shirt with the process of birth, the melancholy farewell with an impending departure in The Evening of life on a boat which (in antiquity) carried the dead after they fulfilled their allotted span (dressing completed).

Then came a startling discovery that enabled me to shake off the chill. It concerned the number over the filing cabinet. Sixty is "hatvan" in Hungarian, and Hatvan was the name of the town in which my brother Lajos, Ali's father, lived. My brother was an ardent Zionist (which placed his life in additional danger under Nazi rule) and it would have fallen to Ali to recite for him, eventually, the prayer for the dead. Have I identified myself with my brother and did the dream portend his death instead of mine?

Ambivalence, equivalence or identification may well be

symbolized by the number 2. There were two youngsters. I was the youngest son in my family and Lajos was my oldest living brother. There were two g's instead of two k's (wrongly as I thought) in *Jisgadal Jisgadash* (two words with an identical syllable), "the boys" were two, so were the newspapers and countries. The letter "g" is the initial of guilt—and I had failed my father with the prayer for the dead. Lajos stepped into my father's place as the head of the family, hence if I was one of the boys in the beginning of the dream, the prayer was said for both father and brother. Surely, I would not use the equivalent of birth and death for a theoretical analytic statement! My literary work on this subject rendered this totally unnecessary. Was the dream attempting to convey a message from my brother?—I have died but I live, just as you lived after you "died" in being born!

I well realize how startling the query sounds. Let us remember, however, that the prayer for the dead is based on the belief that the dead still live and that for their peace of mind it is necessary that we pray for them. It is only our scientific realism which beclouds this issue. By reason, we reject the idea of continued life after death. By emotion, we secretly lean toward it. No other single idea has had such a sway over human imagination as the problem of survival after physical death. The value of a message from the dead would not be the personal content but the proof that there is another plane of existence. It is the undying hope of humanity that such evidence might be forthcoming.

The fundamental issue that stared me in the face was this: has my brother died and when? If he died at the time of the dream, was the message originating from his mind when he was on the point of death, making the dream a telepathic one, or did he die later in which case the dream may evidence precognition, perhaps with a superimposed attempt at comforting me with my own dose of philosophy?

Unfortunately, at the time of the dream no communication existed between Hungary and the United States. A year or more may have passed before the Iron Curtain was lifted and the news arrived that my brother Lajos was dead. He was taken to a concentration camp in Austria, and was killed, around the time of the dream, because of his fearless support of fellow prisoners.

Thus, the issue of telepathy or precognition cannot be settled; but the assumption that the dream presented an extrasensory phenomenon is well supported. The case bears on the universal belief that existed in every culture, at every age, namely, that by visions, hallucinations, dreams, or manifestations of distress, the dying or the dead may succeed in alerting the ones they loved of the momentous thing happening to them. My brother used to worry about my interest in such matters, so—knowing him as I do—he would have tried to reach me if he could. Yet it is equally possible that my unconscious, if alarmed, would dramatize his passing in the way it was presented in the dream. But what was it that alarmed my unconscious? And here we are falling back again to the original question: Was it telepathy or a flash of precognition?

Case 2. On April 22, 1941, I dreamed that an archaeologist drained a pool in his garden to make diggings. He expected to find there the Winged Victory of Samothrace. I was deeply interested and promised to complete the digging for him. A few minutes after I woke up, my wife switched on the radio. It was announced that according to unconfirmed reports, the Germans had occupied the Island of Samothrace.

The Winged Victory is about the only thing I can associate with Samothrace. No personal or emotional interest existed in me for a telepathic reception and dream elaboration, from some hypothetically known announcer, of a news item that was about to go on the air. It looks as if I had "heard" the announcement prior to its being broadcast, or that the whole thing was a coincidence.

I incline to accept coincidence, because the news had no bearing on the content of my dream. Yet, if precognition is to be treated with the same tolerance as coincidence, in retrospect I could see in the dream a prophetic flash of the success of my continuing researches (digging in the garden under the lake) into prenatal determinants of personality development.

Case 3. This is my wife's dream and is dated November 17, 1938, from the time when I was living in London. In the dream my wife saw Hitler with a Charlie Chaplin moustache. She felt that if his moustache were cut off he would lose all his power.

The dream appeared to be a Samsonic fantasy, until three days later the London Sunday papers announced that Charlie Chaplin was going to play a prisoner in a German concentration camp and at the same time he would also play the part of a dictator. Hitler's name was not mentioned, but the conclusion was obvious.

Coincidence is no longer sufficient to explain a dream of this type. Telepathy also fails. Clairvoyance might be defensible on the assumption that photographs of Charlie Chaplin as Hitler may have existed somewhere. It is easier to assume a vision through space than through the barrier of time. But the name is not the thing. The impression of extrasensory perception is very strong. The why and wherefore is difficult to answer unless we just assume that the dream mind is not limited to cognitive material for the building of a dream but may occasionally draw on precognitive ones. I would guess that by the content of the dream my wife was mocking me: the sorry figure a husband cuts if he attempts to be dictatorial. A deeper personal motivation: The killing of her father and mother by the Nazis was five or six years away in the womb of time.

Case 4. On December 22, 1940, I was reading the introductory part of an article in the *New York Times Magazine* by H. L. Robbins under the title: "Santa: A Success Story." After the first few lines, my mind wandered off to a man who called on me the day before to make inquiries regarding analytic treatment. Because he was a man of little intelligence, I mused how I would explain to him the meaning of a symbol. I thought of Christmas (because of the article). I would ask him what it meant to him. If he answered: peace, goodwill, rest, I would say, Christmas is the symbol of that for you. Then I continued mentally: he is a sign painter, I could tell him: if you painted three balls for a pawnshop that would be the symbol of a pawnshop. He would understand that.

Satisfied, I resumed reading. The article explained the attempt in America to identify Santa Claus with Nicholas, Bishop of Myra, in Asia Minor, who lived in the fourth century. It spoke of the wonders of his benevolence as follows:

> He rescued three plump small boys from a homicidal innkeeper who planned to make mincemeat of them. In the dark of the night, he dropped three bags of gold through a poor man's window, thus enabling the poor man to marry off his three daughters in style. And once, cruising in the Mediterranean, he stilled a storm when the sailors thought they were lost.

89

Naturally, on attaining sainthood, Nicholas became the patron of children, maidens and mariners, and later, through mariners, of merchants. Traders in the Middle Ages decorated the prows of their ships with three gold balls, representing the three bags of gold, and when they had become bankers, they retained the symbol.

Here were the three bags of the pawnshop of my meditation. Is this a case of coincidence, clairvoyance or precognition? The origin of the pawnshop symbol was totally unknown to me, and I am quite positive that I stole no glance ahead at the content of the article. If the initial concentration on the article, followed by the relaxation of attention, enabled my unconscious to contact the mind stream of the author, we could talk of telepathy. If I saw, through my unconscious, without looking, the continuation of the text in some such way as half finished thoughts are carried on without conscious knowledge, then it was a case of clairvoyance. If neither of them is acceptable, we can call it precognition; but he who prefers coincidence will not have to wage a very strong fight to defend himself.

Case 5. This case is a nightmare, my own. I was making weird noises and my wife woke me up. This was the dream: I was creeping out of the waters in the dark in a place that looked more like a gorge than a cave. Suddenly, the feeling came over me that there were other animals about and that it was not safe to be on land. I heard some mysterious sounds, and the thought came to me that the best way to scare the animals away would be to shout. So I began shouting. This noise was inarticulate, it disturbed my wife, so she woke me up. She asked me if I had a nightmare. I told her the dream and explained my impression that it represented the first appearance of life on land.

For two days before this nightmare, my wife had been urging me to read Dr. Louis Berman's book, *Glands Regulating Your Personality.* She mentioned that I would be rather interested in what Berman says about the thyroid gland as a primitive sex gland. The day after the dream I took the book in hand and on page 47 found this: CREATOR OF THE LAND ANIMAL. According to this conception, the thyroid played a fundamental part in the change of sea creatures into land animals.

If my wife had not read the book, this would have been

a perfect case for clairvoyance or precognition of what I was going to read. As it is, telepathy from her mind has the advantage. Coincidence is the least probable explanation.

Case 6. This consists of three oddities. The first concerns a patient who arrived at his session with a book. As soon as he entered, I asked jokingly: where is the bell and the candle? I have no idea why the sight of a book should have suggested to me Bell, Book and Candle, a form of exorcism of the Devil in Scotland. But the sequel was curious. The patient showed me a passage in the book: the greatest cause of insanity is too much care by the mother. This represented a vital problem to him; he lived with a psychotic mother and wanted to know whether he should move out, because life with her was undiluted hell. Then he proceeded to tell me of a sister called Belle to whom, before being taken to the hospital the last time, his mother said: "Your father is not human, he appears in different forms, he is in league with the Devil."

The case is amusing. However, it does not argue for anything. I made a facetious statement and the patient found associations that fitted in with it. The net was spread wide enough and I caught what the patient's mind felt provoked to give. Nevertheless, I felt a little puzzled when, after a visit to my barber, I heard him complain of nightmares. I said, nightmares are often due to fears of childhood, they are like mice coming out of their holes at night.

"That's funny," he said. "I dreamed last night that rats were crawling over my face, because my wife accidentally brushed my face with her hand."

The third of such stories is the best and the oddest. I have succeeded in impressing upon a patient the necessity of reading good books and to apply his growing insight to the stories. He already read two and came with a third one. The first was *That None Should Die*, the second *Follow the Leader*, the third *An Hour Before Dawn*, by Somerset Maugham. He chose all three books because of their titles: It suddenly struck him that the very choice of the title must have some significance. He thought that the first title would refer to his desire to survive, the second to save himself by analysis, following his analyst, and that a new life is about to begin for him.

I agreed to the psychological significance of title choosing and said that it would have been equally significant if he had noticed the titles he had rejected. If, for instance, he would reject a book the title of which is, say, Black Skeleton, one could analyze the emotional disposition that made him reject it.

I said Black Skeleton on the spur of the moment. I heard of no such book, and skeletons are not black. Consider then my surprise when the patient produced a dream in which Red Skelton, the comedian, appeared and was being chased by a monster. To make the situation odder still, I had a dream the night before about this patient in which he was running with a knife in his hand. Then I had a vision of a mirror, of the antique type, with panels. This latter part of the dream I recalled only after the patient told me of another dream of his in which his bookkeeper bought him an antique mirror which had four panels in the middle.

The telepathic contact between my mirror dream and his looks evident. Which raises the question: Was my reference to Black Skeleton an indication of continued telepathic relationship during the waking state? Or was it a precognitive flash the ground for which was prepared by the telepathic contact during the night?

To answer with no to any of these questions and brush aside the web of interlocking eelments is easy, but it would not be facing the problem fairly.

Case 7. This case is more startling than the preceding ones. It was, at first, just a wonderful dream without extrasensory implications. It was this:

> Eliphas Levy came into the room, looking about 30, like my husband, but having a beard and a moustache. He said something that I cannot remember, and I answered: I am going to tell my husband to grow a moustache and a beard. Then I started walking and arrived in front of a huge wall which I saw from a distance, with a beautiful sky behind it. The wall looked like the wall of Windsor Castle and was as thick as the walls of Jericho. It was made of cork or honeycake. I entered the wall and I became small and green. I said to myself: am I dreaming this? I answered: no, no, I am not dreaming this. I was like a dragonfly, a fairy dragonfly. I understood the how, why and wherefore of Life.

A miraculous transformation is hinted at in this fascinating dream. Eliphas Levy, the magician, is made to look like the patient's husband who is a natural substitute for the father, the generator of life. The patient's mother was 30 years old when the patient was born—which explains the magician's age. He represents both the father and the mother. That is why he is a magician. In real life, the patient is a fairy-like creature, and is often paid the compliment that she must have been a fairy in a previous life. She identified the dragonfly with a photograph of Pavlova, and confessed as one of her greatest sorrows that her parents had not permitted her to become a ballet dancer. It seems that in the dream she returns into the womb to find fulfilment of that which should have been.

Windsor Castle is a reference to the royal estate of the unborn, and it gives a clue to the patient's abundant royal fantasies. The honeycake and Jericho suggest the land flowing with milk and honey, the impregnable fortress of the womb.

During the afternoon of the same day on which I received this dream, my attention was drawn to the column "This Curious World" in the *World Telegram and Sun*. There were two drawings side by side: a cork tree and a dragonfly. The respective captions said: Cork trees may be stripped of their cork once every nine or ten years; a dragonfly may spend three years in the water before emerging as an aerial insect.

The combination of two such incongruous elements as a cork tree and a dragonfly in the newspaper and in the dream is very odd for coincidence. Could it possibly be more! I was a regular reader of the *Telegram* and always glanced at "This Curious World." But the dreamer never read the *Telegram* and it is doubtful if she ever knew that such a column was run in it. When I showed her the cutting from the *Telegram*, something was brought to her knowledge which could have served as a matrix for a precognitive dream. My own action had created a situation which otherwise would not have come into existence. I was responsible for the dream that followed. But if I was an indispensable agent, in this case, for the content of the dream, the act of precognition may have been as well mine as hers! The dream material might have reached her by telepathy from my own mind. In other words, this could also represent a case for telepathy-*cum*-precognition.

One can only pause in wonderment, particularly after paying additional attention to the fact that the dragonfly illustration plainly refers to prenatal and postnatal life, and it also presents the No. 3 which is the first digit of 30, standing for the age of the patient's mother at the time of her birth and for the age of the magician in the dream. Oddly enough, the cork tree also reveals a birth number: 9, the number of gestation. The stripping of the cork tree is the prerequisite to a new growth, a renewal of life—and a tree is always an excellent symbol for the Tree of Life which appears to be the maternal body in the dream.

What final conclusion can we reach from the study of this group of dreams and oddities?

I do not claim that they establish a case for precognitive dreams. The clinical argument is not sufficiently strong. But I consider the material valuable because it presents food for thought in the direction of extrasensory perception in dreams beyond the range of telepathy and clairvoyance. A presumptive case is all we need for a start. Psychoanalysis will not be able to ignore too long the problem of precognition. Humanity has persisted in believing in prophetic dreams throughout the ages. Psychical researchers have compiled an enormous mass of objective material to prove the reality of glimpses into the future. Psychoanalysis is actually behind times as far as such problems are concerned. The material has long been available for psychoanalytic investigation. If the prevailing analytic disposition is against clairvoyant and precognitive dreams, it is at least incumbent upon us to prove that such dreams mean something other than a transcending of the barrier of space and time. By so doing we may learn a great deal more of the working of the human mind than by persistently refusing the challenge.

She Became a Chinaman

Our dictionaries define transfiguration as a change of form or outward appearance, and quote from the Gospels the scene on the mountain where Christ's face "did shine as the sun and his raiment was white as light." (Matthew 17-2) The scene was witnessed by Peter, John and James; they saw Moses and Elias next to Jesus and were filled with exaltation.

Ever since, transfiguration implies a change of countenance, but subsequent ages have failed to witness a similar miracle.

The only one that somewhat approaches it comes from witnesses of Ramakrishna's transfiguration. The account is given by Romain Rolland.[1] It was the culmination of Ramakrishna's years of burning desire to see the Divine Mother.

From that moment his days and nights were passed in the continual presence of his Beloved. Their intercourse was uninterrupted like the flow of the river. Eventually he was identified with Her, and gradually the radiance of his inner vision became outwardly manifest. Other people seeing him saw what he saw. Through his body as through a window appeared the bodies of the gods. Mathur Babu, the son-in-law of the foundress of the temple and the master of the place, was sitting one day in his room opposite Ramakrishna's. Unobserved, he watched him pacing up and down on his balcony. Suddenly he uttered a cry, for he saw him alternately in the form of Shiva as he walked in one direction, and of the Mother as he turned and walked in the opposite direction.

Transfiguration was always the last stage of the successive visions of this great Hindu prophet. Rolland writes:

First he saw the figures outside himself, then they vanished within himself, finally he became them himself. This ardent creative act is striking, but was natural to one of his outstanding plastic genius. As soon as he visualized a thought, his vision became incarnate.

No better introduction can be found to a discussion of transfiguration as it is understood in parapsychology. It no longer means an ambition to reach the gods but it does involve a plastic genius for assuming the bodily characteristics of deceased people in order to put them in contact with the living. It is a form of mediumship that in earlier years was very popular in England. Its best exponent was Mrs. E. F. Bullock of Levenshulme, Manchester, who in an illumination of red light thrown into her face, used to change into a Chinaman. She was in trance, of course, and the Chinaman was one of her spirit-guides and acted as a go-between for the audience. The transfiguration of Mrs. Bullock's face was said

[1] *Prophets of the New India*, Cassell & Ltd., London, 1930.

to be due to a thin cloud of "ectoplasm" that her body emitted and the red light was said to be necessary because this emanation was too sensitive to white light.

I first saw Mrs. Bullock's demonstration in the summer of 1934 at a meeting of the Great Metropolitan Spiritualist Association in London. I sat at a distance of about 15 feet and my impression was that the lower part of her face became an amorphous mass, that there was an ebb and flow over her face and that new features were forming in place of her normal ones. I was not allowed to leave my seat and approach her for a clearer view.

I invited her to a demonstration before the International Institute for Psychical Research for the purpose of taking infra-red flashlight photographs of her facial transformations. The demonstration proved to be highly successful. Standing on the platform against a black background in a black surplice (which left only her head and hands visible) in front of a 25-watt red lamp shining in her face, Mrs. Bullock showed a series of remarkable changes of countenance. There was a Chinaman, a Japanese girl, a bearded man, another one with a moustache, an alleged African with a ring in the nose, a man fallen in action during the war with a circular wound in the forehead and several others, and the representations were so impressive that they called forth exclamations of wonder from the audience.

The weakness of the demonstration was that the light source used by Mrs. Bullock could cast strange shadows that could be considerably varied by the movement of her head and the play of her facial muscles. She happened to have a very flexible set of features and it was obvious that with due practice her face could easily assume a Chinese cast. Joey Brown had sent me a series of photographs on which he had done the same without any claim to mediumship or ectoplasmic assistance.

However, the study of the light and shade effects and the belief that she was an intermediary for spirit communication alone promised sufficient rewards for a close investigation.

On this occasion I was sitting at a distance of two yards from the medium. I saw nothing that would have suggested ectoplasm or other alien matter. But I saw a moustache. There were shouts from the audience when it appeared. It was formed, I could well see, by the shadow cast by the pursing of her upper lip. I saw a beard too. It was no more substantial than the moustache. The wrinkles of Mrs. Bullock's neck shimmered in the red light and seemed to flow straight from the raised chin. The ring in the nose of the African was represented by a circular depression of the skin from nose downward, the wound on the forehead by a round swelling.

It was a highly dramatic performance. Leon M. Lion, the well-known theatrical producer, was my guest at the demonstration, and paid Mrs. Bullock the compliment: "Whatever the cause, we must pay tribute to the effect."

The camera made Mrs. Bullock nervous. We could only take four photographs. The Chinaman was excellent. The audience did not imagine the Chinese cast. It was there. There was a vapor around the right hand which followed the shape of the hand and appeared to start ⅛ inch away from the surface. Mr. Leon Isaac, the Institute's official photographer, could not account for it photographically. He was emphatic that it was not due to a photographic defect.

The other three photographs were less impressive. The moustache was clearly not a moustache but I could see how, with red illumination from underneath, it could suggest one. There was a problem though in the fourth picture. It was of "Moonie," an African spirit-guide. It showed a curious surging white cloud over the black surplice under the neck. This cloud was not seen during the demonstration, is absent from all other photographs and was not due to a fault in the plate or process of development. Could it have been "ectoplasm"?

The experiments clearly were worth continuing. The following day we sat for our first infra-red cinema picture and for infra-red and ultra-violet "stills." Something unusual happened during the demonstration. I called attention to a shaft of shimmering light that appeared, like a transparent curtain, on the right-hand side of Mrs. Bullock's face. The next impression was an enormous drooping moustache which instantly suggested the picture of Arthur Conan Doyle. The moustache was seen by others before I spoke. Hence, it could not have been an illusion on my part alone. The shaft of light which originated the impression had a direction of its own, and appeared to move downward. That is to say, it did not come from the light box.

Now we had a problem again: was the shaft of light an ectoplasmic phenomenon, seen by a reflection of visible red rays from a cloud of material particles? Would it be transparent to the longer wave-length employed for the flash exposure? In that case it could not be recorded on a photograph by infrared. The moustache could have been there, but was absent as far as a photographic record was concerned.

This was a speculation in favor of the medium because, as we soon found out, the change of her features did not require ectoplasm. After white light had been restored Mrs. Bullock changed into a Chinaman in full visibility. The effect was very striking and it spoke well for her honesty, suggesting that her features could be controlled by both conscious and unconscious efforts and that the conscious change did not in the least dispose of the psychological problems presented by her religious devotion and mediumistic efforts.

One of our scientists, Mr. W. T. L. Becker, Managing Director of Color Photographs, Ltd. and a member of our Council, was asked for a statement of what he observed. This is what he said:

> Changes began and the medium's face appeared to be plastic as if it were dough being kneaded by invisible hands; alternatively, there may have been a rippling of the facial muscles under the skin, such as one notices under the skin of a tiger or a cat about to pounce on prey. The lips remained parted by approximately the same distance, whilst the upper lip lengthened and became less fleshy or thinner. I had an impression of pulsation of the lips vertically up and down from the upper lip to nose and sometimes also from lower lip to chin, just prior to some of the important changes in configuration. After this preliminary kneading, the eyebrows rose sharply, the eyes slanted, and the Chinese face arrived, the transformation being complete in a few seconds: as if the tiger suddenly had sprung. The whole of the change was utterly remote from any conception of conscious or unconscious grimace. I saw no lines or wrinkles or contraction of specific group of muscles but simply a kneading or plasticity of the whole. It may be that a grimace in slow motion would give a similar effect, but it is quite outside normal experience.

Our physicist adviser, J. B. Hoper, M.Sc., stated of the appearance of the Chinaman:

> The Chinese face appeared as the first of the three or

four definite forms produced during the demonstration. This came very suddenly, the eyes, eyebrows, cheeks and chin changing simultaneously. The face appeared to be that of an old man, very much wrinkled, especially about the chin. The chin had that wizened form reminding one of a monkey, the shape of the lips adding to this illusion. Nevertheless, the figure produced was that of a Chinese, and a very good representation, too.

Both this Chinaman and another were successfully photographed by infrared. Indeed, the picture of the second Chinaman gave us a rare thrill. On the right side of the face a long, wide, straight-cut moustache appeared to be hanging. Unhappily, on closer examination and comparison with the first infra-red still photograph taken that afternoon the moustache turned out to be the collar of the medium's dress, escaping from the black surplice and touching the Chinaman's chin at a critical point. The effect was so deceptive that I wondered whether it was purely accidental or whether, in answer to our desire to photograph the moustache, the medium's unconscious produced, by the most economical means, the result we hoped for.

The ultra-violet "stills" turned out to be puzzling, too. In the ghastly greenish-blue fluorescent light nothing was visible in the medium's lap or over her face, yet the photograph of the Zulu spirit-guide showed markings that indicated a flattened nose, tufts of hair over the lips and the mockery of a beard. No explanation was forthcoming for these strange effects. The light was striking Mrs. Bullock full in the face and she could have had no knowledge how things would photograph in ultra-violet light. But fluorescence plays strange tricks. We hoped to settle our problems by an infra-red cinema film. Two days later we shot it successfully by improved lighting and with a noiseless cine-camera.

The film was 400 feet long. I showed it at the Oslo Psychical Research Congress in August 1936. It made quite an impression as far as the facial changes were concerned, but it showed no alien matter on her face. (We made her wash it and rub it with a rough towel before the experiment.)

The following day we photographed the Chinaman again. The result was odd. His nose was sharp and unmoved, but the skin of the face was in a heaving rippling movement. We did have results for our labour but not enough to settle the problem of transfiguration. However, I have elicited one piece of information which seemed to bear, quite definitely, on a biological mystery. Mrs. Bullock told me that during the transfiguration process she had the positive sensation of a hand massaging her womb. This had lent support to a finding that has rarely been publicized in parapsychological research: that the medium draws on her sexual energies for the production of such phenomena, that she acts as if she actually were to give "birth" to the phantoms that lead researchers on such a heart-breaking chase.

Adventures in Spirit Photography

The problem of spirit photography as a mediumistic talent (distinct from accidental markings or faces found on privately exposed plates) has been the subject of wilder controversy than any other psychic claim from the time of its emergence through William H. Mumler, head engraver of a famous Boston jewelry firm in 1862. The reason is obvious. No psychic phenomenon offers a chance for easier simulation than the production of a so-called "extra" (the face of a spirit, present but invisible) on a photographic plate, film, or light sensitive paper for a bereaved sitter who hungers for a sign of continued existence from the Beyond.

I have never done any special investigation in this field, though I have had private sittings with most of my contemporary spirit photographers. The "extras" that appeared on my plates were no departed relatives or friends of mine and meant absolutely nothing to me. Hence, I had no personal bias in favor of this phenomenon; rather the reverse, a prejudice against it. The foundation of my pessimism was the startling demonstration of P. MacCarthy, an engineering student, then Secretary of the Sheffield Society for Psychical Research, later my assistant at the International Institute for Psychical Research in London. MacCarthy had succeeded in proving that spirit photographs can be faked even under "perfect" test conditions.

His *pièce de résistance* was to ask the audience to name a

book in order to produce from it a sentence by the audience on a photographic plate as an "extra" in any language desired. The audience chose the Bible. Conveniently, there was one available on the platform and it was handed to him. He opened it at random (the book had been worked upon to open at a certain page) and asked the audience to choose a passage from above or below, counting a certain number of lines—forcing the choice upon them by well-concealed emphasis. When he got his *right* passage, he asked for the language, knowing well that the popular choice is always between Chinese and Greek. He was given, for the same reason as before, Chinese. Now he had the text he wanted, the translation of which was prepared in advance by his laundryman. (The details of four other "voluntary" choices he imposed upon the audience can be read in the October 1935 issue of *Psychic Science,* a quarterly periodical of the British College of Psychic Science, of London.

Needless to say that he was thoroughly searched by the Committee that supervised the experiment, and handcuffed in order to prevent any sleight-of-hand. No apparatus was found concealed on his body. (Yet, he succeeded in getting one because the Committee could not reasonably deny him admission to a certain place where one is in the habit of retiring alone—a place that has been successfully used by mediums before for vitiating test conditions.) His only condition was that he should be present in the dark room when the plates, exposed on volunteer sitters, were being developed. So he had to be admitted. Concealed underneath his index finger in a ring, painted flesh-color so it could not be seen from above, was his ingenious Psychic Imprinter. All he had to do was to point it at the plates as they were being developed, and so the extras appeared as promised and in the order desired by his audience.

The success of this experiment so dumbfounded the audience that they refused to believe him when he tried to expose himself. Even his own father fell back on the "only" sensible explanation, that his son was a medium, but ashamed to confess it. Seeing that all his protests were futile, MacCarthy finally gave an interview to *Armchair Science,* a monthly edited by my late friend, Professor A. N. Low, and he revealed the technical secret by a diagram and full description of the apparatus used. To quote from *Armchair Science:*

The Psychic Imprinter, as Mr. MacCarthy names his device, is constructed from a small piece of metal tube about two inches long and less than half an inch in diameter. Inside this tube there are three tight fitting sections. One contains filter and lens, another in the center the film slide and pea-bulb, and a third the battery. The battery on the right lights an overloaded pea-bulb through a spring contact at the end of the tube. The two-celled battery is of carbon and zinc in dilute sulphuric acid containing some potassium bichromate to act as a depolarizer. As the E.M.F. of each cell is just below two volts there are nearly four volts for the pea-bulb which lights very brightly and is practically a point-light.

The film carrying the micro-photographs slides in front of the bulb and is kept steady by elastic and held in place by a small hook and stops at the other end. Through the miniature positive shines the bright light which is focused by a short focus lens on to the plate to be imprinted, but in front of the lens a filter is fixed, which stops the visible light and only lets through the violet and ultra-violet rays.

The whole ingenious device was painted flesh color and held in place by two metal rings, also painted, underneath the index finger so that it was only necessary to point the finger over the exposed plate for a second to imprint an "extra." Although the battery held sufficient electricity to light the lamp for several minutes, actually only two and a half seconds of light were required for the five imprints.

No wonder that I felt justified in my skeptical approach to the wonders of spirit photography. I knew of many other simple ways by which spectacular results could be obtained without co-operation by the spirits of the dead. Thus, when it came to the claims of John Myers, called the greatest of all spirit photographers of our generation, I had my natural reservations. This was supported by the furious battle that has been waged in the daily press of London and the psychic press over his demonstration. Lord Donegall was the leader of the opposition in the *Sunday Dispatch,* and Maurice Barbanell, the editor of *Psychic News* was the champion on the spiritualistic side.

It would be far too late to revive the merits and demerits of the case these stalwarts had presented but for me, personally, there was a climax to it in the week of August 17-22, 1943, at Lily Dale, New York, where I made an investigation of the claims of several resident mediums and attended a gala demonstration of spirit photography by John Myers. He had invited, from Chicago Technical Institue, Howard Betz, a physicist, and Norman Bartley, a photographer, to take charge of the photographic proceedings. The photographer brought three plates from Chicago and loaded them in the dark room himself. The first plate was exposed on a young man, the second on the audience from the stage, Myers only signalling to snap. The third plate was not inserted in the camera. Instead, it was held before the audience by the physicist. The experts retired into the dark room to develop the three plates. After a while someone rapped on the door of the dark room and asked: "Any results?" The physicist answered in a low voice: "Unfortunately, yes."

Then Bartley, the photographer, appeared on the platform and stated: "We have developed the plates with standard equipment, including standard developer, brought by us from Chicago with the plates, and found 'extras' on three of the plates. Before these were used, the plates and camera showed everything to be normal. The loading was satisfactory."

So the demonstration was a great success and was reported in the *Psychic Observer* under a five column headline:

POSITIVE PROOF OF SUPERNORMAL PHENOMENA UNDER TEST CONDITIONS

I have taken my quotations from the *Psychic Observer* which, while reporting truthfully that extras were recognized by the audience as their deceased relatives, failed to report that, as it often happened before, John Myers got too excited, in fact, almost hysterical during the proceedings and burst into the dark room. Thereby he broke one of the most important conditions of the experiment. As he later explained, he just could not help himself. That he was in a highly nervous state, I had occasion to observe during the day prior to the demonstration. But I also observed something else. He appeared at breakfast with a bandaged index finger. He said he cut himself during shaving. I could not help thinking of MacCarthy's ring. What was to prevent him from gaining possession of it, or of a duplicate, while he was still residing in England? In that case, his presence in the dark room would have been as sufficient to explain the "miracle," as it was in MacCarthy's case. It was a rather embarrassing situation. No part has been assigned to me in the actual demonstration. The two young men from Chicago were babes in the wood. They knew about plates and development, but they could not possibly explain how the extras got on them by normal means known to them.

The only way out of my dilemma was to find out, by hook or crook, if there was a ring on John Myers' bandaged finger or not. So, on the platform during the meeting, I pretended to stumble, fell against John Myers and grabbed his bandaged hand for support. I pressed hard—and in a split second I had my answer: *There was no ring under the bandage.* John Myers did not use the MacCarthy technique. Hence, his breaking into the dark room may really have been due to hysterical excitement.

Sometime before this Lily Dale adventure I had another strange encounter with Myers and his spirit photographs. I had been invited by him to attend a special demonstration of psychic photography in his apartment at the St. Moritz Hotel in New York before a group of his friends. I went with my wife as an observer. I had no part in the preliminaries or the actual conduct of the demonstration, nor did I want to. By this time, my attitude concerning mediums and their phenomena was more psychoanalytic than parapsychological. My mature view was that mediums do not function exclusively on one level of consciousness and any discipline that tries to keep one level apart from the other is bound to have an adverse influence on the manifestations themselves. I not only hoped that a purely psychological inquiry would eliminate the personal fear element from parapsychological research but also it was my secret hope that eventually I would get a chance of putting John Myers on the analytic couch and find out something about Black Foot, his spirit-guide, and any other psychological quirks that made him click. I did not care about the conditions of control at this particular demonstration for another reason. I knew only too well that every researcher can pick flaws in the conditions which others provide, if not at the time of the experiment, then afterwards on further meditation. If by any miracle he could not find any, other researchers will do the service for him. If they cannot, somebody will be bound to step forward with the accusation that the researcher must have been in league with the medium.

A fresh packet of photographic printing paper was broken open in the dark and distributed, for a few seconds of holding in dim light, to the invited guests. It was brought by a photographer by the name of Mr. Siegel and, according to his testimony, John Myers never handled it. The paranormal aspect of the designs that appeared on the printing papers when collected and developed, hinges on this testimony.

However, I was not interested in establishing, for my satisfaction or for the others, the reality of psychic photography. I was concerned only with what happened to the two printing papers that were handed to me and to my wife, sitting at a distance from me. Something did happen to them, something very strange, if by coincidence, so unusual that it deserves reporting. Let me quote from an article I wrote for the *Psychic Observer*.

My printing paper was the last of the packet, No. 24. My wife, sitting apart from me, had No. 16. The numbers were scrawled on the back of the printing paper by the photographer as he made the distribution in a more or less random fashion. I held it in both hands by the edges, leaning forward from my chair, letting it slump in my lap. Suddenly, an impish thought entered my mind as to what Myers should put on the paper to make it convincing Then I chased the thought away saying to myself: nonsense, it is not concentration that produces psychic results, it is relaxation. My mind wandered off, and presently all the papers were collected and handed, for a few minutes, to my wife to hold. Then the development of the papers began, and this is what was found: *a shell in flight.*

On my wife's paper there appeared to be two luminous circles which, by their relative sizes, suggested the sun and moon, and were presently described in such terms by the medium from an adjoining room.

On my paper, there appeared the luminous impression of a shell in flight . . . judging by a slight light trail at the nozzle. The indentation of the cap is plainly visible, the only puzzling feature being a drop-like protuberance in the middle of the circular back. The medium identified it as a shell in flight.

The sun and the moon had no personal meaning for

my wife, but it had a very curious value for me. It happened that when I received John Myers' invitation for the night, I was under the impression that the day was Tuesday. As I knew I was free for Tuesday night, I accepted. When I put down the receiver, I realized that I made a mistake and that being Monday I was not free. I was booked to take the Master's Chair at the School of Instruction of a fraternal organization.

I was looking forward to that evening, so I asked, in considerable dismay, what should I do now? I had to cancel one of the two engagements.

My wife suggested I should cancel the fraternal one, as I was not indispensible at that demonstration and could have the same opportunity again. I agreed and made the cancellation. All this came back to my mind as I looked at the two luminous circles on my wife's printing paper . . . for a good reason. There is a triplicity of fraternal symbols consisting of the Sun, Moon and Master and they are called the Lesser Lights. That night I was less than a lesser light: none at all, as I did not take the Master's Chair. The two other lights existed independently of me . . . and they were on my wife's printing paper, the only celestial symbols in 24 experiments.

Was this mere coincidence, or had some mind been able to contact mine and convey a subtle and only to myself intelligible hint of such contact?

The question was intriguing and it was rendered still more so when my paper emerged from the developing bath. For remarkable as it may seem, the shell was a correct pictorial representation of what had passed through my mind, and . . . taken together with the two luminous discs on my wife's plate . . . make the representation complete. Further, the luminous trail of the shell seems to be a definite allusion to light and thus can be taken as a cross reference to the light of the sun and the moon.

Is this second set of meanings also a coincidence? Note that both of them concern thoughts of a private character. The matter of my Monday appointment was only discussed between my wife and myself. No one else knew about it, and not even my wife knew the thoughts that passed through my mind while I was holding the printing paper handed to me.

This is the exact wording in which I accounted for my experience in an article I wrote for *The Psychic Observer* at John Myers' request. But I was dismayed by the way it was made into a publicity stunt by Ralph Pressing, the editor. The headline screamed: SPIRIT PHOTOGRAPHY A FACT over five columns, the subtitle shouted: *London Scientist Attends Test Séance,* and the editor's summary which my article, "The Strange Case of John Myers," boosted skyhigh, stated with a finality:

The case for spirit photography settled for all time. No one *DARE* question the authenticity of the signed statements accompanying this article. No one *DARE* attack the mediumship of John Myers.

The signed statements came from the guests who attended the demonstration. I did not know that I would help to establish the case of spirit photography for all time, nor did I want to. Had I suspected it, I would not have permitted my article to be used in the lead. Not that there was anything in my statement that I wished to withdraw. On the contrary, I could have added to it, but I doubt that the editor would have considered the addition printable. To quote from a confidential letter I wrote about it to my psychoanalyst colleague and friend, Francis Regardie, on April 27, 1943:

My printing paper was numbered 24 on the back when it was given to me. When I was holding it, I leaned forward and naturally, the paper with my hand holding it dropped between my legs. It occurred to me, it would be funny to get a picture of the sexual trinity on it. I thought I would concentrate on it. I did for a while, then stopped, thinking: these things never work by concentration, let us leave it alone. So my mind wandered off, and presently, the papers were collected according to numbers. Mine was the last and was either on top or at the bottom of the packet as it was handed to my wife to hold.

Then the papers were developed; darn it if my paper did not show a shell, which is a perfect phallic emblem, and Amarya's paper two balls. These two balls were described by the medium as the Sun and the Moon. The relative size fitted that description.

It also fitted, by the same difference in size, the phallic trinity.

I did not tell this part of the story to John Myers until recently because I had my qualms about it. It was not a very nice thing to do. I only told him when, quite recently, he sent me, for my reading and opinion, a manuscript on the story of his demonstrations of psychic photography. It recalled to me, rather ruefully, that he did have such a booklet in mind as far back as the reported experiment and I answered him May 4, 1943:

As to the booklet, think it over, in the form I told you about it. You would have to take a series of sessions with me and tell me about your dreams and your past. You would gain a great deal of benefit from it aside from what we may find out about spirit photography.

My suggestion was not accepted. I had one or two analytic sessions with John Myers, but he did not continue. Black Foot remained a mystery. But I could not help telling him now: "Do you know that to me you look like a Red Indian? What was your fascinattion in childhood for Red Indian stories?"

I believe that the seeds of his spirit-guide were implanted in his mind on such early levels. I particularly wished to know if the origins of Black Foot reach down to the mysterious experience Myers reported in his biographical note from the time when as a child he found himself locked inside the boiler in the basement and, after desperate attempts to get out, fell into an exhausted sleep. Did his unconscious mind solve the problem of getting out and did he get out in a sleep-walking act? In that case, what about the bearded figure in white who appeared to deliver him? Was he the archtype of the Wise Old Man of Jungian psychology, which explains the white beard, or was this vision a foundation on which a transformation into the more fashionable Red Indian guide was made? John Myers believes that this tall stranger appeared many years later on his photographic plate as a psychic extra, which means that consciously he had failed to make an identification.

As to the question, what can John Myers be expected to prove by his demonstration, my answer is the same as the one I gave nearly 20 years ago: *Must* it prove anything? Is it not just as unscientific and intolerant to look for finalities as soon as we discover something new as to deny the existence of the new? Nothing is final in this life. If we can make a good case for the existence of a new force, we have gone a long way ahead. . . . There are new forces of the mind waiting for discovery. This is the greatest contribution that Spiritualism can make to the science of the mind.

The Great Memory

Museums are storehouses of memory; but they can never give us a complete picture of man's apperception of Nature and his age-old adaptation to Life. Nature is too vast for our comprehension and our adaptation to Life may have an episodic significance only. Nevertheless, we want it to endure. Perhaps it does, and we cannot help it.

There is reason to suppose that every act, physical or mental, leaves an indelible record in the universe; that everything living or dead has a ghostly counterpart, the design on which was formed by the forces of the cosmos.

This is the basis of the Great Memory. In the East it is called Akashic Records. In the West sometimes it is described as the Cosmic Picture Gallery. It is the *Memory of the Universe* or, at least, of our Planet, impersonal, beyond our comprehension, but not beyond our ability to catch glimpses of it when Nature appears to be in a "reminiscent" mood, or contact it if we have the immense mental development that some people claim to have reached.

Some years ago I read a report in the London *Times* by the Duke of Argyle. He passed by a road on which men were working. They pointed to a distant mountainside from which a mediaeval army, in glittering armor, was seen descending. Was the mountainside haunted? The answer is that ghosts do not haunt in packs, much less in army formation. Moreover, English history has a very clear attestation to such a mysterious event. A battle was fought on October 22, 1624, at Edge Hill (near Keinten, Northamptonshire). Two months after the battle a number of shepherds and village people witnessed an aerial re-enactment of the battle with all the noises of the guns, the neighing of horses and the groans of the wounded. The vision lasted for hours, was witnessed by people of reputation for several consecutive days and when its rumor reached the ears of Charles I a commission was sent out to investigate. The commission not only reported having seen the vision twice, but actually recognized fallen friends of theirs among the warriors. Sir Edmund Varley was one of them.

In *Biographia Presbyteriana*, Patrick Walker, the Covenanter, tells us that in 1686, about two miles below Lanark, on the bank of the Clyde:

> Many people gathered together for several afternoons, where there were showers of bonnets, hats, guns and swords, which covered the trees and the ground, companies of men in arms, marching in order upon the waterside, companies meeting companies . . . and then all falling to the ground and disappearing, and other companies immediately appearing in the same way.

But Patrick Walker himself saw nothing unusual. About two-thirds of the crowd saw the phenomena, the others perceived nothing strange. Said Andrew Lang:

> Patrick Walker's account is triumphantly honest and is, perhaps, as old a piece of psychology as any on record, thanks to his escape from the prevalent illusion which, no doubt, he would gladly have shared.

Was a similar sharing of illusions reported by Pausanias? According to him the Battle of Marathon survived aerially in a similar manner. Four hundred years after the great battle, the neighing of horses, the shouts of the victors, the cries of the vanquished and all the noise of a bitter war were frequently heard on the ancient plain.

Capt. Louis Patrick Bowler, author of *African Nights* and a pioneer in Bulawayo at the time of Cecil Rhodes, writes about his reminiscences about a famous spot where a slave convoy had perished:

> I was awakened from sleep by the native witch doctor shaking me and whispering: "Look, they come!"
> At first I could see nothing in the darkness, but gradually I became aware of a string of slaves tied together, wending their way towards the landing place. They were followed by a man in white ducks and a great black dog.

Turning to Capt. Pooley I asked him what he could see. He said:

"There is nothing but a big black dog lurching along down there."

This is in curious agreement with Patrick Walker's inability to share the perception of his fellowmen.

Odder still is the confirmation of the slave convoy story by my friend, Dr. G. B. Kirkland, formerly Government Medical Officer in Southern Rhodesia, in these words:

I had driven hard across country over an execrable apology for a road from a little town called Macheke in the Rhodesian uplands, for about a hundred and twenty miles across the border at Mtoko, intending to stay the night in the very old Portuguese townlet of Tete. The chief things I remember about the place were the ancient square fort, for all the world like P. C. Wren's Zinderneuf which he described in *Beau Geste*, the almost equally antiquated ferry over the Zambesi, and the drinks which were cheap and nasty.

We had been delayed on the road, my brother and I, and we decided to make a night of it in the car. Harubisi, the native boy, at once lit a fire and started to cook a meal. I was reading, I remember—reading in the light of the full moon. We had shot a guinea fowl earlier and my brother was cleaning his gun.

Suddenly Harubisi, who was the most phlegmatic fellow in the world, jumped to his feet in painful excitement. *"Congilla Inkoos,"* he hissed at me in a frightened whisper. "Ape, Ape" (Look over there, over there).

The moon shadows were playing queer tricks among the trees, the Christmas beetles were shrilling, and the frogs were kicking up a frightful shindy.

I looked and I saw—now wait a moment. I have never seen what is called a "ghost" or anything even remotely like the traditional "spook." But what Harubisi and I saw was a long train of men in single file, tied together by their necks, shambling along at a distance of about three hundred and fifty yards. There was no sign of any-one driving the train, which I considered rather queer; but, curiously enough, there was a large, very light colored

111

dog with them. The men were wretched specimens, emaciated to a degree.

I called my brother. "A slave convoy," I said. "Good God, I thought that sort of thing was wiped out."

My brother hurried over, but when I tried to point them out to him they had gone. Perhaps they had passed the little clearing and disappeared among the trees.

Harubisi himself was doing weird things behind a tree. I ordered him to come over the road, but he protested he was too frightened. "Who are those men?" I asked. *"Inkoos,"* he replied, "they are not men, they are the spirits of dead slaves. I have seen them before."

Two other white men known to me have also seen what I saw, and always with the dog. I have tried to collect more data, but failed. Natives are reticent on these things.

I often wonder whether these miserable fellows originally perished on the way and are members of the great "undead" that Algernon Blackwood writes so graphically about.

A critic would naturally object. Dr. Kirkland may have read Patrick Bowler's story and imagined the rest. The objection is not as good as the story. But, of course, we need contemporary confirmation of such experiences, preferably not from savage lands. There is one such story well worth mentioning.

Under the auctorial pseudonyms of Miss Morrison and Miss Lamont a remarkable book was published in 1911, entitled *An Adventure*. The authors were, as revealed later, Miss Anne Moberly, daughter of the Bishop of Salisbury, England, and Dr. Eleanor Jourdain. According to the book they had simultaneous visions, in 1901 and in 1902, on the grounds of Versailles Palace of the place as it was in 1789.

Some time after the first publication of the book testimony was given by people who lived in the neighborhood of Versailles that they had also seen the mysterious appearances, the strange phenomena being witnessed only on the anniversary of the attack on Versailles during the French Revolution. The most inexplicable feature of the story was that the people of the eighteenth century saw, heard and spoke to the people of the twentieth century who never doubted at the time that they were in communication with real individuals.

The anniversary may be a clue. There is a trauma of anniversaries that psychoanalysts frequently find occurring when the date of tragic events returns on the calendar. Why it is difficult to say, but there may be a link in it with the cosmic rhythm, the return of the seasons and the orbiting of the Earth around the Sun. The Great Memory is stirred like our own personal memories are and this stirring endows them with a life that becomes perceptible at times.

It is not easy to follow the reasoning of the theosophists, but perhaps it is appropriate at this point to quote from Annie Besant's and C. W. Leadbeater's *Man, Whence, How and Whither:*

> The mind of a Logos or Word . . . containing within itself all the mental images embodied in, say a Solar System, arranged in order of succession of their proposed manifestation, but all there, all capable of review, as we can review our own thought images . . . the Soul may reach the Memory of Nature, the embodiment in the material world of the Thoughts of the Logos, the reflection as it were, of His Mind. There dwells the Past in ever-living record; there also dwells the Future, more difficult for the half-developed soul to reach, because not yet manifested, nor yet embodied, though quite as "real." The Soul, reading these records, may transmit them to the body, impress them on the brain, and then record them in words and writings.

I only knew of one man who shed practical light on this loss in mysticism. He was my old friend, G. R. S. Mead, the great scholar of Christian origins. This is what he says of Akashic research (in *Did Jesus Live 100 B.C.?*):

> It would be as well to have it understood that the method of investigation to which I am referring does not bring into consideration any question of trance, either self-induced, or mesmerically or hynotically effected. As far as I can judge, my colleagues are, to all outward seeming, in quite their normal state. They go through no outward ceremonies, or internal ones for that matter, nor even any outward preparation but that of assuming a comfortable position; moreover, they not only describe, as each normally has the power of description, what is passing before their inner vision in precisely the same fashion as one would describe some objective scene,

but they are frequently as surprised as their auditors that the scenes or events they are attempting to explain are not at all as they expected to see them, and remark on them as critically, and frequently as skeptically as those who cannot "see" for themselves but whose knowledge on the subject from objective study may be greater than theirs.

Now, although it is true that in the majority of cases I have not been able to check their statements, and doubt whether it will ever be possible to do so, owing to the lack of objective material, nevertheless in a number of instances, few when compared with the mass of statements made, but numerous enough in themselves, I have been able to do so. It can, of course, be argued, as has been done in somewhat similar cases, that all of this is merely the bringing into subjective objectivity the imaginative dramatisation of facts which have been normally heard or read, or even momentarily glanced at, and which have sunk beneath the threshold of consciousness, either of the seers themselves or of one or other of their auditors, or even some permutation or combination of these. But such an explanation seems somewhat feeble to one who, like myself, has taken down laboriously dictated passages from MSS, described, for instance, as written in archaic Greek uncials—MSS, the contents of which, as far as I am aware, are not known to exist—passages laboriously dictated letter by letter, by a friend whose knowledge of the language extended hardly beyond the alphabet. Occasionally gaps had to be left for certain forms of letters with which, not only my colleague but also myself, were previously entirely unacquainted; these gaps had to be filled up afterwards when the matter was transcribed and broken up into words and sentences which turned out to be in good, construable Greek, the original or copy of which, I am as sure as I can be of anything, neither my colleague nor myself have ever seen physically. Moreover, I have had dates and information given by these methods which I could only verify afterwards by long and patient research, and which, I am convinced, no one but a widely read scholar of classical antiquity could have come across.

Many years have passed since my last conversation with G. R. S. Mead, but I am still filled with wonder over this statement of his. I know nothing similar that I consider creditable in this field of research and I confess I am awed by the possibilities that his admission opens up for the human mind.

The Cocos Island Mystery[1]

A recent outbreak of interest in treasure-hunting on Cocos Island sent me searching through papers I had preserved from my old days of psychical research in England. I read the book, *The Lost Treasure of Cocos Island*, by Ralph Hancock and Julian A. Weston, which had renewed interest in the perennial mystery of what has happened to the immense treasures hidden on a scrap of land 550 miles due west from Panama City, and I compared its latest findings with my unpublished writing on the quest for treasure there which Sir Malcolm Campbell (then Captain Campbell) had undertaken in 1926. My writing also told about two mediums through whose help I had tried to find the location of the treasure on Cocos Island, which Sir Malcolm Campbell so conspicuously failed to find. Yes, it would be worthwhile at last to publish the contents of my old paper, for as Hancock and Weston conclusively show, somewhere in the steaming jungle of Cocos Island lies the greatest treasure hoard on earth, yet in 140 years expedition after expedition has failed to find a trace of it. Under the circumstances any possible clue should be given.

The consensus is that there are three treasure troves on Cocos Island, and this is what Sir Malcolm Campbell believed when I happened to travel with him in 1933 from London to Budapest on the Orient Express. We were bound for an international newspaper congress where the great speed king—Sir Malcolm was the first man to travel over 300 miles per hour in an automobile—was to represent Lord Rothermere and the *Daily Mail*. He gave me his book, *My Greatest Adventure* (1931), to read, and talked freely, as the Orient Express sped along, about the mystery of Cocos Island:

The first [treasure trove] is that of Captain Edward

[1] From *Tomorrow* Magazine, Winter 1962. Reprinted by courtesy of the Parapsychology Foundation, New York.

Davis, a partner with Damphier in his privateering adventures, when he blockaded the Bay of Panama and sacked the City of Léon in Nicaragua in 1685.

Hancock and Weston add to the Davis story:

> Captain Davis and his men made Cocos Island their headquarters and raided the coast of New Spain from Baja, California to Guayaquil. From time to time the *Bachelor's Delight* was joined by the ships of other freebooters . . . All these made stops at Cocos Island to bury the plunder of their raids. And when one considers the tons of silver ingots, the chests stuffed with jewels and pieces-of-eight, and the leathern bags filled with gold that must have been buried all over the island, the marvel is that so little of it has ever been found.

Captain Davis "surrendered to his Majesty's mercy," accepted the amnesty offered to all pirates by King James II, and retired to Virginia to await a chance to return to Cocos Island and recover his treasure. He finally started back in a small ship, took to piracy along the way, and mysteriously disappeared.

The second treasure trove was deposited on Cocos Island by Captain Benito Bonito, the notorious "Bonito of the Bloody Sword." He operated in the waters off Central America in the years 1818–1820 and is thought to have buried several large fortunes on Cocos. In 1819 his cutthroat crew came ashore and hijacked a rich cargo of gold that was being taken from Mexico City to Acapulco. This netted treasure estimated to be worth 11 million dollars—all of which Captain Bonito buried on Cocos Island. In 1821 "Bonito of the Bloody Sword" died in a mutiny of his men in the West Indies.

But the greatest treasure trove on this small tropical island—it's only four miles long by three wide—is the "Lima" treasure which is estimated to be worth one hundred million dollars! In 1820 the Spanish Viceroy of Peru became alarmed when a rebel army under José de San Martin invaded his province. He hastily emptied the mint and its storehouse of gold and silver and stripped the churches of their solid gold and silver accoutrements, and transported all this treasure to Lima's seaport, Callao. Here it was put on board the British merchantman, *Mary Dear*, which was commanded by a Scot, Captain Thompson. It was arranged that Captain Thompson should put to sea and cruise for a couple of months. Then, if the Spanish regime at Lima were still secure, he should return to Callao and restore the treasure; otherwise he should deliver the treasure to the Spanish authorities in Panama. A half-dozen men, including two priests, came on board to guard the fabulously rich cargo.

Out to sea went the *Mary Dear* and the next morning the gold-crazed crew murdered the guards and the priests. Captain Thompson headed for Cocos Island in lat. 5° 32′ 57″ North, long. 87° 2′ 10″ West in the Pacific Ocean. He thought that the treasure could be buried without interference in this uninhabited place and that, after a year or two, he could reassemble his men and they could go back to Cocos, recover the treasure and take it home to England.

Only the first part of this plan was affected. The *Mary Dear* anchored in one of the three bays on the north side of Cocos Island and her longboat, loaded to the gunwales, made 11 trips to shore. The immense treasure was hidden in a spot selected by the captain and the mate, and only a small amount of coins was kept back and shared among the crew. The *Mary Dear* sailed away—to disaster.

A Spanish man-of-war picked her up and made acutely embarrassing inquiries about the missing treasure. Captain Thompson and his crew were put on trial for murder and piracy on the high seas. Everyone was sentenced to be hanged and the sentence was carried out until only the captain and the mate remained. They then made a deal. If their lives were spared they would lead the Spaniards to the spot where they had buried the "Lima" treasure. Which in due course they did.

And here thickens the mystery of Cocos Island. For when the *expedicionarios* landed on Cocos, the Captain and the mate promptly disappeared into the thick jungle which comes right down to the water's edge. For days the *expedicionarios* hunted for them, but finally had to sail back, disappointed in their treasure-lust.

The self-marooned men lived on coconuts, birds' eggs, fish and small game for several months and were rescued sometime in 1822 by a British whaler which stopped at the island for fresh water. The captain and the mate said simply that they had been shipwrecked on the island, and to avoid raising any suspicion, they refrained from taking with them even an ounce of gold.

The next item in this fascinating story is the death of the mate in Costa Rica, and then a sequence of stories about the treasure coming from Captain Thompson. But did the mate die at Puntarēnas, as generally accepted until Hancock and Weston came along with their new book? Is there also a chain of evidence coming from him as a source? The Cocos Island story from 1822 to the present is a tangle of legends, fancies, facts and fictions, and scores of unsuccessful treasure hunts, some extremely well organized and some one-man amateur affairs.

This is a business of ancient descent. From time immemorial man has searched for buried treasure. From time immemorial spirits have been alleged to hover over hidden hoards. The air of the supernatural circulates over treasure troves, and uncanny happenings have chilled the blood of many brave adventurers, as happened with Sir Malcolm Campbell in 1926. He discussed with me the unknown into which he felt he had strayed on that little tropical island.

According to him, he had gone there for romantic reasons. As he put it, "What able-bodied man is there with time, money and imagination, who would not trim his sails and set his course for salty horizons tomorrow, if he had a clue in his pocket, a treasure to find!"

He camped on the island with two fellow-adventurers and a mongrel dog. One night, aching in every limb from the day's exertions, he was trying to sleep in the terrible heat.

He writes in *My Greatest Adventure:*

Suddenly the dog, who had been sleeping beside me, twitching occasionally in his sleep as dogs sometimes do, but otherwise normal, leapt to his feet with a terrifying howl and dashed to the open flap of the tent door, barking and chattering with rage and fear. He was almost beside himself. I have never seen a dog in such a paroxysm of terror. It was as though he had seen a ghost. He stood there barking and yapping into the blackness of the night, every hair on end, his voice vibrant with fear and defiance.

Both men awoke and sat up. I took my revolver from the holster and crawled to the tent door, expecting to meet anything from a ghost to a wild pig or an Indian on his belly. There was nothing. The great wood fire, built to keep off the insects, leapt and flickered redly against the velvet background of the tropic dark. Overhead a million stars shown and twinkled like points of fire. The trees, like a tapestry of black velvet, stood brooding and motionless around the tiny camp. A million insects filled the night with a throbbing hum. The sea broke with the swish of silk gently on the beach. There were no other sounds.

I stepped quietly outside the radius of the firelight and sneaked among the trees, expecting at any moment to surprise some lurking enemy. It may seen a little melodramatic to recount it now, but I can only say that Cocos possesses such an indefinable influence of evil that when once you are on it, your nerves are on the edge for anything. It is a haunted island. I could find nothing, although I scouted cautiously round all the camp, slipping and sliding among the trees, finger on trigger ready to shoot. All the time the dog was standing in the tent door, whining and shivering. I had the feeling that somewhere in the blackness someone was watching me, following my every movement. I returned to the tent with a prickly feeling down my spine.

When I got inside the dog quieted down after a time, and presently went to sleep. I lay awake for an hour or so with my revolver handy, waiting for something to happen. Nothing did. Finally I fell off to sleep.

The next night the same thing happened again. Round about midnight the dog sprang suddenly to the tent door, yapping, barking, shivering with fear. He stood there, frothing at the mouth, half paralyzed with fright. Again I reconnoitered, revolver in hand. Again I had the feeling that something was crouching in the bush watching me. But I could find nothing and nothing happened.

Twice after this the same thing happened in the middle of the night. We could not account for it then, and I cannot explain it now. There are no animals on the island, so far as I know, except wild pig, and they are not stealthy beasts. There is no subtlety about them. When they move it is for all the world to hear. They plunge and crash, and do not care who listens to them. I saw no rats, no snakes, in fact, no reptiles or mammals of any sort apart from pig. What then, or who, can have been our mysterious midnight visitors?

In our conversation on the Orient Express, Sir Malcolm would subtract nothing from this account of an extraordinary experience. He knew that psychical research was my pre-occupation, and he assured me that his account was a faithful and unembellished rendering of what had occurred. He was not a spiritualist, nor did he believe in ghosts or evil spirits; but he frankly confessed that he would not like to spend many nights alone on Cocos Island. He also noted that almost every one of the major expeditions that in the last century had landed on Cocos Island and searched for the treasure had met with disaster, and not one had succeeded in finding anything. Even his own party had suffered in a small way from misfortune: one of his companions hurt his leg, and another badly lamed for a fortnight.

Of what was the dog afraid? Sir Malcolm could advance only one explanation. It is romantic, and it stirs one's imagination. (Incidentally, it is not included in the lore that Hancock and Weston put in *The Lost Treasure of Cocos Island*.) There is a legend in the South Seas that at the time of the Spanish Conquistadors some of the Incas of the Peruvian mainland fled from the appalling cruelty of the invader, and found refuge on Cocos. When the pirates came on their irregular visits, these Incas retreated to the top of the highest mountain on the island, nearly 2800 feet high, where, according to one of the pirate chroniclers, there is a crater-lake teeming with fish. Here, the legend says, the descendants of the mighty Inca race still dwell. They are in deadly fear of the white man and the moment their sentries descry a ship upon the horizon, they damp their fires, and every member of the group takes to the high hills.

I frankly told Sir Malcolm that I did not believe a lurking Inca spy could send his dog into a paroxysm of terror. To me the signs pointed to a "supernatural" visitation. We talked long into the night. I told him that, as an experiment, it would be well worthwhile to attempt an inquiry through psychic channels into the treasure's location. Of course, he was rather skeptical, but agreed to lend me the Admiralty map he had used in his treasure hunt.

The map showed a mountainous island of less than 20 square miles in area. It rises almost vertically out of the sea and has only two adequate landing places, Chatham Bay and Wafer Bay, on its north side. It is said that there are only two seasons —the rainy season and the wet season; and the island is obscured much of the time by heavy rainfall or by fog.

I covered a top corner of this map, to hide the name of the

island, and took it to the British College of Psychic Science, where I had a sitting with Miss Jacqueline. I took shorthand notes.

The map was still unrolled when Miss Jacqueline said:

"Is that concerning a place? Is it an initial H or K?"

I said that K, according to the sound, was correct.

She then took the map which could have conveyed little more to her than that it represented an island, and continued:

"I don't know whether it is connected with something hidden. I see three or four people trying to discover something, to look for something. I see very great possibilities. It is almost as if I were going up to hidden treasure."

After I had partly unrolled the map she pointed at various spots on it and asked:

"Has there been any writing on this place? Nothing to do with Glastonbury Abbey? No name of any person like that?"

This was an error, but nevertheless a good proof that the idea of hidden treasure was not conveyed from my mind to hers. The spots she pointed out were different from those Sir Malcolm had picked as likely. I told Miss Jacqueline nothing whatsoever.

Two days later I visited her again. She then said that at almost the instant I had left her, she had heard her "guide" say, "Coco . . . Coco Island."

This time she tried her divining rod over the map. It went into oscillation over certain spots, indicating, as she believed, the presence of gold. She pointed to the highest peak, Mount Iglesias, and said that some people were there. This was in curious agreement with the legend that descendants of the Incas may still be surviving on this mountaintop. I found this interview encouraging.

With the map rolled up, I next called on Mrs. Eileen J. Garrett. When she passed into trance and "Uvani," one of her spirit controls, introduced himself, I asked him if he could put me in touch with "John King," a picturesque old-timer in spirit "controls," who is said to have been in the flesh Sir Henry Morgan, the pirate. "Uvani" said that he would try, and after a little while, said that he had found him. He announced that he would speak in his behalf.

"This contract gives him the impression of a great deal of adventure. This is a map. The map of an island. Off Penzance. I feel an island to which this map takes me. There is some idea of exploration here. He is glad to see that adventure is still left in the hearts of some people. There is treasure. He has the feeling of buried treasure. This was the haunt of pirates in the old days. There have been many shipwrecks here, and nobles fleeing from the court with their jewelry and documents give him the impression that this island has a great history. Legends are current, it even being suspected that many of the royal fugitives had taken up residence here until they were taken off from this hotbed of treasure. I do not know if any treasure has been found, but he is definite that much had been put there, especially under the little church to which there was a path from the water front."

I said that there must be some mistake. The island is no-where near England and is uninhabited.

"Uvani" was puzzled. Was I sure that there was no channel at all? Then to my surprise:

"Is it anything like C . . . O . . . C? "

Then slowly:

"Cocos. He speaks of Cocos Island as connected with the peninsula by an ancient civilization. Peruvian. The habitation of the ancient In . . . [struggling] . . . Inc . . . A religious sect like the Aztecs which he calls White Indians. At one time it was the headquarters of the occult tribe of the Aztecs . . . it was only approachable from two sides. There is an extinct volcano and the remains of a church. For a long time it was thought that there were inhabitants on that island, on the other side of the volcano, on the west where there is no landing place. The western side is sheer cliff. In the old days there was a port on the other side for traders between South America and the Southern Archipelago. The treasure was taken to the western side of the island. It meant days of dwelling there and carrying provisions. There was a time when it was a place of refuge. Many Inca pilgrims went there. No treasure has been taken off. He could help to find it. It would give him great joy, like old days. But one would have to make a safari and take it very seriously."

There are some remarkable points in this statement. Remember that the map was rolled up. Nothing indicated the nature of the roll. If Mrs. Garrett or "Uvani" were reading my mind, how did the confusion at the beginning of the description come about? Moreover, in my romatic imagination I would have preferred that the ancient Incas were still living on the island to their being wiped out by a volcanic eruption.

There are two high peaks on the island, Mount Iglesias, 2,788 feet, and another, unnamed, rising 1,574 feet. Whether they are volcanic I cannot tell, nor do Hancock and Weston tell us. It is plain from the map that the west side of the island is unapproachable. It is curious, too, that another clairvoyant, a Mrs. Pollock, of whom Sir Malcolm Campbell writes in his book, should have said that "the treasure lies high up, perhaps a thousand feet above sea-level."

I was given no precise indication of where the treasure is to be found. But "John King" had said that he could lead to it. He asked for a meeting with the owner of the map.

Had I known the topography of the island, had I possessed myself of all the available information about the pirates and their evil deeds on this island. I believe I should have obtained more help. Why I would have, I cannot tell. All I know is that in mediumistic communications the sitter's imagination, if deeply exercised, appears to act as a reply, and is able to glean more definite indications than does a barren mind. Mrs. Pollock, for instance, gave Sir Malcolm fairly precise indications of the whereabouts of the treasure, indications that were almost as important as the pirate clue which he possessed. Though, owing to shortness of time, Sir Malcolm returned from Cocos with empty hands, he was sufficiently impressed by Mrs. Pollock to write in his book: "Mrs. Pollock's indication will very likely either lead to the subsequent discovery of the treasure, or will be amply justified should it be found without their help."

I wanted to arrange a meeting between "John King" and Sir Malcolm. He had written:

> One of these days I shall return to Cocos, and when I do I shall not give up the search until I have either found the treasure or convinced myself that it is humanly impossible to disvcover it.

But in the nineteen-thirties he was afraid to expose himself to a fresh treasure-hunting temptation. He never again outfitted an expedition to Cocos Island, and the prize piece of the "Lima" treasure—a solid gold, gem-encrusted, life-sized image of the Virgin Mary—still lies unfound on that secretive speck of land midway between San Francisco and Valparaiso.

Tomb-robbing is as ancient a specialization among thieves as the worship of the dead by burial ceremonies. Nowhere had both gained as much notoriety as in Egypt. The Pharaohs had given up the pyramids as burial places because they no longer could protect the bodies of the dead. Rock hewn shaft-tombs were easier to conceal and the practice of carving them from the Nile cliffs continued for four hundred years. The continued war with the cemetery ghouls must have been the origin of the protective curse that was laid was on violators of the tomb. Whether any violators of the long past had died because of the curse we do not know, but the curse had survived and—at least as a psychological force—is still alive.

Many stories have been told of the mummy case of a priestess of Amen-Ra, now in the British Museum. A number of people were said to have met with strange disasters immediately or shortly after they came in contact with it, but the principal source of the fear of the Egyptian curse dates, no doubt, from the discovery of Tut-Ankh-Amen's tomb in 1922. This young Pharaoh died at 18 around 1350 B.C. He was the son-in-law of Ikhnaton who abolished the plurality of gods in Egypt and thereby earned the savage hostility of the priest-craft.

It was Howard Carter who made the discovery, but the expedition was organized by Lord Carnarvon. The magnificent treasures that took eight seasons to salvage are now at the national museum in Cairo, but the intact body of the youthful ruler still lies in the burial chamber of the tomb.

Archaeologists will always have to face the charge of desecration of tombs whenever they make a discovery, because such expeditions are not conducted in a religious spirit. Rumors flew thick and fast when a series of deaths struck down those who were connected with the opening of Tut-Ankh-Amen's tomb. The idea of desecration was heightened by an unfortunate act: Lord Carnarvon gave a lunch party in the tomb: tables were set up laden with dishes and wines, the guests were photographed and there was even talk of a concert to be held in the sepulchral chamber. Dr. Weigall, who was then Inspector-General of Antiquities in Eygpt, is said to have voiced his misgivings by saying: "If that is the spirit in which he is going down, he will not live for six weeks."

Omens connected with the opening of the tomb were widely talked about. As the party descended at the entrance, though there was not a breath of wind about the place, a sandstorm on a miniature scale arose and swept along the desert right to the mouth of the tomb; it hung above it for a while, then disappeared. Almost immediately afterwards a hawk (the emblem of royalty in ancient days) flew up from the East, hovered over the tomb and then swept away. Finally, on the day when Howard Carter made his first entrance into the tomb, his pet canary was swallowed by a snake—the emblem of Tut-Ankh-Amen and of the Pharaohs.

None of these omens deserves any serious consideration. People die constantly all over the world from natural causes, though it must be admitted that every curse implies a malignant suggestion the efficacy of which may depend on the streak of superstition that exists in the people concerned.

This is an easy way of dealing with the curse from Egypt. That complicating elements exist has been admitted by well-known Egyptologists. Dr. Weigall is one of them. To his name is attached one of the strangest adventures in the record of occult happenings connected with tombs. It concerns a porcelain cat, a fresh find which, he thought, probably contained the mummy of the actual animal—sacred to Bubastis, the cat-headed god of Love.

Dr. Weigall took it home for an examination, but was unable to discover the joint between the two halves. That night he found himself unable to go to sleep. This sudden attack of insomnia is one of the common features connected with Egyptian relics. The excitement of his unconscious was indicated by strange fancies. The cat seemed to move and glare at him. After tossing about for hours, he fell asleep, only to be awakened by a tremendous report—a second common feature in these mystery stories. He jumped out of bed and found himself attacked by a huge grey cat which clawed his face and hands, and then flew out through the open window. Dr. Weigall rushed to the window in time to see his own cat in the garden bristling at an intruder that had disappeared in the bushes. The attacker must have been objective enough to be seen by another cat, and so were the claw marks. On turning to the porcelain cat, he found the casing split wide open.

Exposed and standing perfectly upright, a mummified cat was staring at him.

This was the third feature of the adventure: the discharge of energy (the loud report) followed by telekinetic phenomena. The mystery of how to open the porcelain cast was solved, but the mummy suffered no ill effects from the explosion.

Before discussing the merits of the case, let us consider Sir Alexander Seton's story of a human bone (a sacrum) that came from a deep hole from a newly discovered small pyramid in the desert behind the Sphinx.

The bone was taken home as a souvenir and kept in a glass case in the Seton home in Edinburgh. After a series of disconcerting illnesses, a robed figure was seen by the very scared 9-year-old nephew of Seton. Then came a night during which Sir Alexander had "the feeling of absolute panic." This is also a common feature of mummy mysteries. He went downstairs and found the bone out of its glass case, the glass case lying completely shattered at the bottom of a table two feet away. On another occasion a glass vase that contained flowers was found lying on the floor. The glass vase was on the table where the bone had been placed. Nobody had been in the room. In a third instance, a chair in the drawing room was found upside down after a "thump" when Sir Alexander was alone in the house. The table on which the bone stood was also moved and the vase was thrown eight feet away from it.

In his account before the Edinburgh Psychic College of these odd happenings, Sir Alexander voiced the conviction that the bone "wanted to go home" to its resting place. He was quite willing to believe that there was something in the curse of the Pharaohs.

Let us now turn to a third story, that of Mrs. Eve Brackenbury, Rebecca West's secretary and a seasoned parapsychologist. She was, for years, Assistant Research Officer to the Society for Psychical Research in London, and—at the time she told her story in a lecture—Honorary Secretary to the Medical Committee of the International Institute for Psychical Research of which I was then Director of Research.

Some years before, Eve had been given the present of the mummified head of a beautiful Egyptian woman. Nothing was known of its history—and she would not have believed it anyhow.

The first night after its arrival, the mummified head remained wrapped up as it came. Nothing happened, except that neither she nor her husband (an engineer and inventor whom I have also personally known) could gain a wink of sleep.

Next day the head was unpacked and placed on a bureau by the side of a dainty porcelain figure of a Chinese goddess. The bureau stood next to the wall which adjoined their bedroom. For some reason, again, neither of them could go to sleep. They sat up, smoked and talked. Then suddenly, there was an appalling crash in the next room. It sounded like the crack of a revolver. Both Mrs. Brackenbury and her husband received a shock. In the wake of the shock they were assailed by stark, unreasoning fear. They could not summon up enough courage to go into the next room and find out the reason of the crash. They could not help thinking of the mummy. Stories of evil forces and ancient curses came surging into their minds. The fearful crash appeared to be evidence that some mysterious power was abroad in the next room. There was no doubt that the crash came from there. The apartment below was empty. The house was occupied by them alone.

Eventually, as no other phenomenon followed the crash, the tension relaxed and they fell into sleep. Both of them were disturbed by nightmares. Mrs. Brackenbury found herself in a dark cave pursued by a horde of headless men. She woke with a scream and found her husband in an almost cataleptic state. They spent the rest of the night awake. At 6 o'clock in the morning they still would not enter the next room, something seemed to stop them before the door. With the stirring of traffic and other increasing street noises they felt the atmosphere becoming more normal, so they passed into the next room.

The mummied head stood on the bureau as before. But the Chinese goddess was dethroned. Something had thrown it over and flung it under the bureau into a position into which it could not have rolled by just falling over. Strange to say, the delicate figure with outstretched fingers was completely unharmed.

The uncanniness of the mummy was felt by a dog. Before its arrival, the dog would frisk gaily about the flat whenever its owner brought it up; now it refused to enter and fled howling down the stairs.

After this Eve gave the head away. None of its subsequent owners suffered from any disturbance, except one on which it inflicted nightmares. He who likes may ask the question: Was the Chinese goddess responsible for the crash? Did ancient Egypt rise against China? Could the clash arouse some mysterious dormant power in the mummified head of the Egyptian Princess?

When I posed this question I did not realize how near I came to a theory of explanation. Only after I had formulated my hypothesis of the Family *Gestalt* to explain ancestral haunting in old British families[1] did I realize that the Chinese goddess and the Egyptian head may well have been possessed by antagonistic powers. I could not imagine the source of this power until I came to realize that the worship of ancient religions, with the appropriate rituals and sacrifices, must needs create a *Gestalt*, a collective psychological entity on a higher and more powerful level than the Family *Gestalt* exists. No one should underestimate the power of religion. It still can move the world. The gods of Old are asleep but not dead. The power invested in sacred rights, buildings and objects can be released by an act of sacrilege against the persons who channelize it and against their environment.

Sacrilege demands punishment or propitiation. This is an elementary principle, the existence of which the possessors of religious objects removed from burial places, temples or from bodies buried with appropriate rites do not yet suspect. In absence of propitiation, the power of the *Gestalt*—popularly called the curse—springs into action.

The common feature of the three cases discussed is sacrilege. Dr. Weigall committed it when he took home a mummified cat —a representation of cat-headed Bubastis, the god of Love— and handled it with irreverent fingers. The sacrum in Sir Alexander Seton's possession was torn away from a burial place and "demanded" a return in much the same way as ghosts in haunted houses will not be at rest until their un-covered skeleton is buried in holy ground. The mummified head was "roused" by the close spatial relationship with the symbol of another *Gestalt*, the figure of the Chinese goddess.

The *Gestalt* is not human; the Group Soul is—to a great extent. The ghost that once was man may gravitate into it through the particular pattern of his earth life. Both Gardner

---

[1] *The Haunted Mind,* Helix Press, New York, 1960, pp. 43-54.

Murphy[2] and Prof. H. H. Price[3] agree in postulating this in their field theory and world of images. If we fear the dead by instinct, the more we should dread the wrath of the *Gestalt*. We do not lay food out on the graves of the dead, like savages, but we do bedeck them with flowers in loving memory and we are anxious to speak well of them. This is symbolic and verbal worship, the nearest we dare to come to a rite of propitiation. *Gestalt* or Group Soul, curse or malignant suggestion that releases a psychic storm—we should never take the risk of running against it.

Dreaming True

Having dreamed that he was a butterfly, Chuang Tzu, the Chinese sage who lived 2500 years ago, asked himself on awakening:

> Now, am I Chuang Tzu who has dreamed that he was a butterfly, or am I a butterfly which is now dreaming that it is Chuang Tzu?

Many people have asked since: which is our true home: the world of dreams or the physical world?

On the face of it the question is preposterous. Psychoanalysis has disposed of a large part of the mystery of dreams, proving that dreams are built on forgotten memories, ideas and desire that the unconscious weaves into the pattern of a crazy quilt.

Yet, there are dreams regarding which the tools of psychoanalysis prove to be of little help. Some of these dreams are famous and have often been quoted in books. One is that of Professor Agassiz, the famous paleontologist of bygone days.

He had been striving for two weeks to decipher the obscure impressions of a fossil fish on a stone slab in which it was preserved. He failed. In a dream he saw the fish with all the

---

[2] *"Field Theory and Survival," Journal of the American Society for Psychical Research*, Oct. 1945, p. 202.

[3] "Survival and the Idea of Another World," Proceedings of the Society for Psychical Research, Jan. 1953.

missing features perfectly restored. The image escaped him on awakening. He went to the Jardin des Plantes in the hope that an association with the fossil would recapture it. No such thing happened. Next night he again dreamt of the fish and, in the morning, the features of the fish were as elusive as ever. For the third night he placed paper and pencil near his bed. Towards the morning the fish again appeared in his dream. Half dreaming, half awake, he traced the outlines in the darkness as best he could. On full awakening he was surprised to see features in his nocturnal sketch which he thought impossible. He hastened to the Jardin des Plantes, began to chisel on the surface of the stone, taking the sketch as a guide, and to his surprise, he found the hidden portions of the fish as indicated in the drawing.

Psychoanalysis might submit the suggestion, with a smile, the Professor Agassiz had seen the same fish somewhere before but that he could not sufficiently stimulate the latent memory to rise into consciousness. While he was asleep, his subconscious mind did the trick.

Professor Agassiz alone could have told whether the explanation was correct. It does not much help us in dreams of a more complicated type, as that of Professor Hilprecht, the Babylonian scholar. He tried to decipher two small pieces of agate and, tired out by vain speculation, went to sleep. In a dream, a tall, thin priest of the pre-Christian Nippur appeared, led him to the treasure-chamber of the temple and went with him into a small low-ceilinged room without windows in which there was a large wooden chest; scraps of lapis-lazuli lay scattered on the floor. Here he told him:

The two fragments which you have published separately belong together, and their history is as follows: King Kruigalzu (c. 1300 B.C.) once went to the Temple of Bel, taking with him as an offering, among other articles of agate and lapis lazuli, an inscribed votive cylinder of agate. Then we priests suddenly received the command to make for the statue of the god Nidib a pair of earrings of agate. We were in great dismay, since there was no agate as raw material at hand. In order to execute the command there was nothing for us to do but cut the votive cylinder into three parts, thus making three rings, each of which contained a portion of the original inscription. The first two served as earrings for the statue of the

130

god; the two fragments which have given you so much trouble are portions of them. If you will put the two together you will have a confirmation of my words.

The continuation of the story is given by Mrs. Hilprecht who saw the professor jump out of bed, rush into the study, and cry out: "It is so, it is so!"

It is difficult to escape the feeling that at least an element of clairvoyance is mixed in this extraordinary dream which many, no doubt, would put down to the direct intervention of a long dead priest.

We could easily solve the problem of dreams of this type if we could carry our waking consciousness and reasoning power into the dream world. This is the gift which Peter Ibbetson possessed. Is George duMaurier's charming story the product of imagination or is there a germ of truth behind it?

Occultists will tell you that a great truth is behind it. They claim to know a definite technique whereby you can "dream true", *i.e.* retain your consciousness in the dream state. You must keep, they say, control of yourself up to the moment of falling asleep. When you have learned to do that, construct mentally a definite scene, hold it firmly in your mind and, at the very last moment, before you fall asleep, transfer yourself into the scene, step into the picture and you will find that your consciousness remains unbroken, that you will have perfect continuity of thought and, on waking, you will remember everything that happened while you were asleep.

This sounds very tempting. But who can do it? I have tried and failed. I pictured myself going up in an elevator; then the elevator stopped and I stepped into a mental picture. So far so good, but . . . I was awake. I found it impossible to go to sleep while I was holding on to my consciousness. If I allowed my consciousness to slip, the mental picture faded away.

I gave it up; but I am asked to believe that some people can do the trick. They find themselves in a dream body, which is remarkably free from physical limitations. In fact it can only act on matter by dint of a terrific effort. Dr. Van Eeden, a Dutch physician, tried to move definite objects while thus asleep. All he achieved was a dual consciousness. He remembered clearly that he was asleep in bed, with his arms folded across his breast and that at the same time he was looking out of the window and saw a dog run up, look at him, and run away.

Mr. Sylvan Muldoon, of Wisconsin, the author of an unusual book, *The Projection of the Astral Body,* claims to have succeeded where Dr. Eeden failed. The odd thing was that in reality the object did not move until two seconds later. There was a metronome in another room on the piano. He started it with the hands of his dream body. Then he returned to bed and woke up. A little time elapsed and then the metronome began to tick.

The same curious time-lag was observed by Sir Oliver Lodge in his experiments with Eusapia Paladino, the famous Italian trance medium. She could move objects without physical contact when she was six or seven feet away, the time interval between the movement of her hand and that of the object was something like two seconds. An accordion began to play by itself. The fingers of the medium, at a distance, were moving in a thoroughly appropriate manner. Sir Oliver says:

> It is as if Eusapia were dreaming that she was fingering the instrument, and dreaming it so vividly that the instrument was actually played. It is as if a dog dreamt of the chase with such energy that a distant hare was really captured and killed as if by a phantom dog; and, fanciful as for the moment it may seem, and valueless as I suppose such speculations are, I am, I confess, at present more than half disposed to look in some such direction for a clue to these effects.

Could we but establish that a dream body existed, many bewildering and apparently supernormal dreams would be reduced to the normal order of things. Simultaneously, this would open up an avenue to fascinating adventures, and we would paraphrase Gertrude Stein by saying a dream is a dream is a dream.

Numerous attempts have been made in the past by psychoanalysts to illuminate the intriguing psychological problem of *déjà vû*—that strange familiarity which unexpected landscapes inspire on coming into view. A curious depersonalization accompanies the experience. Reality becomes vague and undefined. In Freud's term, a derealization or repudiation of reality ensues. A feeling of historicity, of having lived somewhere else in a distant epoch takes its place. The sensation is short-lived but unforgettable. It inspired Jung to describe his life as "a historic fragment, an excerpt from which the preceding and succeeding text was missing."

Jung actually believed that he had a parallel life in the 18th Century and the first time the experience came to him was at the early age of 12. He felt emerging from a dense cloud behind which "there was not yet an I" because everything merely happened to him but now he happened to himself. "I am myself now, now I exist." Nevertheless, he was bewildered by his repeated historic experiences.

A terra-cotta piece portraying Dr. Stuckelberger, a physician of the 18th Century, had buckled shoes, writes Jung:

> Which in a strange way I recognized as my own. I was convinced that these were the shoes I had worn. The conviction drove me wild with excitement. . . . I could still feel those shoes on my feet, and yet I could not explain where this crazy feeling came from. I could not understand this identity with the 18th Century. Often in those days I would write the date of 1786 instead of 1886, and each time this happened I was overcome by an inexplicable nostalgia.

Bergson speaks of *déjà vû* as the memory of the present: a sudden duplication and projection of the present into the past. Tennyson calls it "mystical similitude," psychoanalysts explain it by false recognition, involuntary repetition, unconscious fantasy, memory of a forgotten dream, or prenatal memories in which a beautiful feeling is symbolized by the beauty of a landscape. But *déjà vû* is not restricted to sight. It may take the form of *déjà entendu* (already heard), *déjà lû* (already read), and *déjà éprouvé* (already experienced). Some take the sensation for evidence of a previous life reincarnation. Others speak of ancestral memories, due to a molecular orientation in an ancestor's brain under the effect of strong emotions. Spiritualists take it as an impression conveyed by a discarnate entity; in Charles Fort's fantasies it is the memory of a forgotten teleportation, and in Dr. Wigan's medical opinion[1] it was described, as early as 1860, as apperceptive weakness, due to an independent function of the two hemispheres of the brain, one perception lagging behind the other, thus giving the sensation of time elapsed.

Most stimulating perhaps is the view that *déjà vû* is not a memory of the present but a memory of the future, that it is really a precognitive sense perception which is automatically retrojected into the past because the human intellect is not capable of accepting foreknowledge. This fascinating view involves us deeply with the mysteries of time whether the experience comes through a dream or otherwise.

I was told by a patient that when he was handcuffed in the last war as a prisoner, in a flash it came back to him that he had dreamed of the scene four years before but did not recall the dream until the event actually came to pass. (Maeterlinck calls this terrestrial realization.)[2] If the dream had been recalled at the time, it would have remained a dream. Only the fulfilment invested it with a sense of wonder.

Here is a similar dream just communicated to me by a nephew in Budapest:

> Reading your paper, *The Place of Premonition in a Crisis of Life,* I recalled a recurrent dream from the years of 1909, 1910 and afterwards before the first World War.
>
> I dreamed that I was an army officer in Italy. My orderly was bring me my midday meal, and suddenly the lady of the house appears. She is a beautiful woman and I converse with her while eating. Then I saw her in a

---

[1] *The Duality of the Mind,* 1860.

[2] *The Unknown Guest,* by Maurice Maeterlinck, Dodd, Mead & Co., 1914, pp. 211-216.

black nightgown which promisingly revealed a beautiful body.

The dream occurred perhaps five or six times. Then came the war. When the Italians joined it, my corps was the first to be taken to Italy from Galicia. We were advancing on the Piave, and suddenly I found myself in a familiar setting. Everything seemed to be known as if I had been there or had seen it before. I felt at home.

I was having dinner on the terrace of a castle. As my orderly was bring the meal, it occurred to me: the only thing missing is the beautiful woman. And she appeared! I recognized her in an instant and greeted her as an acquaintance.

The best of the story is that I was also familiar to her, as she told me later. Hold on now: the black nightgown also became real. I have often wondered how could I have dreamed four-five years before that which actually happened.

At the time of fulfilment there was a memory of the present. But the dream of four-five years before was the memory of the future. The dream could be a daydream, not of the idle kind but a creative one, the type that writers, inventors, musicians, painters, poets and dancers have in their moments of inspiration.

The two satellites of Mars were discovered by Professor Halle in 1877. Some 150 years before, Jonathan Swift wrote in *Gulliver's Travels* of the astronomers of Laputa: "They have discovered two small stars, or satellites, which revolve round Mars. The inner one is three diameters distant from the centre of the plant, the outer one five diameters; the first makes its revolution in ten hours, the second in twenty hours and a half." These figures, taken at the time as proof of Swift's ignorance of astronomy, show striking agreement with the findings of Professor Halle.

In the automatic writings of mediums we find similar memories of the future. Andrew Jackson Davis wrote in his *Penetralia* in 1856:

I am almost moved to invent an automatic psychographer—that is, an artificial soul-writer. It may be constructed something like a piano, one brace or scale of keys to represent the elementary sounds; another and

135

lower tier to represent a combination, and still another for a rapid recombination, so that a person instead of playing a piece of music may touch off a sermon or a poem.

The typewriter was yet in the distant future, but Andrew Jackson Davis had a "memory" of it in 1856. And let us not forget that science fiction of the last few decades has proved to be a storehouse of memories of the future.

I have recently discovered an unusual instance of the memory of the future in the Hungarian Frigyes Karinthy's book: *A Journey Around My Skull*.[3] In describing his first meeting with Dr. Olivecrona, a brain surgeon of Stockholm (who was to operate on him for a brain tumor), he was struck by a feeling of familiarity. He felt he had seen him or known him from before. Long after the successful operation, he described Olivecrona to an actor in Budapest: his appearance, his manner and his behavior. After the third sentence, the actor interrupted him:

"This man, he is a perfect description of . . ."—and he mentioned a name, the hero of a Hungarian stage play.

"It is I who have written that play," continues Karinthy, "exactly twenty years before. It was about a very talented but emotional engineer who suffered from inner struggles and indecision; he invented an automatic, pilotless bombing plane (since then this became a reality), but a sceptic friend wanted to prove it to him that unconsciously he wanted to revenge himself on humanity because his beautiful wife had left him and went to live with an elegant dandy.

"To prove his selflessness, the engineer decided that he himself will go up with the plane on the day of demonstration. But he suffered from terrible fears of death. At this moment, an alter-ego appears, a surgeon from the North, a representative of the Solweig motive, and suggests to him a brain operation in which he will excise the center of the fear of death in his small brain at the back of his head. The engineer accepts the operation, and the next day when the plane goes up, not dreading death any longer, he has the courage to stay alive.

"My actor friend knew the role and had played it. What I have told him about Olivecrona recalled to his mind Olson

[3] Hungarian reprint in *Circus*, published by Szepirodalmi Konyvkiado, Budapest, 1956, p. 145.

Irjot, the surgeon of the title role actor whom he had played in exactly the manner and character in which I have depicted Olivecrona to him."

To answer the objection that Karinthy might have been spinning just another story to make his book more wonderful, let me quote from a letter from Dr. Lila Vészy-Wágner, a London psychoanalyst, which I received the day after my lecture on déjà vû.

> I was very interested in what you quoted for me from *A Journey Around My Skull*. I remember both the earlier play and the book, and endorse the actor's testimony. He could not have been more "identical" with the later Stockholm brain surgeon about whom neither he nor Karinthy himself knew anything at the time. As far as I remember, the only "difference" was that the real one was a Swede and that the one in the play a Finn. Both Nordic; one, however, "nearer" and more akin to the Hungarian.

That even a pure fantasy may leave us with a highly disturbing problem of the déjà vû, let me now speak of Alexander Woollcott's story[4] about a young woman from Catonsville, Maryland, who, while in France on her honeymoon, recognized a house as one she had seen in her recurrent dreams throughout the years. Greatly excited, she decided to explore the house—and had frightened a priest, a gardener and the elderly lady inhabitant of the house out of their wits. They had recognized her as the ghost that had haunted the house for the last ten years! This is, on the most charitable assumption, much more than déjà vû. Like my nephew's case of the Lady of the Castle in Italy, this memory of the future casts a creative spell on people of the past which is a logical absurdity.

Woollcott gave credit to André Maurois for the story, but he claims to have heard it before reading that piece and concluded that "only a hide-bound and bumptious fellow would venture to say that it could not have happened."

Well, it did, at least if we are to credit with the truth Prof. Augustus Hare's autobiography.[5] It did not happen in France, but in England, to a Mrs. Butler who lived in Ireland. For

---

[4] See *Long, Long Ago*.

[5] *The Story of My Life*, Vols. I-IV, 1896-1900.

many nights in succession she had a recurrent dream of finding herself in a very beautiful house furnished with all imaginable comforts. The following year, Mrs. Butler and her husband moved to London and went to see a house in Hampshire. At the gatekeeper's lodge, Mrs. Butler exclaimed: "This is the gatehouse of my dreams!" When they reached the house, she recognized it in every detail, except a certain door which, it turned out, had been added to the place within the last six months—after her dream period. Being for sale at a very low price, the Butlers bought the house, but afterwards began to suspect the bargain. The agent then admitted that the property was haunted. The ghost was Mrs. Butler herself.

Assuming that this fantastic story rests on some factual foundation, did Mrs. Butler see herself in her future occupancy as a memory of the future and had time just gone out of joint when her future began to haunt the past?

Let us now return to the past. A cathartic fulfilment of a racial nightmare has been described by a patient as follows:

When the Germans had driven us into the ghetto, and we saw the enclosure around it, we felt fallen back into the Middle Ages. Then a strange thing happened to me: an old oppression lifted from my mind. There was a Jew Street in Pressburg. I always hated it, though I never lived in it because of a foreboding that one day it might swallow me. I used to give it a wide berth—and now I was back. With this realization the nightmare lifted. For this reason I have no regrets for what I had been through.

A similar experience, with a feeling of elation, is recorded by Jung from the time when he was on way to Nairobi. On a jagged rock high above his train, he saw a slim, brownish-black figure motionless, leaning on a long spear.

I was enchanted by this sight—it was a picture of something utterly alien and outside my experience, but on the other hand [inspired] a most intense sentiment of déjà vû. I had the feeling that I had already experienced this moment and had always known this world which was separated from me only by distance in time. It was as if I were this moment returning to the land of my youth, and as if I knew that dark-skinned man who had been waiting for me for five thousand years.

138

The feeling tone of this curious experience accompanied me throughout the whole journey through savage Africa. I can recall only one another such recognition of the immemorially known. That was when I first observed a parapsychological phenomena together with my former chief, Prof. Eugen Bleuler. Beforehand, I had imagined that I would be dumbfounded if I were to see so fantastic a thing. But when it happened, I was not surprised at all; I felt it was perfectly natural, something I could take for granted because I had long since been acquainted with it.

I could not guess what string within myself was plucked at the sight of that solitary dark hunter. I knew that this world had been mine for countless millennia.

A practicing New York psychoanalyst, who used to be known in his earlier years as "the Hungarian prophet," claimed to have the memory of many incarnations and interpreted in this sense his experiences of déjà vû.

It occurred to me to ask whether he had met me in any of his previous lives. To my surprise he answered: a good many times. I was always a Hungarian peasant. He chose me as his analyst because I was Hungarian, but:

> When you opened the door for me, I knew I saw you before. I knew you from the Szilágyág. You were then in Sunday pants, a pipe in your hand, and the picture was so vivid that it embarrassed me. I was perturbed by it all through the first session. I had to make an effort to keep reality and fantasy apart. I have called myself schizophrenic for a long time. It is possible that I sniffed after you like a dog until I found you. I never knew about your *Encyclopaedia of Psychic Science,* but it is possible that I wanted you to prove to me that I am not crazy.

This analyst came from Hungarian peasant stock and his mother was the Wise Woman of her village. It is possible that by his reincarnation fantasies he was trying to raise himself to my level as a prophet must needs be greater than those of the common herd.

Prenatal memories, in a sense, also belong to a previous life. Freud acknowledged them in The Uncanny[6] as a reference to the mother's genitalia:

---

[6] From *Collected Papers,* Vol. II, pp. 398-399.

"This unheimlich place . . . is the entrance to the former heim (home) of all human beings, the place where everyone dwelt once upon a time and in the beginning. There is a humorous saying: "love is homesickness"; and whenever a man dreams of a place or a country and says to himself, still in the dream, "this place is familiar to me, I have been there before," we may interpret the place as being his mother's genitals or her body.

As the majority of people dislike Freudian plainspeaking, they often objectify prenatal longings in the mother and develop a tremendous feeling of nostalgia for her. A beautiful illustration is Louis Anspacher's poem *The Pilgrim:*[7]

It's somewhere hereabouts that she was born.
    She told me once and I have not forgot.
    Her eyes, when they first opened, saw this spot
That is now sacred to me. Here the morn
Was sunnier and the nights less forlorn
    Because of her. I pondered: Is there not
    Some music clinging, or I know not what
Of footfalls somewhere on some pavement worn
Ever so lightly by her passing? So
    I wandered through the clangor of the street,
    I was so still. I listened, walked so slow,
Looked everywhere among the hurrying feet
For some dim traces of the long ago.
    An ache came over me, but an ache so sweet
    I would not change for many a joy I know.

Finally, there is another Ultima Thule of *déjá vû,* so far not touched upon. Between the prenatal state and a previous life there stretches a dim region antecedent to conception the existence of which all believers in reincarnation, ancestral dreams or of the immemorially known must needs grant: the prematernal state, or pre-existence.

In my *Conception Fantasies*[8] I have examined a number of dreams in which references appeared to "other waters," to a reality more remote than life in the uterus. The mental as-

[7] From *Slow Harvest,* Brentano, 1943.
[8] *Samiksa,* Calcutta, 1951.

surance that such a reality as waters outside existence appeared in the dream of a young girl as "swimming under water into lots of beautiful places. It was like . . . flying from great heights. I had a definite feeling about what I was going to do as I approached the house into which I was going to enter. I felt that all my plans had been made."

The house into which she was going to enter was the womb of her mother. The dream is an example of *déjá senti* or *déjà éprouvé* (already known) as the descent of the spirit followed a definite plan: the dreamer knew that she was leaving the prematernal state for a mission on earth.

Unhappily for the reality of a prematernal existence, science has nothing to offer and the visions of mystics, saints and other psychically gifted people have only psychological value. Moreover, the prematernal state may be so alien to our comprehension as to defy any attempts at verbal expression.

Bibliography to Parts I and II

ANSPACHER, LOUIS: *Slow Harvest*, Brentano, 1943.

ARLOW, J. A.: "The Structure of the Déjà Vû Experience," *Journal of the American Psychoanalytic Association*, Vol. VII, 1959, pp. 611-631.

DUCASSE, C. G.: *The Belief in a Life After Death*, Charles C. Thomas, Springfield, Mass., 1961, pp. 232-233.

ELLIS, HAVELOCK: *The World of Dreams*, London, 1911.

FENICHEL, O.: *The Psychoanalytic Theory of Neurosis*, W. W. Norton & Company, Inc., 1945.

FERENCZI, SANDOR: *Further Contributions to the Theory and Technique of Psychoanalysis*, Hogarth Press, London, 1950, p. 422.

FODOR, NANDOR: *Conception Fantasies*, Samiksa, Calcutta, 1951.

——: *Encyclopedia of Psychic Science*, Arthurs Press, London, 1934, p. 109.

——: "Extension of the Self," MS., unpublished.

——: "I Dreamed that I Dreamed," *International Record of Medicine*, Feb. 1957, pp. 100-102.

——: *Mind Over Space*, Citadel Press, New York, 1962, p. 87.

———: *New Approaches to Dream Interpretation*, Citadel Press (paperback ed.), 1962, pp. 93-110; orig. hardcover ed., 1951.

———: *The Place of Premonition in a Crisis of Life*, Samiksa, Calcutta, Vol. III, No. 3, 1959.

———: *The Search for the Beloved*, Hermitage Press, 1950, pp. 208-218.

FREUD, SIGMUND: *Basic Writings of Sigmund Freud*, Modern Library, 1938, pp. 171, 394.

———: "A Disturbance of Memory on the Acropolis," *Collected Papers*, Hogarth Press, London, 1924, Vol. V, pp. 302-312.

———: "Fausse Reconnaissance in Psychoanalytic Treatment," *Ibid.*, Vol. II., pp. 334-341.

———: *The Psychopathology of Everyday Life*, Fisher Unwin, London, 1914, pp. 320-324.

———: "The Uncanny," *Collected Papers*, Vol. II., pp. 398-399.

HARE, AUGUSTUS: *The Story of My Life*, Vols. I-VI, 1896-1900.

JUNG, CARL G.: *Memories, Dreams and Reflections*, Pantheon, 1963, pp. 34-35, 235, 254-255, 291, 219.

———: *The Psychology of the Unconscious*, Dodd and Mead, 1946, p. 47.

———: *The Structure and Dynamics of the Psyche*, Pantheon, 1960, pp. 522-523.

KARINTHY, FRIGYES: *Journey Around My Skull*, Hungarian reprint in *Circus*, (p. 145), Szepirodalmi Konyvkiado, Budapest, 1956.

LOCKHARDT, JOHN GIBSON: *Life of Sir Walter Scott*, London, 1837.

MACROBERTS, RUSSEL G.: *Something Better than Reincarnation in DeWitt Miller's Reincarnation: the Whole Story*, p. 105.

MAETERLINCK, MAURICE: *The Unknown Guest*, Dodd and Mead, 1914, pp. 211-216.

MARCOVITS, E.: "The Meaning of Déjà Vû," *Psychoanalytic Quarterly*, Vol. XXI, 1952, pp. 481-489.

MARTIN, EVA: *The Ring of Return*, Philip Allen, London, 1927, pp. 173-174.

RANK, OTTO: *The Trauma of Birth*, Brunner, 1952, p. 80.

RHINE, J. B.: *The Reach of the Mind*, William Sloan, 1947, p. 81.

SCHNECK, J. M.: "A Contribution to the Analysis of Déjà Vû," *Journal of Nervous and Mental Diseases*, 1961, Bo. 132, pp. 91-93.

——: "The Psychodynamics of Déjà Vû," *Psychoanalysis and the Psychoanalytic Review*, Hinter 1962, pp. 48-54.

SIDGWICK, MRS. HENRY: "On the Evidence of Premonitions," *Proceedings of the S.P.R.*, Vol. V., London, 1888-1889, pp. 288-354.

STEKEL, WILLIAM: *Sexual Aberrations*, Liveright, New York, 1930, Vol. I, p. 149, Vol. II, p. 199.

SCOTT, SIR WALTER: "Diary, February 17, 1828."

WIGAN, DR.: *The Duality of the Mind*, 1860.

WOOLLCOTT, ALEXANDER: *Long, Long Ago.*

PART III.

OF GHOULIES AND GHOSTIES

Of ghoulies and ghosties,
Of longleggetie beasties,
Of things that go bump in the night,
Good Lord deliver us.

(SCOTTISH PRAYER)

This is the story of a demon lover and his beloved—in the 20th Century when such things are supposed to be the superstition of past ages. The heroine, or rather victim, is not a witch, just an ordinary young woman, a writer by profession, and the demon is not a minion of the devil but the "spirit" of a suddenly deceased friend bent on a love affair with the living.

Are such things possible?

The answer was given a few hundred years ago by a famous mediaeval cleric, the Rev. Joseph Glanville, in these words: "Man does not yield himself to the angels, nor unto death utterly, save only through the weakness of his feeble will."

My story began on Jan. 28, 1961, following my television appearance on Long John Nebel's program. An S.O.S. came on the telephone from a young lady of 26 who was being visited by an incubus and felt on the point of losing her mind.

The immediate question was: had she lost it already? Was she psychotic, hysterical or just psychic?

She came with her mother and made a very personable appearance. No wild eyes, no hysteria, no scattering of speech and mental reactions. She was logical and extremely rational. She knew of my interest in the paranormal and wanted immediate help. She did not even know that I was a psychoanalyst.

We had two professional sessions. She cancelled the third one as if she had sensed the very searching question I was about to ask. But I continued to be in friendly contact with her on the telephone. I was tremendously interested in the case, visited her at her home once and gave her whatever advice I could free of charge.

Because I was a psychoanalyst, she felt no restraint in talking to me about the very intimate matters involved, even though she was not committed to analytic discipline. In fact, she confided in me more than in her own mother who only found out from me that she had a spirit lover in the full meaning of the word. If she was to be given any help, it was impossible to keep the secret as the "affair" involved the mother and necessitated the same plain speaking on her part as was demanded from the daughter in talking to a psychoanalyst.

I shall tell this totally incredible story, extracting from my dated interviews and telephone conversations as it developed, changing the name of victim for her own protection, and of the spirit to avoid a national scandal for besmirching the reputation of an all-American hero. Jean and John will have to do.

John died shortly after his 34th birthday. Jean knew him through his organization, admired him, loved his books and was corresponding with him. But John had never paid court to her. They were, in no sense, intimate.

On the day John died, she felt a presence in her room and heard a voice in her mind: "I am not dead." Gradually, the voice became more distinct. If she sat down on her bed she felt somebody sitting next to her. When she challenged the feeling, the seat bounced as if somebody threw himself up and down. Slowly the invisible presence became more intimate. Touches on her body followed, she felt his manhood, accepted his lovemaking and experienced an ecstasy from which "wild horses could not drag her away." Soon, however, the enormity of the situation dawned on her mind and she tried to protect herself by prayer. As it was of little help she hung an iron crucifix, wrapped in soft paper, over her vulnerable part. She wore it on the day she paid me her first visit. It hurt her. Toward the end of the session she went into the bathroom and took it off. She showed it. It was a heavy crucifix, at least five to six inches long. It was astonishing that she could wear it at all. It was the crudest chastity belt that anyone could devise. She told me:

> Every time he came near me I felt the pain of a wound in my chest, I would become terribly over-heated, desire water, my pulse rate would double, in my thyroid gland a churning sensation would develop and the hair would rise all over my body.
>
> From his book I found out subsequently that he was hyperthyroid, had a wound in his chest, which became malignant and necessitated an operation.

This was in line with the claim one always meets with in research work with mediums, that the recent dead, in trying to communicate, transfer the conditions of their dying on the medium. Jean was psychic, not a medium as far as she knew, but it seemed as if she were drifting in that direction.

John gradually began to manage her life; urged her to participate in the work of his organization (which she did by sending contributions) and to study shorthand. He also acted as her medical adviser. She has been suffering from acne since the age of 10. Jean heard him say: "Why don't you take pirodixin?" She found out that pirodixin was the recommended therapy, took it and it helped.

I was looking for a book, said Jean. Before mother could answer me I heard John say: "It is in your bookcase." I looked and said it was not. He said: "Yes, it is." I went back and found it lying flat on top of other books, out of the line of my vision.

If I was stuck for a word in my own writing, he gave it to me. One particular word was *burgeoning*. I never heard of it. I looked it up in the dictionary. It fitted. But he did not want me to carry on with my work. He urged me to continue with his and made me apply for a job.

As the days passed he began to be more affectionate. He resented my dating. He imposed upon me his wishes. He did not like my curtains and wanted chintz. I assumed he did not know he was dead and wondered if I should tell him.

Every time he touched me we got a terrific static on the radio. It never happened when he did not. Sometimes an odd odor accompanied his visits. It was disagreeable. I could feel his body. He was a man all right, but his body was very light and exceedingly hot. The crucifix seemed to stop him from molesting me. But this morning I went into the tub and took it off. As I got out he was rubbing against me and I had to put on the crucifix in a hurry.

I told him that he was using me as a prostitute and that I resented it. He protested that he had a deep affection and admiration for me. I answered: "That does not make any difference; you are in one world, I am in another. Go to your father and mother and ask them to pray for you."

Yesterday afternoon he was back again; pawed me on the breast and other places. When I protested he said: "I love you."

I told him that I had tachycardia. I would have to commit suicide if he did not stop. I felt his hand under my blouse over my heart; he appeared to be listening. My heart was beating like a sledge hammer. He took his hand away and it gradually quieted down.

Jean claimed that by this time she found many evidences pointing to John's identity. She urged him to play Chopin, and found out from his books that he was very fond of Chopin and Rachmaninoff. He was a competent doctor. He came to her constantly at dawn. She found out that he used to rise at dawn. When she put on snow boots she heard him say: tie your laces tight. She discovered that he had tripped over his own shoelace once, fell down a cliff and injured himself in the chest.

This is the extent of the revelations I had from Jean in her first session. What was I to do to be of immediate help? I have read in magical literature that the visualization of an egg-shaped luminous aura surrounding the body helps to protect against psychical invasion. I suggested that she should resort to it and take herself very firmly in hand against unconscious sexual attraction. Was she sure she could feel his body?

Once I made a sudden movement and he said: "Oh boy, you just kicked me in the face."

Mother came to my bed. We spent a terribly restless night. She could feel the rustling of the sheet. Someone was stirring it. I took up a long back scratcher and kept hitting the sheet. I got the impression that he was a little weaker. I don't think we slept more than an hour.

I was at peace after I left you. Both mother and I concentrated on the aura. But the trouble started in the evening. I sensed his heart beat, but the terrible heat of his body was less. Although his body is very light I can tell where his arms and legs are.

What about the odor?

It is a male sex odor. Possibly like that of a dog in heat. I felt his head on my chest for a while. I had the impression he was sobbing. The pain in my chest lessened to a very tight feeling. My desire for water also diminished.

149

Later in the day I had a second telephone call. Despair.

No more odors. I cannot feel his body, except the part I object to. It is very active. I will be all right for 10-15 minutes, then I feel an approach again. My chest vibrates. I feel a cool breeze. The harder I fight the harder he fights back. The crucifix and the Bible that I placed there no longer stop him. But he was stopped for a while when mother took the back scratcher and began to hit out with it. Then he came around the other side of the bed. Again I felt his head on my chest.

For the first time since a week Jean and her mother had a peaceful night and slept all through. She wanted to cancel her session but changed her mind and came.

March 2nd, 1961

Right after I stopped talking to you John went wild. I felt a rising vibration in my thighs and got up immediately. But I felt as if invisible reins were trying to hold me down. His strength was less than before. I walked around the room and refused to sit down. But something was tugging me from head downwards as if I were encased in something. I wanted to get out of the house but I could not. I did not know what to do. I turned on the television and after a while a feeling of peace came over me.

I was in a state of anxiety when I visited you. I know what paranoia is and I was afraid you would diagnose my case as such. I never had any mental aberration. But I had pyschic experiences since I was a child. At times when the telephone rings, I can tell who it is before answering.

When he first came I asked: "How do I know it is you and not my imagination?" He said: "You will know it is me. Tomorrow morning, when you come back from the store with your mother, the first thing she will say: your hair looks nicer that way, I like it loose. From this you will know that it was I talking to you.

Next morning it happened exactly as he told me. I was shocked and told mother what happened. He was not yet destructive. He was not yet hurting me. He was helping me with my shorthand.

I enjoy cooking. He stood by my shoulder in the

kitchen, grabbed my arm and said: "This is John." I had a swirling sensation around my ankles, it was mounting higher and higher, to my throat and to my head like a vapor or live ribbon. Every time I would do something he did not like, I would get this ribbon sensation strongly on my arm. When I asked: do you disapprove, the sensation got stronger.

Why did you come to see me so late?

I was ashamed of the sex angle. Otherwise I would not have been frightened. I am not easy to seduce. Ever since childhood I had a slightly abnormal thyroid. I was being constantly checked by doctors. I had a slight adrenal disturbance too, that darkened my skin. I was producing too much cortisone. The doctor gave me hormones to balance it. My skin still bothers me, the acne. It disappeared after he made love to me.

Was the psychic strain in Jean due to these physiological aberrations? I warned her not to play around with psychism.

I made a grab last night. I tried to emasculate him. It worked. I had peace after that. But I am afraid that others may come in his guise and try to use me as an astral whore.

March 5, 1961

Jean's mother on the telephone:

We had a terrible night. Jean could not sleep at all. John was in constant possession of her body.

Jean took over the telephone:

Yesterday was not bad until the evening. Then a terrible vibration started in the chair in which I was sitting and when I went to bed the whole bed started shaking. No heat, no sensation of his entire body on me, but the bed sheet was alive and something was pricking me all over, on the soles of my feet and in the crotch.

We have been praying at home, father in church. But

151

sometimes praying makes the situation worse. The crucifix no longer helps. I cannot even contact John mentally.
Grabbing only relieves me for a little while, then he takes
me again. It is as if a demon would follow me everywhere. During my menses nothing bothered me. In the
beginning even that made no difference.

She felt there was no longer any identity attached to the attacks. Her fear was getting stronger that others had stepped
into John's place.

March 10, 1961

Things have improved a little. I have taken heavy
sedatives for the night, as you suggested. An hour later,
the invisible man sat down next to me. Mother saw the
depression it made on the bed. It was not my imagination.

I forgot to tell you, the other night he came behind the
chair in which I was sitting. The small hairs on the top
of my head rose as if an electric comb had been placed
over it. Mother could see it.

Jean's mother:

We feel much better. He is still around, but in a light
vein. We are able to sleep at nights. When I think back
it seems like a nightmare. I cannot believe it happened.
If I had not seen the bedcover move and form a depression, I would not have been convinced. If we had not
found you we would have gone mad.

Jean took over:

I do not have much to report. He is still around,
though. I get a slight kiss on my cheek and neck. Sometimes he approaches me below, but it is lighter. I reason
with him and he leaves. Sometimes I feel him in bed and
hear his heartbeats. I move to the opposite side. I am so
used to him now that I feel he is a boarder in the house.
The pressure of his hand is so light that it no longer scares
me.

I am near-sighted. Occasionally I wear a contact lens
in one eye. It irritates me in the wind. Once it bothered

me in the subway. I was tearing. I felt him come near me. This sounds crazy I know. But I felt a very light touch in the eye and the lens fell into place.

He is back. He is now annoying me in the rear. I think he is psychotic. What happens to crazy people when they die? Do they stay insane? I found out that he pretended to be a devout Catholic while alive. But last Sunday I went to church (I am a Lutheran). He came and annoyed me sexually. I think he was a ruthless sadist, so different from what the public thought him to be.

I asked Jean to tell me frankly whether the incubus was able to make love to her at the beginning because she wanted him to.

I thought he was a good person and I did not deter him. If he was a good man he would not harm me. After a while, however, I felt mesmerized. I began to fight him and he became violent. I was, by this time, repelled and disgusted. Before it did not matter. Now he is repugnant to me.

Mother cut her finger while cooking. I ran for a bandage. I felt him come up behind me. My hair rose up, and I heard him say: "Hurry up, wash the wound out." Some instinct of the doctor is still operating in him.

What shall I do now?

I suggested: Imagine that you have a blow torch in your hand and shrivel him up with it.

The blow torch did not work. It made him more violent. It seems better to placate him and be nice to him. He responds better. Once in a while he comes just the same and touches me in the rear. I yell at him: "You abnormal." He seems to understand it and changes to the front, but not as strongly as he used to.

I rarely hear his voice now. But it became quite clear in church. "Why aren't you singing in the choir?" he asked. The fact is that I have a good voice and I was trained in professional singing, but my heart was not in it. I was amazed to hear his question.

I did visualize the blow torch. I tried to burn him up in every part. But he annoyed me so much more. He approached me when I was talking to my friends in church. It was uncomfortable but bearable. Every two or three days he appears to be weaker. He sleeps now on the lower side of my bed on top of the cover. He is not so affectionate as before.

April 16, 1961

Things are getting worse. Mother was in bed with me two nights ago. This demon pushed something into her thigh. It was a burning sensation. In the morning he woke her by poking her very hard in the back of her shoulder. He does not want her near me. The beast has been attacking me in the rear constantly. It makes me sick. I have been praying so hard that I cannot pray any more. Each time I pray it is getting worse.

Jean's mother took over:

I am a nervous wreck. The harder we pray the worse it gets. What are we to do? He is getting stronger, using her in the rear and in the front and picks on her skin. I wrap a band around her to keep him away. One night I felt a burning sensation on my thigh and leg. I felt a movement, an attempt of penetration into my muscles. Do you know anyone, a medium, who could exorcise him?

The question made me recall the name of a medium who was recommended to me in case I want to make any investigation. I gave her the name. Jean was electrified and lost no time in contacting her.

She told me that the same thing happened to her some years ago. She was going to ask her spirit-guide to protect me. She is not feeling well now, but as soon as she recovers she wants to come to my house.

154

I said I wanted to be present also.

Believe it or not, this "gentleman" went to see Rosie, the medium, annoyed her and tried to grab her by the throat. Her spirit-guide yanked him away. She thinks there is some perversion there. She told me to call on her and her spirit-guide, Minnehaha, if he again annoys me. I did so. Within a minute or two I felt a rustling on the bed as if two men were rolling around and fighting. It was very strange. Right after that there was peace. Rosie told me that this is quite a common occurrence. If a spirit-guide comes to take an entity away, there is wrestling and a fight. They struggle with each other. This is the most fantastic thing in the world, but evidently these things exist. She promised to arrange a séance for the purpose of getting rid of him whether or not he knows what he is doing.

Rosie called me and said of the incubus:

I saw him the first day Jean called me, from the stomach down, stark naked. I have never seen a spirit naked before. Next day I saw him again. He had a whip in his hand and this time he was dressed. He was in uniform or wore boots or leggings. I told Jean that my big band of Red Indians would see to her protection. Years ago I was myself bothered by spirits. One night I woke up and there was a man's hand holding my breast. It was solid and warm and I had a hard time to pull it off. There were others. They kept close to me, kissing me at night. I even felt a man's body lying next to mine. But nothing further happened.

Jean called shortly after.

If that was a horse whip Rosie saw, it was John. He was crazy for horses.

He is behaving better. Believe it or not, he is producing perfumes in various rooms of the house. It is a lovely oriental scent. I asked him for another perfume. Sure enough, I smelt a fresh spray.

The séance at Jean's house was a "frost." Rosie jumped up and down in her armchair, gave an awful lot of initials, none of which made sense, and called on Minnehaha to dislodge the incubus. Nothing else happened and Jean was disappointed.

Jean reported that John was back, jumping up and down on her bed to show that he was not exorcised.

I am a little mixed up about Rosie. For a week the trouble was less, but the trance revealed a lot of discrepancies. She told me what a terrible night she had with her exorcism. As far as I can see, she did nothing. If the disturbance lessened, it was due to its natural decline. There is no mental communion any more between John and me, but he is on the bed every night. Today I went out on a date. He annoyed me in the lower region. I forgot to tell you, at the beginning when I asked him why he came near me he said: "We can have a life together;" also: "I am trying to protect you so you would not be taken over by a lot of people."

Jean seemed to sense an underlying meaning. In my mind the query arose: was she playing the role of a succubus? Is it really she who is holding onto the ghost, instead of the reverse?

Jean called off her professional appointment I made with her after the last session. She was afraid I would hypnotise her.

Jean gave up Rosie. Wanted me to recommend her another medium.

I am disturbed at nights dreadfully. It is not the sex angle. I am not sex-starved. John tells me now that he did not want to die. He is hanging onto me because I represent life on earth. He does not want to go on in the afterlife. The minute I talk to somebody he resents he stabs me in the arm and buttocks, sometimes on the head. When mother tries to protect me he will shove her aside and burn her skin. Whenever he touches me the area gets very hot. He can regulate his size over my body.

Sunday night I dreamed of a friend of the family. He came and said: "I have been trying to get through to you, but John is blocking me."

Did not hear from Jean for some time. Then I was away on my vacation. Returning, I called her:

At the end of June and early in July the persecution became bad again. I did not know what to do. Through a friend my father met a man in the advertising business of whose private psychic demonstrations fabulous stories were told. I was invited to one of his séances. I was dumbfounded, spellbound and started to cry. He brought through Adele, an air hostess and friend of mine who lost her life in an air crash four years ago. She called me Cookie, a nickname no one else knew. Then Adele brought through another girl whom I knew in school. She told me I was getting an awful lot of misinformation. She said that Rosie's only contact with spirits was with those in the bottle. They talked about you by calling you Dr. F. They said that you were very age-conscious and will stay young if you worry less about the exterior than the interior; that you were not getting proper nourishment. They reproached me for not telling you a lot about myself. I did not tell you that I had a husband, a devout Catholic, whom I am suing for an annulment.

Then John came through. I felt terrible because I

blamed him so much. I asked him: "Were you poking my mother?" He said: "Yes, I was, I was sore at everybody who blamed the happenings on your mind. I wanted to convince her that I was around."

Then I was told by the spirit-guides that I had very unusual abilities for mediumship. They did not want to help me sooner because I would have lost the chance of finding things out about myself and would have lost the desire for mediumship. It is up to me now. From that day on I have slept wonderfully. I am able to go to work and have no trouble whatever.

Did John admit his love making to you?

Yes, he had me blushing.

Sept. 14, 1961

No trouble. Read my book *On the Trail of the Poltergeist.* The incident on vampire visitation elicited this comment:

Whenever I would lie down there would be a terrible shaking of the bed and the incubus would be on top of me. Only I did not get a cold sensation like your subject, but an extremely hot one, the feeling as if someone would be breathing in my face.

March 21, 1962

I cannot complain. Things get better and better. John came back and made himself known in many ways. A very strange thing happened some time ago on Long Island. I was driving with some friends. The driver got sleepy. The road was long and winding. All of a sudden I felt someone sitting in my lap just as when John used to be around. Suddenly the driver touched the back of his neck and said: "Something punched me. Do you know, I was falling asleep and it awakened me?" The car was going off the road. If he had not been awakened we would have had an accident.

Occasionally John still comes back and talks to me and looks after my health. He told me no wonder my skin breaks out. I should not touch fish or chocolate.

* * *

It must be wonderful to have a spirit-doctor look after you free of charge. But was it free? Jean was going through hell for many a month. Whatever role her own love starvation may have played in the story, whatever latent psychic gifts grew on her physiological malfunctions, the reality of her tale of horror—shared by her whole household—cannot be doubted. Whoever prefers hysteria, paranoia or any other form of mental disorder is welcome to the diagnosis. I would not make any. After all, I was an outsider to the story. My advices availed her little. I just kept the records. In an abbreviated but faithful form this is what I have been presenting in this study. As a human document the record is invaluable.

Vampire Abroad

People engaged in the investigation of the paranormal must be prepared for everything. They are natural targets for the discharge of emotions caused by strange experiences or a psychotic attack. They must be prepared to investigate stories however odd they appear and regardless of their own reservations.

In this spirit I paid attention to a hysterical tale that was poured out to me over the telephone a few years ago at night. The caller gave his name as John Benderi, of Park Ave., New York City. He had read my book *Haunted People* and had tried to find me for some time. The Hungarian Counsulate said that I was on Fifth Avenue and the telephone operator gave him my number. He lived with his brother who, seven months ago, in the woods of Hungary was bitten by a weird fox-like animal and now it had bitten him in the neck while he was asleep. On top of this, the apartment resounded with unbearable animal noises and things were flying about, with plaster falling from the ceiling and wounding his brother. They badly wanted help. Would I call?

The story smelt to high heaven. First, there was no Hungarian Consulate in New York at the time and Hungary was not open to visit by tourists. I was in the Manhattan telephone book; besides I could have been found very easily through my publishers. More than that, foxes have never been tied up with the vampire legends of mediaeval Hungary. If

Benderi's brother was suffering from rabies, he needed medical help. The story was clearly a hoax; nevertheless, there existed a vague possibility that psychosis may be hidden behind it. In that case the vampire fantasy would reward the trouble of an investigation.

I offered to go immediately, but I was put off by 24 hours. The hoaxers were not prepared for such an immediate response. I fell in with the suggestion and called the following day. I did not go alone. I was accompanied by my friend, Richard Baron von Touche-Skedding, who lived in my house and was very keen for a vampire hunt. He is six feet tall, broad-shouldered and looks the perfect picture of a movie detective.

I assume we must have been watched from a window. The threat of disturbing the peace hung thickly in the air once the assumption was made that I had a detective with me. We had difficulty in finding the house and could not locate the right apartment. But we were lucky to find a mail man making deliveries, and were assured by him that there were no Benderis in that house. We rang bell after bell, and either had no answer or were met wtih screaming protests. It seemed that *we* were the disturbers of the peace.

I never heard of the Benderis again and the assumption was more than legitimate that the would-be hoaxers had beaten a retreat. I regretted it because I had some experience with vampire fantasies from a previous investigation in England the story of which was published in my book, *On the Trail of the Poltergeist,* three years after I heard of the vampire fox. The story was one of sheer horror, rivalling that of Dracula, imperfectly remembered, but still revealing vague traces of identification.

The dramatis persona was a Mrs. Forbes around whom a tremendous upheaval had been reported by what is called a racketing spirit. The investigation had been on for many weeks and I was conducting it as Director of Research of the International Institute for Psychical Research, of London.

She reported a vampire visitation during the night. She awoke feeling something like a human body lying beside her on top of the cover. Something cold and hard which she took to be a head was touching her neck. She felt paralyzed. After a few seconds the thing left her with the flapping of a bird's wings. In the morning she found two punctures clotted with blood at the back of her neck.

Respectable vampires bite people in the jugular vein in front of the neck and they do draw blood. Mrs. Forbes was pale as a ghost but judging by a belated medical check-up in a hospital lost no blood. However, the puncture marks were real and deep, behind the sternal mastoid muscle, a little more than an eighth of an inch apart. I thought that the two ends of a hairpin could well have inflicted the wound. But why? Was she playing a game or acting out an unconscious fantasy?

The answer is that she was doing both and the unconscious element was the most fascinating part of the story. In a gruelling cross-examination by myself, by Laurence Evans, my assistant, and by Dr. Wills, our medical adviser, we were told the following tale:

I went up before my husband to go to bed. I heard the fluttering of a bird. . . . I did not light the lamp and did not draw the curtain. I thought that the thing might come again and I would see what it was. . . .

I could not keep awake. Something like chloroform put me out. I fell into a heavy, unnatural sleep. It may have been around midnight that I woke up with the sensation that there was something ghastly on my left-hand side (which is away from my husband) on top of the cover. It felt like a human body. Pressing against my neck was something cold and hard, about the size of a man's head. I could not move, I could not shout, I was paralyzed with fear. I felt getting weaker and weaker, sinking. I imagine that bleeding to death would give the same sensation. There was a smell—the smell of rotten meat . . . Directly it left me I heard the same flapping noise, a sudden swish through the air with a regular beat. It went towards the window. Yet I saw no shadow crossing it. The top of the window was open. The light in the street was still on. I felt too weak to get up and I dared not wake my husband. He has been complaining of feeling terribly weak every morning. He has a recurrent dream that someone is cutting his throat. He told me the night before that there was a bird in the room. He heard it settle on the chair beside my bed. . . . There might be something else tucked away in my mind that I cannot bring forward. For the life of me I cannot think of it now.

Presently she thought of several relevant things. As a child, hanging onto her mother's skirt, she had visited a dying man. He had a growth in his head that burst. The smell was similar and terrible. When she woke up after the vampire visitation she had a taste of blood in her mouth. She recalled a recurrent dream in which she is in a hall of coffins:

> It is a big, stony place, but not a cellar. . . . I stand and watch, and see myself rising from one of the coffins. Before I leave it fully everything goes misty. I try to wake up and get back to my body, but I cannot.

A perfect setting for a vampire rising from her coffin in a vault. But then, judging by the recurrence of the dream, the fantasy had an incubation period. Indeed, Mrs. Forbes reminded me, while reporting on the telephone, that she had spoken to me of a similar incident three weeks before. I remembered. She had a nightmare in which something bit the back of her neck and she found some tiny red marks on her neck in the morning. She had asked me to look at the marks when she saw me, but I dismissed the story thinking it was an erotic dream. My notes confirmed that my memory was not playing tricks with me.

Moreover, of her mental dissociation there was no doubt. She said:

> Sometimes I feel that I am not here, that I am not really alive. I feel as if I had died on the operating table. It seems to me as if another person had taken possession of my body. . . . You know that I am always kind to animals. Yet I have the awful feeling that I wish to hurt them. Last Monday my cat had an accident. I found his back toe sliced off at the joint. I have a horrible feeling that I did it without knowing.

Add to this the nightmares of her husband about his throat being cut and the deep hostility that I knew existed between the marital partners—and you can see why I was frightened that the vampire fantasy is a prelude to a drama of homicide. The strange fact also emerged that each time the vampire visitation took place—and there was a third, diluted repetition three weeks later—she had her menstruation and I could not help wondering whether she was trying to retaliate for assault fantasies.

It took a while to discover that it was not against Mr. Forbes that the homicidal build-up was being used. It was against me. *I was the vampire* who had assaulted her, not sexually, but by exposing her fraudulent phenomena.

When the first vampire visitation took place, she had a greater fall than Humpty-Dumpty ever sustained. We found a linen wrapper dropping on the floor from under her skirt and there was evidence that it was used for "apporting" objects by vaginal concealment. This was a shattering blow to her occult reputation. But the investigation continued and I caught her *in flagranti* before the second vampire attack. She was throwing a small stone from her purse behind her back —an "apport" for which the Poltergeist was responsible. Also a living bird flew up from under her skirt, and I was pretty well convinced that it was hidden there in a small sack.

Remember, too, that Dracula was a Hungarian Count. Vampires were supposed to abound in Hungary and *I was a Hungarian*. She denied ever having heard the Dracula story and association tests seemed to bear her out until she recalled that her husband had seen the motion picture made of Bram Stoker's story and had warned her not to see it.

In that motion picture Dracula was played by Bela Lugosi, another Hungarian, and moreover, an old friend of mine.

As a medium, Mrs. Forbes had a slowly emerging "spirit-guide" called Bremba. When it first appeared Mrs. Forbes had difficulties of articulation. She was in trance and, very faintly, the name came as Brember. We simplified it to Bremba. Note that the sound contains *BRAM* and *ER*, the first name of Bram Stoker and the last syllable. Further, when Bremba was asked (the medium being in trance) to explain the meaning of the bites, he said that the medium's soul has been cast out of her body, but it comes back to gain sustenance from the blood of its former body and in coming back it takes the form of a bird. The bird has to be killed, then the entity that possesses her body would have to leave it and her own soul would return. We should wait up for the bird. It was a bat. It would appear again in about three weeks when the medium had recovered the blood that she had lost. He should open the windows, turn the lights out, catch it in a net and wring its neck. The hour should be 12:30 A.M. In the meantime we might take the medium to the zoo, show her the vampire bat and watch her reactions.

The macabre fantasies of Mrs. Forbes were now in full flower. Murder has entered into it. Heaven only knows what would have happened if I had been stupid enough to go along with her vampire fantasy. I bowed out.

Goblin of the Loaf[1]

A magic wand, by a wave of which duties around the house would be performed, the dinner made ready and served piping hot, may be the dream of many housewives. In fantasy, the idea may be very attractive. In practice, however, magic never works out so well. A disconcerting element is usually reported, something unearthly and puckish, something that puts the joke on you and, perhaps, frightens you out of appreciating it.

The Websters, a family with seven children living at Raikes Farm, Beverley, England, certainly did not like the way it worked.

Not being blessed with too much worldly goods, bread was an essential element in their bill of fare; but the magic abroad in their house would not let them have it. The case created considerable excitement 60 years ago and never was solved. Nor can I, as a psychoanalyst, throw any light on it.

As reported in the London *Daily Express,* and subsequently in *Light,* October 24, 1903, the farmhouse was said to be haunted. Strange noises, footsteps and mysterious choir singing were heard in the night, but the thing which mostly disturbed the family was that the bread, from the first week of March 1903, crumbled away each night.

It looked as if it had been gnawed by rats or mice. All sorts of precautions were taken but nothing could arrest the dwindling of the loaves. They were set in a closed pan, with a rat trap, and with another trap on top of the lid, the floor was sprinkled with flour, two lengths of cotton were stretched across the room, and the doors were locked. In the morning

[1] First published in *Fate Magazine,* December 1961; reprinted by permission.

everything was found intact, but one of the loaves had entirely disappeared, the other had dwindled to half its original size.

For nearly three months the Websters kept this mystery to themselves. But the situation became more desperate. Mrs. Webster saw the end of a loaf waste into nothingness on the kitchen table within an hour. So the services of ex-police constable Berridge, of Bishop's Burton, were requested and he was put in sole charge of the dairy for several days.

Berridge frankly confessed that he was baffled. He came to the farm with two loaves of bread and locked them in the dairy with his special lock. The next day they appeared to be all right, but a day after, on cutting them open, he found the loaves quite hollow. He suspected faulty baking but the cavity gradually grew wider and wider, and the second loaf began to dwindle before his eyes. He secreted pieces of bread in other places about the house and in every instance they wasted away to nothing.

Ten leading chemists of Beverley and Hull visited the farm and analyzed the bread. The microscope did not reveal the presence of any microbe or fungus and they pronounced the bread absolutely pure.

When Mrs. Webster resorted to baking cakes for the household she was relieved to find that, though they lay side by side with the blighted bread, they showed no sign of shrinkage. However, when the last crumb of bread disappeared the Goblin of the Loaf attacked the cake as well.

The decay of the bread or cake was immediately arrested if it was removed from the precincts of the farmhouse. Thus the blight was proved to be purely local. The Goblin was attached to the house or to the family.

In magical practice this devouring of things is not unknown. Ibn Khaldun, a remarkable early parapsychologist who died while Chief Justice at Cairo in A.D. 1406, in an introduction to his *Universal History*, said that in India there were some who would point at a man and he would fall dead. It would then be found that his heart had vanished. They would point too at pomegranates, and all the seeds would be found to have vanished.[2]

The latter sounds similar to the work of our Goblin.

[2] *The Religious Attitude and Life in Islam*, by D. B. MacDonald, p. 114.

A still closer parallel is found in the story told by Père Labat, in *Nouveaux Voyages aux Isles d'Amerique,* of a black sorceress who, on board Count Gennes' boat en route to the French Islands in 1696, could waste the hearts and livers of her negro companions. She was tied to the guns and severely whipped. The Surgeon-Major struck her several times with a rope's end. The woman told the surgeon that, because he was ill-treating her without reason, she would eat his heart also. Two days later the surgeon died in agony. His body was opened and his heart and liver were found to be as dry as parchment. Thereupon the Captain made a bargain with the sorceress, promising to send her back to her country, provided she would hold her peace. Père Labat wrote:

> In order to impress this officer with a sense of her power, she asked if he had any fruit or anything else eatable on board. He answered that he had some watermelons. "Show them to me," she replied, "and without touching or coming near them I engage to have eaten them before 24 hours are over." He accepted the challenge and showed her some watermelons, which he placed in a box which was immediately locked, and of which he placed the key in his pocket. The next morning the woman asked him to look at the melons; he opened the box in which they had been placed and, to his great satisfaction, found them seemingly untouched. His joy, however, was of but short duration and was changed to extreme astonishment on attempting to take up the fruit; they were entirely empty, and nothing but the skin remained inflated like a balloon and dry as a parchment. The ship was accordingly obliged to return to land, and take in water and fresh supplies.

We can criticize this story as being far too marvelous to be taken for more than a tale. But it is odd that the Goblin at Raikes Farm should act so similarly in modern times and that no one should have been able to solve its mystery.

* * *

I found another story in a manuscript left by Father Sinistrari of Ameno, a Franciscan monk and lecturer on Sacred Theology at the Convent of the Holy Cross in Pavia,

Italy. He died in 1701. The extraordinary events which are recorded in *Demoniality* and *Incubi and Succubi* (Paris, 1879), concern Hieronyma, a married woman of the town "of unimpeachable morality." Here is an incident, in Father Sinistrari's words, which reads like a fairy tale from *The Arabian Nights*:

On St. Stephen's Day the husband had asked some military friends to dinner and, to do honor to his guests, had provided a substantial repast. Whilst they were, as customary, washing their hands before taking their seats, the table dressed in the dining room suddenly vanished; all the dishes, saucepans, kettles, plates and crockery in the kitchen disappeared likewise, as well as the jugs, bottles and glasses. You may imagine the surprise, the stupor of the guests, eight in number. Amongst them was a Spanish captain of infantry who, addressing the company, said to them: "Do not be frightened, it is but a trick; the table is certainly where it stood, and I shall soon find it by feeling for it." Having thus spoken, he paced round the room with outstretched arms, endeavoring to lay hold of the table; but when after many circuitous perambulations it was apparent that he labored in vain and grasped at nought but thin air, he was laughed at by his friends; and it being already high time for dinner each guest took up his cloak and set about to return home.

They had already reached the street door with the husband who, out of politeness, was attending them, when they heard a great noise in the dining room; they stood to ascertain the cause thereof, and presently the servant came up to announce that the kitchen was stocked with new vessels filled with food, and that the table was standing again in its former place. Having gone back to the dining room they were stupefied to see the table was laid, with cloths, napkins, salt-cellars, and trays that did not belong to the house, and with food which had not been cooked there. On a large sideboard, all arrayed in perfect order, were crystal, silver and gold chalices, with all kinds of amphoras, decanters and cups filled with foreign wines, from the Isle of Crete, Campania, the Canaries, the Rhine, etc. In the kitchen there was also an abundant variety of meats in saucepans and dishes that had never been seen there before.

At first some of the guests hesitated whether they should taste of the food; however, encouraged by others, they sat down and soon partook of the meal, which was found exquisite.

Immediately afterwards, as they were sitting before a seasonable fire, everything vanished at once, the dishes and the leavings, and in their stead reappeared the cloth of the house and the victuals which had been previously cooked; but for a wonder, all the guests were satisfied so no one thought of supper after such a magnificent dinner. A clear proof that the substituted viands were real and nowise fictitious.

Father Sinistrari ascribed this charming miracle to a demon who was tempting and persecuting a woman of unequalled virtue. One may wonder in which direction he displayed greater credulity.

Demon or Goblin, serving dinner or eating your bread, which would you like to have at your service?

I think you will choose drudgery!

The "Living Machine" of Rev. John Murray Spear[1]

To discover and scientifically control the principle of life has been the dream of many men, but few ever have become involved in such a weird adventure as the Electrical Infant and New Motor Movement of John Murray Spear.

The story has been buried in the early chronicles of American Spiritualism. But it is of fascinating interest and worth bringing back to the light of day as John Murray Spear's followers acclaimed it "God's last, best gift to man . . . destined to revolutionize the whole world" and "infuse new life and vitality into all things, animate and inanimate."

This combination of a *homunculus* and of a *perpetuum mobile* or a "living machine," originated about 100 years ago

[1] First published in *Fate Magazine*, December 1961; reprinted by permission.

with John Murray Spear, a famous Universalist minister who had distinguished himself in nearly all the benevolent but unpopular reforms of his day. John Murray Spear received his given name from John Murray, the founder of Universalism, and throughout his life claimed to be acting under the influence of the older man's spirit.

Electricity fascinated John Murray Spear. Hopelessly unscientific and dominated by superstitious ideas, he combined copper and zinc batteries in the form of an armor around spiritualistic mediums of his day and expected to make phenomenal discoveries. The idea had such a hold on his mind that he passed into states of dissociation in which "spirits of the dead" spoke through him and announced the coming of great discovery along his line of search.

Gradually the dream took definite form. John Murray Spear needed a Mary for his New Dispensation. He found her in the person of Mrs. Semantha Mettler, the wife of a Boston doctor and a well known medium of the day. In her presence he passed into the "superior state" and enunciated this message.

How fondly, how constantly, how widely is this one [Mrs. Mettler] beloved! How beautiful is the influence this woman exerts! Wherever she is she attracts! In this particular she possesses a most remarkable character. Her friends know no bounds to their affections for this one; and there is nothing which they would leave undone to gratify her. There passes from this woman a very marked influence. It is not precisely the religious influence; it is not precisely the moral influence; it is not precisely the practical influence; but it is, so to speak, a compost [sic!] of all; and these are charmingly intermingled, imparting a most adhesive influence.

This medium [John Murray Spear] has been commissioned to wisely instruct this woman for a high purpose. There is before this woman a new and beautiful labor. At 10 o'clock tomorrow the purpose of his mission to this place will be unfolded. Let this woman be in the region of the tranquilities at that hour.

Note how time was allowed for this message to sink into a very receptive and believing mind from which flattery and the promise of a "new and beautiful labor" were likely to sweep every resistance. Mrs. Mettler had every reason to be thrilled. She believed that spirits were speaking through her when she passed into a state of trance. Now she heard the spirits speaking to her directly through a famous person for whom people had very high regard. No one who came into personal relationship with John Murray Spear ever doubted that he honestly believed in the spiritual origin of the various missions which he undertook. There was nothing of the charlatan about him; he never labored for monetary gain. His fearless disregard of popular opinion and his unwavering adherence to ideas which he believed to be instigated by "the highest wisdom" gained for him a respect which stood him in good stead in some extraordinary undertakings.

As announced, at 10 o'clock on the following day John Murray Spear passed again into the "superior state" and, on bended knee, pronounced these words:

Father of Fathers, and Deity of Deities! Thy will be done on the earths, as it is done in the heaven of heavens. This fondly loved one [Mrs. Mettler] shall be consecrated to the charities. Thou shalt thenceforth be called "Charity." Receive now this blessed power!

Here he closed Mrs. Mettler's hand and breathed upon it. When she opened it, he said:

This hand shall be unfolded to dispense blessings. It is done!

It would be difficult to explain the events that followed without understanding the extraordinary dedication of Mrs. Mettler to a service, the particular nature of which she had yet no knowledge. This dedication, the desire for service and the belief in spirits bound her into a psychic affinity with John Murray Spear. As a result she had some remarkable psychological experiences and prophetic visions at or about the same time that the Universalist minister began to build, at High Rock, Mass., the modern Frankenstein, the machine that was to be animated by a living principle which Mrs. Mettler's maternal functions were to provide.

The building of the machine cost $2,000. The money was contributed by John Murray Spear's followers. They never questioned his authority and the high purpose which the money was to serve. The machine was not built after a prepared design. Parts were added to it bit by bit according to measurements given through the entranced preacher. It was said to have analogies to the human brain, heart, lungs, etc., but in reality it was nothing more than an agglomeration, a curious combination of zinc, copper and steel.

When "the appointed time" arrived Mrs. Mettler received her summons. She came to visit the machine and was received by Spear's followers in a state of hysterical excitement. She passed into a state of true convulsions and her frenzy spread over the rest of the assembly. All persons present recognized a correlation between themselves and parts of the strange machine. This psychological identification produced scenes of hysteria with which we are familiar from a study of religious revivals. At the height of the emotional crisis a miraculous pulsation and undulation was claimed to take place in the extremities of the weird machine.

Amidst mad shouts of victory, it was declared that a living principle had been communicated to the machine and that the mechanical infant was born. By the resolution of all present the modern Frankenstein was solemnly handed over to the Mother for nursing into increasing life.

It was expected that the 'child" would grow into a machine that would move the wheels of the world and would replace all other motive powers. S. Crosby Hewitt, editor of the *New Era* of Boston, the principal paper behind the New Motor Movement, wrote as follows:

> We must confidently assert that the advent of the science of all sciences, the philosophy of all philosophies, and the art of all arts has now fairly commenced. The child is born; not long hence he will go alone. Then he will dispute with the doctors in the Temples of Science.

It is almost impossible to comprehend the spell under which the strange experiment at High Rock held a large number of people. But as the news of the living machine spreads, disquieting rumors arose. It was whispered that strange practices had taken place and that Mrs. Mettler was indeed the mother of the strange machine. In vain did Dr. Mettler, the husband of the lady, strip from the story the gross mask of absurdity. The public mind was aroused against the machine which exposed motherhood to ridicule. Resentment grew to such a pitch

171

that at Randolph, N.Y., where this modern Frankenstein had been transported to enjoy the advantage of a lofty electrical position, the populace marched on the machine, tore it to pieces and trampled it under their feet.

John Murray Spear was heartbroken. He never attempted to rebuild the machine but he did write the following:

> Thank God, the principles which have been presented and the philosophy which has been communicated are beyond the reach of the mob and cannot be harmed by the slanders of the pulpit or the misrepresentations of the press. "Truth crushed to earth shall rise again: the eternal years of God are hers."

The Rage that Burns
the House Down

A psychoanalyst colleague who comes from a small village in Transylvania told me a strange story of incendiary storks. If the stork, on returning from winter migration, finds its old nest on the roof destroyed, it is likely to repay the owner by setting the house on fire. This it does by picking up burning sticks from an open fire and dropping them on the thatched roof.

My friend insists, from his own knowledge, that the story is true. Whether the storks in Translyvania are specially vindictive or not; this is a good start to begin the discussion of another type of rage that can, and sometimes does, burn down the house. I have in mind the case of the incendiary Poltergeist. The chief motive behind Poltergeist disturbances is repressed aggression in the psyche of adolescents before puberty. It manifests itself by stone throwing, crockery breaking and other destructive activities for which an unconscious projection of energy, due to a temporary abnormality of the nervous system, is responsible. Generally, the rage of the Poltergeist is spent in the pandemonium it creates. On rare occasions, however, the production of fire, out of the air as it were, appears to be the "gift of the spirit." This is a more serious threat to the family of the unhappy victim of the visitation than the rest of the phenomena lumped together.

The public usually accuses a ghost because of the perpe-trator's invisibility. This helps to confuse the issue between the Poltergeist and the ghost in the haunted house. The Poltergeist is a man-haunter that works in daylight. It follows the victim wherever he goes. It is strictly personal and has a limited life-time. With the outbreak of puberty, its energy seems to return to normal physiological channels and the disturbance stops. The Poltergeist is not a spirit, it has no identity, it brings no messages from the dead; it is a bundle of projected repressions bent on destruction and mischief because it is born out of rage and frustration. In contradistinction, the ghost of the haunted house is bound to a locality. It works at night. It is often automatic and dreamlike, like a nightmare that floated away from the mind that conceived it, enduring like a gramo-phone record or television picture in the presence of certain mysterious vitalizing factors. The ghost is much more out of this world than the Poltergeist. Its lifetime is not limited and not dependent on the inhabitants of the house. It may carry on in an empty house. It is only interested in echoing some-thing that happened way back in the past. If things go bump in the night, think of the ghost, not of the Poltergeist. Move out of the house and you are out of reach.

Sometimes, however, even experienced parapsychologists get confused in the use of the two terms. Harry Price speaks of Poltergeists at Borley Rectory, and in his book, *Poltergeist Over England,* instead of ghosts. The reason is not due to ignorance but to the fact that ghosts can do everything that Poltergeists do, though they rarely show any sign of activity in daytime. A further complication arises from the spiritualist claim that the ghost is more than the dream of the dead, that it may be an earthbound spirit. It appears that a spirit can do everything that the Poltergeist and the ghost does. It has identity, it can send messages, it has a purpose.

This three-fold situation is rather bewildering, and it be-comes still more so when attempts are made to get in touch with the Poltergeist (through a trance medium or automatic writing) as if it were a spirit. The somatic dissociation in which it originates, begins to turn into a mental one and initial phases of mediumship will manifest themselves as it happened in the case of the Thornton Heath Poltergeist.

Poltergeist, ghost or evil spirit, Borley Rectory was burned down as promised in a message through the planchette. Similar threats were made in the Great Amherst Mystery in Nova

Scotia. A voice (which is not heard in Poltergeist cases) announced that the house would be set on fire. Lighted matches were seen to fall from the ceiling on the bed and fires were continuously started. This ghost had a personality and persecuted unhappy Esther Cox with a ferocious hatred. An invisible hand cut words directly into the plaster of the wall, while everyone heard the words: *Esther Cox, you are mine to kill.* It did stab Esther Cox in the back with a knife that came out of nowhere. The Poltergeist character of the persecution appeared when Esther Cox moved to a farm. It set fire to a barn when Esther Cox passed by. She was arrested for arson and sentenced to four months in jail. However, due to the pressure of public sentiment, she was released a month later.

Ordinarily, the Poltergeist is *sui generis* and can clearly be identified as such. In the case reported by Judge Koloman Tóth, of Hungary, it only played with matches, but did not light them. It was satisfied with attacking a two-year-old little girl with needles and pins all over her body. A young peasant girl's rage against her duties seemed to be the focal point of the malevolent manifestations. Aksakoff, Imperial Counsellor to the Czar of Russia, saw a phosphorescent spark fly through the air, bursting into flames on a cotton dress in the bedroom and, on another occasion, on the body of Mrs. Schnapoff. The Tribuna of Rome reported the persecution of an 80-year-old woman by invisible blows and water splashes on her bed and body all over the house. A 16-year-old niece, Maria Fiore, seemed to be the unconscious aggressor. When the rain ceased, the old woman's dress began to burn. Her bed and clothes and a quantity of hay in the loft also caught fire.

One wonders whether the mysterious cases of spontaneous combustion of the human body may not be due to the deadly activity of an incendiary Poltergeist. Charles Fort collected many stories of this type and while his conclusions are of no scientific value, his documents well repay studying. One may wonder also whether the germ of a Poltergeist story is hidden in the story of the shirt of Nessus that caused the death of Hercules. The motive of rage and jealousy on the part of Deianeira, his wife was clearly present. Nessus was a centaur whom Hercules had killed in the act of raping his wife. The mixture of his blood, seed and olive oil was the poison that Deianeira smeared on the shirt she had sent to her husband with the injunction that on no account should it be exposed to light or heat until Hercules wears it at a sacrifice to the gods. The heat melted the poison and the flesh of Hercules corroded as if attacked by gangrene. The *Tunica Molesta* of Nero, in which Christians were clothed before they were tied to the stake, may have been inspired by the memory of the shirt of Nessus.

We may also query whether the priests of the Old Testament who prayed down fire from Heaven as a sign of acceptance of their sacrifice, were not helped by an incendiary Poltergeist.

Dr. Ervin Benkalo reported in *Fate Magazine* (June, 1953) the extraordinary story of the *Kada Codex*, lost through a fire in the ancient convent of Cinta, Portugal in 1952. The *Codex* was printed in Hungary in 1620. On its cover, and on the first seven pages, the burning imprint of a hand was visible. Subsequent pages showed less and less sign of burn until page 100. The imprint came from the ghostly hand of Bishop Stephen Kada. The story was traced by Dr. E. Friedrich, a professor of history. According to this, the ghost of the Bishop appeared to Father Franciscus Hanacius at the monastery of Privigye of the Calasantine monks, and asked for a Mass and prayers for the release of his soul from Purgatory. Father Hanacius recognized the voice of the deceased Bishop but wanted more proof of identity. The ghost said: the devil has no power over sacred books—and as if an invisible hand had been placed on the cover of his *Codex*, smoke and smell from burning leather and paper filled the room and billowed out of the monastery window. Two and a half centuries saw no change in the imprint of the burning hand.

Can a ghost be harmed by fire? The problem had arisen in the case of the Bell Witch of Tennessee. A priceless story is told by William Porter with whom the Witch went to sleep "to keep him warm." We read:[1]

> The cover continued to slip in spite of my tenacious grasp, and was twisted into a roll on the backside of the bed, just like a boy would roll himself in a quilt, and not a strip was left on me. I jumped out of bed in a second, and observing that the Witch had rolled up in the cover, the thought struck me: "I have got you now, you rascal, and will burn you up." In an instant I grabbed the roll of cover in my arms and started to the fire, to throw the cover, Witch and all, in the blaze. I discovered that it

[1] From *Haunted People*, *op cit.*, p. 159.

was very weighty and smelled awful. I had not got half-way across the room before the luggage got so heavy and became so offensive that I was compelled to drop it on the floor and rush out of doors for a breath of fresh air. The odor emitted from the roll was the most offensive stench I ever smelled.

The means of self-defense employed by the Witch is most interesting and well supports the evil character, bent on murder, of this greatest American ghost story.

Excessive cold as an opposite to the heat of fire, is observed in many haunted houses. Miss Goodrich-Freer recorded excellent testimonies of this phenomenon in her record of the haunting of Ballechin House.

Personally, I only had a short and not very satisfactory experience with the incendiary Poltergeist. It was at the house of Lillian Fisher, a New York Spiritualist minister. She complained of odd doings and the scorching by fire of various objects in her house. I saw evidence of smoke and charring, but the scale was light and it rested on her unsupported testimony which, however, I had no reason to doubt.

The most recent case of Poltergeist arson comes from Talladega, Alabama, in 1961. It is reported by R. E. Hogan in full detail in *Fate Magazine* of the same year. The story is well supported by testimonies including that of Fire Capt. S. H. Joiner who had no explanation to offer. The cabin of Calvin Tuck was on fire 22 times in three days. The Tucks had six small children, aged from 3 months to 9 years. The fire had virtually gutted the structure, the family lost nearly all of its personal belongings and was driven out by fire from several successive homes. In nearly all cases, the fire erupted near the ceiling. Leslie R. Hutto, Talladega County Road Commissioner, and Otis Horton, a local contractor, saw the fire start before their very eyes. Hutto started scraping the mantel piece with a knife, and it flamed up in his face. He also raked his knife in a circle on the wall, and it started blazing in the same way. Part of the flame stuck to the blade of his knife. While they were in the house, a fire would start every fifteen minutes. Police Lt. Ben Cooley saw a quilt hanging on a tree in the yard start burning. He commented: "I would not have believed it if I had not seen it."

In due course, the 9-year-old Calvin Tuck, Jr., was accused and made to confess having started the fires. He was told that a witch doctor was after his Daddy and would get him (the son), too, because he was not telling the truth. The boy then confessed. But the confession did not fit the facts and Fire Marshal Frank Craven did not consider the case of the mystery fires closed.

The truth must be that the young boy was, indeed, responsible for the fires but not consciously, and the fires were started by no means known to him or within his power. Poltergeist victims usually have an uncanny feeling that they are somehow involved and are terrified. It is unfortunate that no psychologist was invited to find out the relationship between the boy and his parent. We can, nevertheless, assume that the burning hatred of the son for his father may have been the motive on which, by a concentration of nervous energy, the incendiary phenomena had erupted.

The Baltimore Poltergeist

On January 14, 1960, at the house of Mr. Edgar J. Jones at 1448 Meridan Drive in Baltimore, Md., a typical Poltergeist outbreak was reported in the local press the mental background of which promised to be rewarding for psychoanalytical inquiry.

I left for Baltimore on Wednesday, January 20, and arrived shortly after midnight. On the train, from the meagre information in my possession, I tried to form a picture of the motives that could have activated this Poltergeist. I was told of a young boy of 17 who was not a Jones but went under the name of Ted Pauls. It was not clear to me that he was a grandson and, pardonably, I derived the wrong impression that he had given up his family name.

The assumption that he was trying to escape from his family by a change of name was erroneous. But I was informed that he was an ardent science fiction fan and devoted all his time to this particular interest. It seemed to conform to my first impression of escapism. Basically, science fiction serves well for an escape from mundane limitations. In the case of a writer of science fiction there would be a sublimation of the need of escape by turning it into creative channels through

177

story telling of the magnificence of far-off worlds whirling in the depth of space. In the reader, however, the relaxation and entertainment found in such fantasies may well be a screen for the archaic yearning of returning into the prenatal state. A distinct planet, in the womb of space, is an excellent substitute for the "fetal island" (the child being in its own universe) where earthly (postnatal) ties had not yet existed. One would be hard put to find a better escape from reality than a journey into space.

Ted Pauls did not write science fiction. He was satisfied with editing a multigraphed discussion sheet called *Fanjack*. I thought that this might bear on the escape motive. Then it occurred to me that interstellar space and the worlds scattered in it are also the habitat, in science fiction stories, of nonhuman life. There is a corresponding facet to that in embryonic evolution antecedent to the fetal stage. The thought intrigued me because the linguistic equation of Ted Pauls with tadpole does take back to the nonhuman stage. What is in a name? Shakespeare had asked the question but did not answer it, at least not to the satisfaction of psychoanalysis. I have dealt with the problem in a comprehensive manner in an essay entitled *Nomen est Omen*.[1] Could Ted Pauls have fallen under the spell of his name? (I found out afterwards that his father did pronounce his name as Poles instead of Pauls.) An impish thought followed and I began to chuckle: it would be funny if he had long legs like a frog to leap off into space. As a science fiction fan he would be acquainted with Abraham Merritt's *The Moon Pool*, an outstanding classic in which giant frogmen from Lemurian times stalk the earth in underground caverns.

On my arrival, this fantasy was nurtured by local information. Ted Pauls had long legs; moreover, he walked like a frog with widespread feet and when sitting in his favorite rocking chair, the chandelier, set swinging by the Poltergeist, always moved from North to South. This seemed to be a secret signature as North and South are determined by the poles. Ted Pauls? The rocking, of course, hinted at cradle days or at the undulating movements of the maternal body during the period of gestation. I was told he assumed the rocking position automatically and seemed to derive a great deal of pleasure from it.

[1] *Samiksa*, Calcutta, Vol. X, No. 1, 1956.

There it was then, a wonderful fantasy of escapism, which turned out to be entirely my own fancy. Observations in the haunted house quickly pushed it into the background. The chandelier could well act in unison with his rocking as the living room, where the rocking chair was, was longitudinal to the dining room in which the chandelier was hung. Hence, North and South was a natural direction. The kitchen was latitudinal, but it was not a place for continued stay. It was therefore unnecessary to connect the swinging chandelier with rocking memories. The topographical situation was sufficient to account for the preferred movement.

Moreover, Ted Pauls' interest in science fiction was not devoid of a creative and sublimatory element (to which I shall presently return). I brought up the question of Merritt's *The Moon Pool* in a discussion of science fiction books. He could not have had any idea that the question was baited. He answered that he had never read the book. (I inspected his library later. There was one book by Merritt in it,—but it was definitely not *The Moon Pool*. The reality situation soon disposed of the fancy that Ted Pauls was a frog. The natural narcissism we have for our names must have completely blinded him to the tadpole interpretation.

So my fancy did not expose him. It only exposed myself as a fantasy fan of strong mystical inclinations. And that was precisely the approach I used with Ted Pauls.

I took with me to Baltimore a science fiction book: Asimov's *Nine Tomorrows,* and inscribed it to him "as from one science fiction fan to another." It was a first and fortunate meeting point between us. For, as I found out, by this time Ted Pauls was getting bitter and hostile to publicity, to the presence of a crowd of journalists and to the nuisance he and his family was exposed to. One frustrated journalist demanded that he should confess to a conscious responsibility for the flight of objects and for the explosive manifestations that accompanied it. He was roused and wrote a letter of angry protest to his editor, a protest very well composed and completely ignored. There was a distinct possibility that the situation would become further aggravated unless a face-saving was presented to the baffled journalists.

My appearance on the scene as a "Poltergeist expert" fulfilled this need. They did not have to have an opinion of their own. They could quote me and hang everything on my statements.

So I had an ideal opportunity to release the pressure in both camps. The journalists were easy. They were courteous and respectful. The problem was Ted Pauls. Could I win his full confidence?

Frankly, I did not know. I was floundering in a sea of uncertainties. While I had not witnessed any disturbance, I accepted the record. It was carefully compiled by a fellow researcher, Douglas Dean. He examined every witness and arranged for a number of scientific tests to rule out the recondite physical factors that people like to fall back on. A prima facie case was established for Poltergeist activity. Hence, the key to the mystery had to lie in the psyche of Ted Pauls. He was above the pubertal age but things had been happening in the house before, at Christmas time, for instance. Twice in the preceding years the decorative blue balls on the Christmas tree exploded with no known reason. I thought he must have had a strong grievance against Christmas. His birthday was on December 16th, but his grandfather assured me that they never pooled his birthday and Christmas gifts. Christmas is a universal birthday symbol. His own birth preceded it by nine days (the term of gestation in months), but I was assured that his birth was normal, and that he had suffered no injuries during delivery, hence the existence of a trauma of birth could only have been proven from Ted Pauls' dreams. He did not have any to tell me.

Nevertheless, the Christmas mystery cannot be dismissed too easily. Birth can be a crippling experience. It survives in the unconscious as such. It may strongly reinforce other feelings of imperfection and provide, through a rebellion against Fate, an unconscious motive for Poltergeist activity. As far as I was able to find out, Ted Pauls had no physical defect, just little peculiarities like his walk, his pixie looks and the odd slant of one of his eyes, making him appear slightly Chinese. I had no time to consult his family doctor or his school psychiatrist (a job with which Douglas Dean had charged himself), but I did find out, from a careful conversation, that he was not crippled in his sexual development. While he had no girl friend, he did have fantasies about girls and only his shyness kept him away from their company. His sexual development was apparently quite normal, hence the cripple motive could be disregarded.

But before more is said of his motivation, let us place emphasis on the fact that the pubertal disturbance might have been responsible for the Poltergeist activity, restrained as it was, at Christmas time. It is an important stage of transition, that well may have mobilized the unconscious imprint of the greatest transition we ever make until death; the entrance into postnatal life. No doubt an explanation could be found for the dormancy period, but I did not have the time to pursue this line of investigation.

The question is often raised why such disturbances should be confined to one person in the household only. Could not there be a contribution from other sources; a kind of pooling of paranormal talent?

We can safely rule out the grandparents because of their age. (At seventy or more one has no vitality to waste.) We can also rule out the parents because they are away during the day. Could we consider the dog?

Hardly. There are no Polterdogs. Kristy, the three-year-old female Schnauzer was not an agent but a victim of the Poltergeist. She cowered and tried to hide before the phenomena took place. She crouched at the door and scratched frantically in order to be let out. This used to happen a few seconds or minutes before something flew or exploded. Her behavior was the best evidence that something spooky was going on in the house.[2]

Had I told Ted Pauls that the Poltergeist activity was due to a projection of his repressed aggressions against someone in the house (parents or grandparents) he would have turned indignantly against me and would have withdrawn into a shell. It is a delicate matter to tell somebody that he is guilty of something he knows nothing about. However, it is not enough to speak of aggressivity in general terms. Specific reasons should be found. He was not a chronic bed-wetter or sleepwalker in childhood. He had not been exposed to humiliation

---

[2] Kristy's distress in the presence of Poltergeist phenomena is not unique. I reported similar terror exhibited by a dog and a cat in the case of the Chelsea Poltergeist (*The Haunted Mind*): "The dog cowered in a chair shivering. The cat ran around like mad and hurled itself against the window several times in an effort to get out, then ran to the door and started scratching on it." There was a dog called Mona in the house of the Talking Mongoose. It was old, senile and only useful for fleas. It never paid any attention to the odd doings in the house. But then "Gef" clearly stated that he was no ghost, just an "extra, extra clever little mongoose." Nor was any distress shown in the Forbes household by the favorite cat. Mrs. Forbes did not know that animals are the best witnesses of the paranormal or she would have made up stories about the cat.

on either account. But his toilet training could have been over-severe. I know at least of one instance within my clinical experience in which a psychotic disposition developed on this basis alone. His mother was not available for an interview and Ted knew too little about himself. He was not a loquacious young man. He had no friends and lived in his room like a monk in his cell. And there was nothing visible to indicate a disturbed relationship with his parents or grandparents beyond the fact that they did not approve of his quitting school at 16 and living for science fiction alone.

Grandfather was a retired fireman of 70. He served the Fire Department for 37 years. No doubt he must have regaled his grandson with plenty of stories of his exploits. Like a war horse ready for the bugle, his short-wave radio was going all day to receive signals of fire. He had an easy way to become a hero ideal for his grandson. Proof of it could be seen in Ted's extraordinary interest in fires.[3] This interest caused me anxiety when told about it on my arrival. The thought occurred to me that he may be studying for arson. There have been incendiary Poltergeists in the past. Spontaneous combustion is a far more dangerous phenomenon than the hurling or smashing of objects. It could easily result in loss of life in a gutted house. But I found that his interest in fires was open and above board. It was most unlikely to become an idea for the Poltergeist. While it is true that in one case a can of fruit dislodged from a shelf full on grandfather's head, this single incident was not enough to suggest that his aggression was directed at the old man. But the old man owned the house and the house was shared by Ted's parents. Any destruction in the house would hit both parents and grandparents. Against this stands the fact that material damage was slight. More valuable items were avoided and when removed to a safer place were not singled out for destruction.

Before discussing further the problem of motivation, let us consider the question of the mechanics of Poltergeist activities. This is the central mystery. It is not enough to say that the Poltergeist is a bundle of projected repression. We should want

---

[3] To quote items from his library: *Fire Prevention*, by P. J. McKeon, *School Fires*, reprinted from various sources, several issues of *The International Fire Fighter, Firemen's Record* for 1926. These books may have belonged originally to grandfather. That he took them over with pleasure, appears from a statement in his magazine: "Yes, I am a fire buff."

an answer as to how this projection takes place. What is the nature of the energy involved? Is it muscular, nervous, electric or electronic? How does it work?

We do not know. Therefore, the best we can do is speculative approach. I would call the Poltergeist manifestation the result of somatic and psychic dissociation. Somatic dissociation is something new. It has never been postulated before. It means that the human body is capable of releasing energy in a manner similar to atomic bombardments. The electron shot out of its orbits round the proton is like a bolt of lightning. It can be photographed streaking through the air in a cloud chamber. It is a purely mechanical energy. The atom, as such, has no power to impart direction to it. A human being has. It appears that under strong emotions not only does such a discharge (happily without chain reaction) take place but that the energy thus released is under control. A Poltergeist-thrown object can travel slowly or fast, it can change course as if part of the psyche of the projector would travel with it, as if the somatic dissociation that releases it would not free it from mental control. But even that hypothesis leaves a great deal unexplained. The explosive effect may be due to pressure in the unconscious, it may partly release it or it may act as a S.O.S. calling for help. But in the Baltimore case the force was apparently able to enter Coca Cola and soda bottles that had not been uncapped and burst them from within. In one instance, a flower pot of plastic material, wide open at the top, was cracked on both sides by an explosion within that left the plant in the middle undisturbed and the pot itself standing. It indicated that the bilateral explosion was exceedingly well balanced. It hinted at brain activity similar to that of an electronic computing machine.

So much for the physical aspect, the elucidation of which fell within the range of Douglas Dean's investigation. My job was to find motives and then decide on a course of action.

The theory of projected aggression could not be dismissed just because the cause of it was not apparent. An unconscious storm may well rage behind conscious compliance with an existing situation Ted Pauls *was* subjected to too much pushing around. He was not suffered to have a goal of life of his own choosing. The fact that he had no friends strongly suggested that the relationship between himself and his schoolmates was not a good one. He might have been subjected to too much teasing and name calling. There was his walk, his pixie looks, his tendency of withdrawal and his intellectual superiority. (He claimed that the school could no longer teach him anything. This was not due to a swollen head because school authorities describe him as a brilliant boy.) Bitter against his schoolmates, smouldering for not being understood at home, tension must have been growing deep within. He was a well-mannered boy, exceedingly courteous and careful to preserve appearances and not lacking in courage if he was provoked. When I first saw him, he faced a crowd that he hated, but he faced it and the only sign of the tension in him was the whiteness of his knuckles as he gripped the arms of the rocking chair. To tell him that he was a monster inside would have been considered a preposterous accusation. I just did not know what to do until, out of the blue, a key was presented by the reading of a page of his editorial writing found in the cellar near the multigraphing machine. To my utter amazement I found that this young boy had a great talent for writing. At 17 he was an accomplished journalist. His vocabulary had left nothing behind and his editorial handling of *Fanjack* showed a rare maturity. He was bursting with a rage for writing and no one in his immediate surroundings understood or appreciated him. They considered his preoccupation nonsensical and drove against it with all their might. Was it, I queried, that the Poltergeist activity arose from his frustrated creative rage?

At this thought I began to breathe easily. I found a therapeutic approach to the problem of the Poltergeist. The boy had talent that clamored for expression. Playing the editor was the only balm for his crushed ego. It elevated him above his readers. If then a depressed ego was hiding behind the Poltergeist rebellion, raising of his self-feelings to a higher level would stop the release of his creative channels into abnormal channels. If frustrated creativity was responsible for the explosive manifestations, increasing self-confidence and acceptance of his personality by people around him would cancel the Poltergeist. He would be lifted to the heights instead of sinking into the depths.

I explained this to Ted, and he drank in the explanation with relief. But I realized that I had yet to prove my sincerity. He may have had his mental reservations about me. So I went out on a limb and stated on television and on radio that I had discovered a boy-wonder who had surprising literary gifts and that recognition of his talent would seal the breach in his psyche and stop the Poltergeist for good. I suggested that he should be commissioned to write the story of the Poltergeist and give his own treatment to the subject. It would be not only a worthwhile document but also one of scientific value. His unusual somatic talent was not necessarily evidence of madness; on the contrary it may have heralded a gift that the race may possess in the future.

One thing I was certain of, that what I did was good therapy. That was more important to me than to be too scientific. I know I was taking considerable risks. I could not be sure that I was right and that the Poltergeist phenomena would stop, but I knew that my publicly expressed confidence in him would pay dividends.

It did. I became an angel of the Lord for Ted Pauls. He was walking on air, beaming with happiness and basking in the sudden change of parental and grandparental attitude. Suddenly they were proud of him and respected him. He was no longer an irresponsible boy of 17. He was a man with a great future ahead. He became the pride of his family.

No room could be left for the Poltergeist with such an uplifting of the ego. His psychic energies could no longer explode downwards. He was out to reach the heights. However, I had failed to take into consideration that Ted Pauls might not willingly consent to my departure at such a short notice, that he may well stage a tantrum through Poltergeist activity against the severance of the important emotional tie formed with me.

The result was that the Poltergeist activity did not immediately cease, rather it reached a crescendo of rage and frustration. Psychoanalytically, this was part of the working-through process. While it appeared to go against my therapeutic approach, actually it did not do so. The protest from Ted Pauls' unconscious level was not maintained too long. It gradually died.

The case is important because accidentally I tumbled on a novel cure of the Poltergeist psychosis. (So described by me in my book, *Haunted People*.) It is as simple as the egg of Columbus. Find the frustrated creative gift, lift up a crushed ego, give love and confidence and the Poltergeist will cease to be. After that you can still proceed with psychoanalysis, release the unconscious conflicts, but whether you do it or not, a creative self-expression will result in a miraculous transformation.

Haunted by the Living[1]

In *Haunted People*, my joint book with Hereward Carrington, a chronological entry appears, in the chapter titled, "The March of the Poltergeist." The entry reads:

> 1662. Related by Cotton Mather. The home of George Walton, of Portsmouth (U.S.). Stone throwing, windows broken, etc., but the stones only hit *people* gently. Not explained.

Recently, I came across a record of the Walton haunting and discovered that it has some unusual features that are worth discussing. I found it in *Myths and Legends in Our Own Lands*, by Charles M. Skinner.[2] Under the subtitle Stone Throwing Devils, I read:

> There is an odd occurrence among American legends of tales relating to assaults of people or their houses by imps of darkness. The shadowy beleaguers of Gloucester, Massachusetts, kept the garrison of that place in a state of fright until they were expelled from the neighborhood by a silver bullet and a chaplain's prayers. Witchcraft was sometimes manifested in Salem by the hurling of missiles from unseen hands. The "stone throwing devil" of Portsmouth is the subject of a tradition more than two centuries ago, but, as the stone thrower appears rather as an avenger than as a gratuitously malignant spirit, he is ill-treated in having the name of devil applied to him. In this New Hampshire port lived a widow who had a cabin and a bit of land of her own. George Walton, a neighbor, wanted her land, for its situation pleased him, and as the old woman had neither money nor influential friends he charged her with witchcraft, and, whether by legal chicanery or mere force is not recorded, he got his hands upon her property.

[1] From *Exploring the Unknown*, Aug. 1963. Reprinted by permission.
[2] J. B. Lippincott Co., Philadelphia, 1896, Vol. II, p. 305.

The charge of witchcraft was not pressed, because the man obtained what he wanted, but the poor, houseless creature laid a ban on the place and told the thief that he would never have pleasure nor profit out of it. Walton laughed at her, bade her go her way, and moved his family into the widow's house. It was Sunday night, and the family had gone to bed, when at 10 o'clock there came a fierce shock of stones against the roof and doors. All were awake in a moment. A first thought was that Indians were making an assault, but when the occupants peered cautiously into the moonlight the fields were seen to be deserted. Yet, even as they looked, a gate was lifted from its hinges.

Walton ventured out, but a volley of stones, seemingly from a hundred hands, was delivered at his head, and he ran back to shelter. Doors and windows were barred and shuttered, but it made no difference. Stones, too hot to hold a hand upon, were hurled through glass and down the chimney, objects in the rooms themselves were picked up and flung at Walton, candles were blown out, a hand without a body tapped at the window, locks and bars and keys were bent as if by hammer-blows, a cheese-press was smashed against the wall and the cheese spoiled, haystacks in the field were broken up and the hay tossed into branches of trees. For a long time Walton could not go out at night without being assailed with stones. Bell, book, candle, and witch-broth availed nothing.

Vengeance implies aggression, which is the chief characteristic of Poltergeist disturbances. The aggression, in this case, is ascribed to a curse. If the dispossessed widow was still living, the charge of witchcraft could have been well supported by the events. Obviously, this was no pubertal disturbance, as it involved a widow, though for all we know the widow—or, for that matter, George Walton—may have had a son or daughter in the pubertal age. But the Poltergeist works in daylight. The haunting of George Walton started in moonlight at 10 o'clock and it was at night, right to the end of the trouble, that he was assailed by stones. Typically, we hear of stones coming in through the window without breaking the glass, and of stones that are too hot to hold, as apports are supposed to be. The hand that tapped the window, without a body, suggests materialization (though poetic license may be involved) which is not in the range of Poltergeist manifestations, and the locks and bars and keys that were bent recall the shuddering verse from the Ingoldsby Legend:

> Fly open lock, to the dead man's knock,
> Fly bolt, and bar, and band!
> Nor move, nor swerve, joint, muscle, or nerve
> To the touch of the dead man's hand.[3]

Regrettably, we do not know whether the manifestations simply faded out in the ordinary routine of dissipated psychic energies, or whether a repentent Walton had paid compensation to the widow. The interest of the story does not lie so much in the Poltergeist characteristics but in the haunting by the living from a distance, as no indication is given that the widow or any members of her family were near the scene of the ghostly events. However, the house had belonged to the widow and may have stayed saturated by her emotional residue.

[3] *Author's note:* I have seen versions of this which contained the additional couplet:
> "Sleep all who sleep, wake all who wake,
> But be as dead for the dead man's sake."

The Talking Mongoose[1]

The story of the Talking Mongoose is one of the most enchanting mysteries of our time. It resided within the double panels of a lonely farmhouse on top of Dalby Mountain on the Isle of Man, and it had kept the British press agog for a considerable time by its fantastic activities. Through the invitation of James T. Irving, the owner of the house, I spent a week in trailing this fabulous animal in 1936. I reported on my findings in my book, *Haunted People*.[2] Before this book was published, Marie Armstrong, the first wife of the late Ben Hecht, and an excellent writer on her own, took interest in the story. Her version remained unpublished for many years, until the editor of *Exploring the Unknown* requested per-

[1] From *Exploring the Unknown*, March 1960; reprinted by permission.
[2] *Op. cit.*, pp. 175-212.

mission to print it. This is the story as told in an interview with me.

The Isle of Man is windswept and bare save for a few spots of such beauty that tourists flock to them. Manxmen are farmers—with difficulty. And the locale of Doarlish Cashen is especially bleak and bare and bony.

Doarlish Cashen means Cashen's Gap. It stands on Dalby Mountain 750 feet above sea level. It is the only house for miles around. It stands utterly alone—no trees, no shrubbery, only the endless sod hedges that divide the fields and mark boundaries to relieve the landscape. It is 25 miles from Glen Maye, near Peel. To reach it is a stiff, difficult climb up the mountain over paths worn, not by human feet, but by the rush of gully water down the mountain.

The house itself is bleak. It is made of grey slate slabs joined with concrete. Its windows are few and narrow. The exterior is on a par with the desolate landscape and the interior—darkish and paneled throughout with brown match-boarding. This paneling is one of the important features of the house for reasons peculiar to our little animal friend Gef. Mr. James T. Irving, the householder, put it in for added protection against the raw winds that at times crash about the old farmhouse. Gef claims he came and saw and approved it as an ideal habitat. "This house suits me," he has graciously stated. "It is my home." And he has identified every inch of the space between the walls and attic that runs across the house with his own strange, half-human little existence.

Now for the Irvings, a family who have had, by reasons of proximity, time, and imposition so to speak, the most contact with Gef. And it may as well be stated here and now that their good faith, honesty, and absolute truthfulness have never been challenged even by those who think Gef is a fake. Gef adopted James Irving, his wife and his youngest daughter Voirrey.

They had nothing to say about the matter. In fact, when James Irving tried to get rid of Gef, he discovered that this small, unseen but voluable mite of mystery was in reality his master.

James Irving moved into Doarlish Cashen in 1917. Gef arrived, as far as the evidence goes, in 1931. He found the place to his liking. Its hidden spaces, the peep-holes through which he avidly spies upon his human "family," the sod hedges in the fields behind which he can run for miles and follow whomsoever he likes, unseen—it all suits Gef.

Mr. Irving was a commercial traveler before the war. His neighbors like and respect him to a man. They may disagree with him about his mongoose, but not one of them but acclaims the entire Irving family as like unto Caesar's wife—"above suspicion."

Voirrey was originally suspected because one does suspect a child of possible mischief, for one thing. And Spiritualists considered her as being the center of a Poltergeist disturbance according to well-known Spiritualistic theories. But it is more and less that. Gef is no Poltergeist. Also, in the beginning, Gef was devoted to Voirrey and she was, in her typically restrained British way, fascinated by Gef. But as time wore on and Gef found more food for thought and opportunity for learning in James Irving, Voirrey grew bored with Gef and Gef quite calmly transferred his premier allegiance to the man of the household. He still followed Voirrey to and from school and assured her parents he was her protector, but he grew less and less interested in her as a person.

Let James Irving tell his story of the first manifestations of Gef:

One night in September of 1931, we heard a noise—"tap-tap-tap." It came from our attic which is boarded in. I thought we had mice. The next day I opened up the attic through the ceiling and found there a little Indian wood carving which I recognized as my own. How it got into that enclosed attic I could not tell. When I dropped it, it made the same sort of sound we had heard the night before.

That same evening we heard the same noise but this time louder. Then it changed into a running noise. I said to my wife, "That is no mouse." Next we heard animal sounds—barking, growling, hissing, spitting and blowing. This was followed by a crack that shook the place and started the pictures on the wall swinging. By this time we were sure some animal had somehow gotten into the attic, but that crack was strange. I didn't see how any animal could make it. While I was wondering about this, something more happened that made us speechless with amazement and apprehension.

This strange animal—whatever it was—was making

gurgling sounds like a baby trying to talk for the first time! It sounded like this—"DOMADOMADOMA—BLUMBLUMBLUM."

Then followed a bark with a note of inquiry or pleading in it. I was stunned. Almost mechanically, I repeated the noise of various animals. "Bow-wow . . . dog! Meow . . . cat!" And back from the somewhere came this same sound and the human word for it, in a shrill and high-pitched voice that issued from a very small throat indeed.

I was carried away with wonder. Some animal was actually taking lessons from me in human speech! It was too amazing to be true! Not actually understanding or believing in the crazy thing I was doing, I nevertheless persisted, or rather, this insatiable little creature persisted. He seemed to follow me around inside the empty space between the walls, and kept at me for "lessons." He questioned me continually and incessantly; he seemed crazy for knowledge.

"One more question, Jim" his voice would implore me, "then I let you go to sleep!"

And in a few weeks' time he spoke fluently, using all our words and phrases and plenty of others that were strange to us. I could not help thinking that Gef (as he wanted us to call him) knew how to speak all the time and only pretended to learn from me lest he should scare us out of the house. But Gef denied this. He said: "For years I understood all that people said but I couldn't speak until Jim taught me."

James Irving, once during these hectic first weeks, whispered to his wife, "What in the name of God can he be?" And the words were flung back at him instantly from behind the partition, in Gef's unmistakable tones: "What in the name of God can he be?"

Gef's hearing was phenomenal. Nothing that happened in that house could be kept from him if he wanted to know. Most naturally, the question was raised in the family, "Is Gef a ghost?" That seemed the simplest explanation, if ghosts can be said to offer simplicity in any form. He has a flair for the dramatic and resounding phrase, as shall be seen. He obliged at once when the question was raised. "I am a ghost in the form of a weasel. I shall haunt you with weird noises and clanking chains."

Whereupon he further obliged with sound effects—a rather ineffectual noise as if he were knocking a spoon against iron. He did impress Voirrey. The child (she was 11 then) turned pale with fear.

Gef had decided to accept the Irvings and make them accept him.

"If you are kind to me," Gef stated in one of his streaks of somewhat childish grandiloquence, "I will give you good luck. If you are not kind, I shall kill all your poultry. Don't think you can hide it from me—I can find it wherever you put it! I am not evil. I could be if I wanted. You don't know what damage or harm I could do if I were roused. I could kill you all if I liked but I won't."

In the light of all the knowledge that has been gained of Gef's character, this speech is pathetic: little, hidden, dreading the sight of man yet craving his companionship; afraid most appallingly and still as brave as a lion.

Disturbed by his manifestations, the Irvings declared war on Gef at first. Irving confessed to me that in the beginning he was both spiritually and physically afraid. Although he showed a brave front, he was not altogether sure how far this monstrosity of nature could go. Gef had already demonstrated that he could pitch things about with considerable accuracy. Suppose, thought Irving, that Gef should take to throwing knives?

So the farmer tried to eliminate Gef by rat poison and gun.

Gef quite easily fathomed all this and screamed his rage and imprecations. He made the house resound with bangs and thumps. Terrified, the Irvings moved Voirrey's bed from her room into theirs for protection. This enraged Gef to the point of squeaky fury. He dashed about like mad, and protested.

"I shall follow her wherever you put her!" he swore to the parents.

And when Irving sat up in his bed in the dark to listen for Gef, Gef screamed, "Lie down, you devil!"

The war ended with victory for Gef. Irving saw sense. This animal was too human. He could not be got at. Moreover, he had shown them that he knew how to handle and light a match. His weird little hand had three fingers and a thumb, and he could use them like a monkey. If he knew how to light matches, what, save his protested good nature and desire for friendship and cooperation, would keep him from burning down the house if he chose? The idea deeply worried the

Irvings until they began to understand that Gef needed them desperately. They were his only human "friends." He could learn from them. They were asked to feed him. Their house he had proclaimed as his ideal residence. He had fundamental social cravings which they satisfied. And finally, he was at this stage attached to Voirrey as one child to another.

"Let Voirrey go back to her room," he announced in May, 1932; "I won't harm any of you."

So Voirrey was moved back and the bewildering cohabitation, on terms of friendship, began in earnest in one house between three human beings and an animal that talked and could reason.

Gef was shy and endured human gaze nervously. For years there was only his voice and the noises he made and the evidence of his actions. His voice is described as shrill and high-pitched—one or two octaves higher than human speech. Then he permitted the Irvings to see his shadow by the light of a candle which they held up to his hiding place. The shadow was that of an animal . . . an animal that was fast growing more human in his thoughts and ways. Irving related:

> I placed a saucer of stewed bilberries, sugar, milk, and bread on top of the staircase. Gef ate and spoke to me while eating—he showed me the shadow of his front paw or hand holding the spoon. Then he rattled the saucer and blew out the candle.

Gef's fingers were actually seen through a slit near the ceiling. Gef told the family to watch while he showed them his hand at this point. You can guess how eagerly they obeyed. The fingers edged through the opening. They were short, yellow, and the nails were curved. Later Gef permitted them to touch his fingers. Mrs. Irving was even allowed to stroke his fur and put her own finger in his mouth. She related:

> My long finger seemed to fill Gef's mouth. His teeth were tiny and sharp. He drew a little blood from my finger. I was indignant. I said, "I don't want blood poisoning here!" He answered impatiently, "Go and put ointment on it." His mouth seemed about an inch wide.

Now and then Gef bestows his favors with his usual flair for the unexpected and grandiose. "I will permit my picture to be taken," he said several times. Then he made an appointment with Voirrey Irving to meet her at the gate. She was instructed to have her camera ready and photograph him when he leaped to the top from behind a hedge, several yards from the house, and he warned Voirrey to be quick—for he would be!

He was, too! The wonder is that Voirrey got anything at all. The pictures are distinct enough to show a small animal much like a mongoose. It bears out the legend that Gef offers his public—that he is an Indian marsh mongoose. He seized upon the identification that was tentatively offered by a visitor, who, when the Irvings were indulging in hopeful speculation, reminded them that a number of years back another farmer had let loose on Dalby Mountain a number of mongooses, to kill the rabbits. Whether from his inferiority complex, which leads him to tell tall stories, or from some other obscure reason, Gef went the whole idea several degrees better. He claimed to be 80 years old and to have tucked away in his brain a store of amazing wisdom plus a command of languages that would do credit to a university staff.

Speaking of language . . . It grieves and delights me to mention that Gef makes use of a vocabulary of curses and descriptive remarks that would do credit to a sailor. He is drolly expressive, and extremely rude when he feels like it. If called when he is unwilling to come, he yells: "Go away, clear to hell! We don't want you here!"

His gift for caricature is equally strong and he is a great traveller. One of his early haunts was a nearby quarry. Here he liked to hide, listening to the workmen, observing them, and gathering unto himself a fine fresh store of invective and expressions. The workmen were not natives—they were brought there from another part of the island. Their names and personal idiosyncrasies could only be known to someone who worked among them or a spy who overheard them among themselves. Gef would report back to the Irvings after a day with the workmen and deliver a wealth of sometimes spicy and always amusing information.

"Who is that man," he remarked to Irving, "who is walking about with eye-glasses and knock-knees, doing nothing?"

He meant the overseer, or boss.

The humanization of Gef proceeded apace.

And still James Irving communed with himself in secret doubting, which he shyly confessed:

I don't think of Gef as an animal. I sometimes wonder if he isn't a spirit in animal form. He does not feed like a mongoose. We give him biscuits, chocolate, and lean bacon. He eats vegetables, we know. He poaches them. One day I heard him gagging. He cried out to me, "Jim, Jim! I'm sick." Then we heard him vomiting. That was during the night when we were in bed—he talks most freely to us then. Sometimes he keeps us awake until all hours, too. Anyway, this one time when we looked under our bed in the morning, we found half digested carrots which he had thrown up. We had no carrots in our house.

Gef, from the beginning, adopted a free and easy manner. He had no intention of letting anybody put it over on him just because he was a small animal, thank you. The head of the house was "Jim" from the first. Mrs. Irving, who quite daunts the beholder with her air of breeding and dignity, was "Maggie." Often, with his cleverness for the perverse, Gef calls her "Chicken," which annoys her and delights Gef. He seems really fond of the household. When Voirrey was younger he followed her to school unseen, and boasted to Irving that if anyone molested the child he would fight them. This assurance was received by Irving with polite skepticism at first until several things happened that gave them occasion to think. For instance, one day shortly after his original declaration of protection of Voirrey, Gef was waiting at the bus stop to Peel, hiding as usual, having arrived there slightly ahead of Voirrey whom he was escorting. He heard a schoolboy say to another who was waiting for the bus, "The Dalby Spook is late this morning. I hope she misses the bus." By "Dalby Spook" the lad meant Voirrey—applying broadly the common phrase for the mystery at Doarlish Cashen to the girl. But Gef took exception to this. He related the scene to Irving. "I threw a stone at him," Gef declared with satisfaction. "What happened then?" asked Irving. "Oh," said Gef smugly, "nothing much." That boy wheeled about and shouted at another boy, "Stop that, Stinky!" Irving inquired and found out that one of the boys waiting for that bus had indeed been a local lad with the beautiful nickname of "Stinky."

Gef did not disappear or even grow less in manifestation after Voirrey passed the age of puberty, as he should have done had he been a Poltergeist. Voirrey, after the first fine flush of excitement was over, grew increasingly indifferent to Gef.

195

The Irvings learned to rely on Gef for such small services as keeping an eye on the poultry, the sheep, or general usefulness. Gef assured Jim of his fidelity in this respect.

"Oh, you needn't bother, Jim," he would say, "if anyone breaks into the house, I'll tell you."

He always gave warning if a strange dog or visitors are about. He was the errand boy of the family. When the Irvings awoke and wondered what the time was in the mornings, it was Gef who raced downstairs, looked at the clock and reported. If they grew anxious about the fire in the stove during the night, Gef trundled obediently down and came back with the information desired. If someone had to awaken early, Gef was the alarm clock. If a sheep got lost, Gef, not Mona the dog, found it. If the goats did not return early enough, Gef ran into the fields and barked like a dog to scare them on home. When the mice grew numerous, he meowed like a cat and frightened them away. He offered warnings and reports on the weasels, and told Irving that the polecat was "a blasted enemy." He killed the mice but never ate them. On the whole, he preferred the less sanguinary method of meowing at them and scaring them away. One night Irving heard a scraping sound. He called out, "Is that you, Gef?"

Gef denied the soft impeachment in a tone of surprise. Both the farmer and his small satellite listened then. Suddenly Gef screamed out in the dark and said.

"Jim, it is a Goddamned mouse!"

Gef's principal contribution to the somewhat meagre budget of the family was catching rabbits. The Irvings had long set traps for these vermin, for the meat and the pelts are important items in swelling the income. At first Gef was tireless at hunting them and delivering them. Then . . .

"Gef is getting lazy!" Mrs. Irving scolded. "Formerly he would leave the rabbits in front of the porch and shout 'Got a rabbit.' Now he just leaves them wherever he kills them and asks my husband to fetch them in. He used to let Voirrey go but now he won't have it."

I asked what this meant and it was explained to me that when Gef announced the first rabbits killed, and Voirrey went to fetch them, it was suspected that she played a trick and killed them herself. This insinuation Gef chose to regard as an insult. So after a kill, which as often as not occurred when Voirrey was otherwise accounted for, he would insist that she not be permitted to get the body.

One night Irving heard him in one of his rare and somewhat touching conversations with his wife.

"I like you, Maggie, and I want you to like me," said Gef. Irving, who had been pretending sleep, felt he needed a little assurance.

"What about me?" he demanded, as he turned over.

"Oh, I like you, too!" Gef hastily added.

Gef's omnipresence and spying often proved embarrassing. One night as Mrs. Irving undressed, Gef, like a mischievous Peeping Tom, loudly named each article of clothing as the poor woman took it off. Mrs. Irving was furious, and left the room and finished her undressing in the darkness of the stair landing.

It was Voirrey's custom to rise first and make a cup of tea which she took up to her father. Gef, the little devil, watched her as she carried the tray up and often squealed:

"Jim, she is drinking your tea! She is tasting the butter! She is eating the biscuits!"

Once when Voirrey had returned from Glen Maye eating chocolates from a bag, Gef's shrillness was heard from behind her:

"Hey, leave me some, you big, greedy vulture!"

One moment one disliked Gef for his naughtiness. The next his real helplessness and eerie lovableness touched one. Often he came home and confessed he is very tired and whispered with gentle confidence, "Hey, Jim! How about some grubbo?" And Jim somewhat shamefacedly obliged with grubbo.

There were times when no one seemed to be around to help Gef to his dinner, so Gef helped himself. He found out with his half-human brain and little hands, how to open the meat "safe" in which some food supplies are commonly kept. On such occasions he pleaded with Mrs. Irving, "Maggie, I hope you won't mind. I have eaten the bacon." Like any housewife who plans her meals, Maggie did mind and expressed herself vigorously. Whereupon Gef demonstrated a little-boy trait. He hid until the storm passed.

Gef was afraid of ghosts. This in spite of the fact that on occasions he airily protested that he may be a ghost himself. The story is this.

James Irving had been out in the rain and come home soaked to the skin. He went to his bedroom to change his clothes and while there heard Gef chatting away, with his wife and daughter in the kitchen below. A prank, directed at all of them, occurred to the farmer. He wrapped a sheet about himself, covering his head, and slipping off his boots, crept noiselessly downstairs. As he entered the kitchen, Gef uttered a scream full of the agony of fright and followed it with his scream of rebuff—"Clear to hell!"

Kind-hearted Irving immediately revealed himself, and Gef, when he saw who it was, sobbed like a child with relief and nerves.

Gef adored making himself more mysterious that he was. And like precocious children, he greatly admired big words. For instance, he said grandiloquently, one day:

"I am a freak. I have hands and I have feet. And if you ever saw me you would be paralyzed, petrified, mummified, turned into a pillar of salt."

And again:

"I am the fifth dimension. I am the eighth wonder of the world. I can split an atom."

And even more modestly:

"I am the Holy Ghost!"

He picked up words as smart children do—by listening. Then he came running home and overwhelmed Irving with questions.

"Jim, what is 'countenance'? What is 'loco'? What is a nun?"

Once Irving wondered how far Gef's intellectual processes carried him. He asked the talking Mongoose where he expected to go when he died. Gef replied with a shudder in his voice: "I'll never die."

"But supposing you did—where would you go?"

"To hell—to the Land of Mist," was Gef's summing up of his own theology.

One day Gef had an adventure that inflated his ego and pleased him no end.

He was sleuthing about down in Peel and heard two people talking about him (Gef) and how prominently he was figuring in the British Broadcasting Libel Case. Gef, inordinately pleased, hurried home to Irving with them. Certainly it is not given to the common garden variety of small animal to be the cause of a man's dismissal from a good job, a libel suit, and plenty of sulphuric debate in the austere British House of Commons.

It all happened this way: R. S. Lambert was the editor of "The Listener," the official publication of the BBC. Mr. Lambert and Harry Price were some of the early army of more or less official investigators, when the Mongoose mystery first became known. They both hurried to Doarlish Cashen and studied the evidence and returned to write a book about the case. The book was in happy due time published—and then the storm broke.

John Lavita was the direct superior to Lambert. He read the book and evidently concluded from it and from remarks by Lambert later that the gentleman had "fallen," hook, line and sinker, and was an ardent and true Gef-ist.

Whereupon Lavita blasted a blast of utter scorn and denounced Lambert to the officials of the BBC, and shortly thereafter Lambert was "given notice." The deposed editor promptly blamed Lavita for his dismissal because of this same championing of Gef and sued his erstwhile boss in a British court of law.

In the meantime, a member of Parliament who was interested in Gef and indignant at Lambert's summary dismissal if and for such a cause, demanded of the House of Commons that, because the BBC was a government agency, there should be an inquiry into Gef, his existence, his ways and means, and his manners and morals. Someone else popped up and threw a derisive challenge to the member and for some time thereafter the air of the House of Commons was blue with a most torrid discussion.

One enthusiastic report had it that two gentlemen were even involved in a fist fight.

But before such an official inquiry could be gotten under way, the libel suit itself came up and the world became Talking Mongoose-conscious for the first time.

Mr. Lambert charged that his alleged belief in Gef had caused Mr. Lavita to refer to him (Lambert) as "mad," thereby causing his dismissal. And the Court, after listening for days to as crazy and impossible a cause célèbre as ever delighted a British courtroom, and after showing considerable speaking interest in the pros and cons of Gef, awarded Mr. Lambert the staggering damages of $35,000!

Gef was quite proud of himself after that!

Gef listened and learned, but he also learned to read. Mr. Irving thought he did this by going to school with Voirrey and crouching on a tree outside a window from which he could hear the lessons in the schoolroom. That all ties in with Gef's thirst for human knowledge. Irving could hardly believe this talent at first. He tested Gef out by indicating words and pictures, and Gef could, if he felt in the mood, give the correct answer. But he preferred his own news by word of mouth. Irving was reading his mail once and Gef shouted indignantly: "Read it out, you fat-headed gnome!"

"Now surely, I don't look like a gnome!" Irving protested plaintively to me. But Gef liked to fix exaggerated and amusing descriptions to people. In a frivolous mood he naughtily called Mrs. Irving, "Maggie, the Zulu Woman, the witch woman, the Honolulu woman!" Seeing James with braces hanging, he called out, "You have a tail like a colt!" Of someone else he said, "He has a face like a frizzled onion."

When I decided to spend a week at the house of the Talking Mongoose, it was with two objects. My first, and most personally intriguing, was to engage in repartee with Gef. I put in dozens of hours lining up what I fondly believed to be a platoon of irresistible subjects guaranteed to overwhelm any Mongoose, talking or silent. I had been told that is was extremely unlikely that Gef would favor me with his conversation. It was quite true that for the last nine months he had been growing more surly and resentful of the visitors, investigators, and the plain garden variety of curiosity-mongers. Perhaps Gef was reflecting the Irving attitude of "Well, if we must, we must!" The facts were that visitors meant more work for the family and confusion on all sides.

But there was actually an important and fundamental reason for my visiting Dalby Mountain. A number of important investigations had been made prior to the one I intended to make and I wanted badly to check up on some of the most vital points of them. And of all the reports of wonder that had come from the Isle of Man, that of Captain James Denis seemed most important. Captain Denis is no wishful and wistful follower after spooks. He is a hard-headed, sporting, practical man—a racing motorist, and a member of the Council of the National Laboratory for Psychical Research. He made, in all, three visits to Doarlish Cashen—the first, with his tongue in his cheek, the second out of annoyed frustration over being unable in the first visit to solve the mystery, and the third because he was frankly intrigued and as yet had come to no conclusion beyond the fact that so far there *was* no conclusion.

Much important material was recorded by Captain Denis in his first and second visits. In re-reading my diary notes on my visit to the Irvings, each page reveals more amusing and confusing mystery than the page before. Gef had packed so much concentrated excitement into his small life that a choice of stories about him is simply a dip into a hat, because each one is as delightful as the last. But also, because they were comparatively recent, I wanted to check on Captain Denis' visits. I did. I came away with the conviction that Captain Denis had decidedly understated rather than overstated his experiences.

But before I go into the Denis saga, I want to touch briefly on a few other reports that I personally checked on and followed back to their sources.

There is the still continued story of a Mr. Charles Morrison, a retired cotton broker, and godfather to Voirrey Irving. Mr. Morrison has been a close friend of Mr. Irving for 30 years and has the highest opinion of the latter's integrity. He first heard of the Talking Mongoose from press reports in October, and noting with amazement that it concerned an old friend, he put on his hat and hurried to Doarlish Cashen to see what all this nonsense was about.

He did not find out, and he speedily asserted that it was not nonsense, whatever it was. Gef gave him the shivers. He heard Gef's voice from behind the paneling while Voirrey and her father were seated with him at the table, and Mrs. Irving irrefutably miles away. He wrote down many of Gef's quaint sayings and habits.

Gef quickly accepted Mr. Morrison. He piped at him, "Charlie, Charlie, chuck, chuck, chuck! Charlie, my old sport!" Mr. Morrison was shocked and indignant at the familiarity from a mongoose. Whereupon Gef thundered, as effectively as his small range of tone could manage:

"Clear to the devil if you don't believe! Vanish!"

Gef carried his resentment of the moment over to young Arthur Morrison, a son. He stormed:

"Tell Arthur not to come. He don't believe. I won't speak if he does come. I'll blow his brains out with a three-penny worth of cartridge."

Mr. Morrison finally, and with reluctance, came to the tentative conclusion that Gef was an animal. His son Arthur was just as sure that Gef was supernatural—an earthbound spirit.

There is a big manor house called Ballamooare, 20 miles away in the north of the Island, owned by a Mrs. Ward and jointly inhabited by a Mr. Berry. It was this impressive place to which Gef travelled underneath a lorry and where he had to "watch like hell" for fear of dogs, etc. Mr. Irving told me, and investigations backed up his statement, that neither he nor any member of his family or friends had ever been there. In view of the relative social status of the simple and middle-class Irvings and the wealthy, sporting landowners of the manor, this is entirely believable.

In October Gef paid two visits to his manor and returned bursting with impressive information of the detail of the grounds and the internal arrangements of the house. Gef went into considerable detail about the cars in the driveway, the servants, their livery, visitors, and the decorations. He said, for instance, that there was a fireplace in the house heavily ornamented with lions. I promptly hired a car and called on the owner. She was none too pleased to see me. Mr. Berry also was quite nervous and called me a "spooky man." He was quite eager to prove both to himself and to me that Gef was all wrong. But in the list of data that Gef had given, less than 10 percent was wrong and of that some might be due to easily understandable mistaking of one thing for another, or even for the reluctance of the owner to admit everything.

When I came to the description of the fireplace and mantel and the lion decorations, the owner was all smiles.

"That's entirely wrong!" she asserted. "I have no such fireplace in my house!" Mr. Berry chortled approvingly.

I prevailed upon them to let me see for myself.

To the consternation of all hands, I found the fireplace exactly as Gef had described it—heavily decorated with lions and lion motifs. The owner shamefacedly smiled and admitted she had never done more than glance casually at her own hearth.

Captain Denis tells us that on one occasion he was sitting with the family in the kitchen. At 9:30 P.M. the geese in front of the house went into flurry of noises of alarm—something they always do when Gef is on his way into the house. Gef, however, held his peace until Voirrey was sent to bed at 11 P.M. Half an hour later came a few raps, then a shower of them from all different points of the house, delivered with rapidity. These were followed by two violent bangs of the bedroom door upstairs and the usual Gef screech "Go and look!"

Captain Denis did look. He found Voirrey's door fastened on the outside. As I have noted, the catch cannot be operated at all from the inside. Denis was satisfied that Voirrey could not have so locked herself in her room and the Irvings had

202

been downstairs with him all the time. Q. E. D. Gef did it! With his little hands. His paws, or hands, could have turned the catch had he jumped up and grabbed it. I myself could find no other answer to this problem.

Then came the high spot of the evening.

Gef descended the dark, walled-in staircase. At the bottom was the open door of the kitchen and in the kitchen sat the Irvings and Denis. They were breathless with excitement. Gef was in a mood for drama. He signalled the stages of his progress down the stairs by thumping on the panelling. Several times he whooped out shrilly, "Hello, everybody!"

At any moment, his snout or tail might be expected to pop into view. The mounting tension was too much for Captain Denis. He forgot his resolution to let Gef make all the advances and flung himself out of his chair and towards the door, at the same time shooting a beam of light towards the staircase and up it. But as quickly as he moved, Gef was even quicker. He turned in a literal flash and was heard scurrying upstairs. His angry scream echoed through the house:

"You damn sleech!" (Sleech is Manx for "sly man.")

Then there was a loud bang. Captain Denis saw nothing. Gef was a bit smug later on about how he had avoided being seen. He deigned to explain:

"I flew upstairs like hell. I forgot that Voirrey's door was fastened and I banged into it." (That was the loud bang that we heard.)

"Then I had to jump into Jim's and Maggie's room. He nearly saw me."

Voirrey's door was still fastened. No human being could have beaten Captain Denis' mad dash for the dark stairway. It is really too bad he could not have restrained himself. Gef might have emerged to take a bow. As a result of all this, the mongoose lost confidence in Denis.

He did vouchsafe the Captain one last token of his mysterious existence, however.

"I'll throw pebbles now at the window," he said. Almost at once pebbles were heard rattling against them on the outside. Mrs. Irving was nervous and ordered Gef to stop it before he broke the windows. At the same time Gef chattered away from the attic, apparently, and stones fell on the roof.

This incident puzzled the good Captain no end. He rather regarded it as supernatural in its portent. How, he asked, could Gef talk inside the house and yet how could pebbles fall on the roof and strike the window?

They asked Gef. He obliged with a quick reply: "That is Hindu magic."

My time at Doarlish Cashen was up. I had sifted the evidence and not found it wanting; I had searched out and searched into the minds, motives and even the morals of witnesses, and satisfied myself. It must be remembered that a good part of these witnesses were "hostile witnesses." They would have been delighted beyond all measure to have either proven Gef a fake, or destroyed him if he could be caught in animal form. Everywhere the evidence held up. Nobody crawled, changed their story beyond the slight and natural changes in telling, and the Irvings emerged from the ordeal as sensible folk, not given to cheap tricks and not at all craving publicity.

That the entity which is called Gef exists, and talks, and acts according to his own ideas—this I hold proven. But as to just what Gef is . . . there you have me. I have spent more hours analyzing and studying this history than I like to admit. I went to Doarlish Cashen originally to investigate what I thought was an occult phenomenon. That was, at the time, part of my business. Although a practising psychoanalyst, I was then the chief research officer of the International Institute for Psychical Research, and Gef seemed to come under the head of things to be seen and found out about.

I cannot say that I *know* what Gef was. I can and do herewith give my reasons for thinking Gef was *not* certain things. For instance:

Gef was not a Poltergeist.

Poltergeists are always invisible. Gef never claimed to be that. Several times he has, with as much decorum as the act permits, performed a natural function under circumstances where the necessary evidence could be seen and examined. When he did this once, he said: "I want to show Captain Denis I am an animal." I sent Gef a book on Poltergeists, hoping to bribe him and prove my good faith prior to my visit. Irving read it to him and he promptly squealed "I am not like those."

He has fingers and a thumb to pick up things and he has been heard to handle matches, spoons, cups, etc. And once Gef did a most un-Poltergeist thing. Let James Irving tell it:

One day when my wife was at Liverpool, Gef was talking to me. I reproached him with his lack of confidence. He then said that he would come into the room and touch me if I buried my head in the cushions of the sofa and promise "truly, faithfully, and honestly" that I wouldn't try to see him. He also insisted I lock Voirrey in the parlor. I promised. I bolted Voirrey in as he demanded. Then I tied a towel over my eyes and buried my head under a cushion. I was curious. After a little, I felt six gentle tugs at my trousers. There was a pause after each tug. Gef was, I knew, giving a pull, then bracing himself for one of his lightning dashes if he saw I was not going to keep my word.

Gef was not a familiar.
A familiar, in the parlance of the supernatural, is, or was, a familiar spirit that took on animal form and could whisk through closed doors, walls, appear and disappear, and was always more or less given to small talk and large deeds. A familiar was highly useful to a witch. It waited upon its mistress and was most diligent fulfilling orders.

Gef's record in some ways is more characteristic of a familiar's than Poltergeist or ghost. But Gef was not a phantom but flesh and bone. If a door was closed and Gef was on one side, there has never been any evidence that he could get on the other side unless he opened it or someone opened it for him. When he raided the "safe" he opened it or someone opened it for him. A familiar is cognizant of everything and anything supernaturally. Gef acquired his knowledge through normal perceptions.

Was Gef really an animal?
Gef ate, drank, and slept. He left his teeth marks in the butter and in the bacon fat. He vomited food which did not agree with him. He talked in his sleep. He had natural functions of which evidence has been seen. He even had colds.

"Jim, I have a Goddamn cough!" he called plaintively one day after he had been coughing. "I have a hell of a cold. You will have to get me something."

He had himself photographed, and the photos show an animal. He had the abnormal hearing, eyesight and natural suspiciousness of a wild animal.

As I said in the beginning, a fantastic story presupposes a fantastic solution. And the best I can do is to say that by process of elimination I think Gef was a mongoose or a similar animal that learned to talk. There have been other remarkable creatures. The Elberfeld horses could draw cube roots and communicate thoughts by tapping with their hoofs. Dogs have been taught to read and spell. Birds can speak.

In lieu of any more positive information, and because I have not been in all honesty able to deny Gef, I am forced to, if not accept, at least not negative his own quaint definition of himself:

"I am just an extra, extra clever little mongoose."

POSTSCRIPT

Some years after my visit Doarlish Cashen was sold. The new owner claimed to have shot a weird looking animal and said it must have been Gef because the house was no longer haunted.

James T. Irving is now dead. The last news I had of the family is dated from 1953. It came from Charles A. Morrison, Voirrey's godfather who accompanied me to the Isle of Man in my search for adventure. He is the man whose diary of the doings of Gef first attracted attention to the mystery of the Isle of Man. In *The Haunting of Cashen's Gap,* by Harry Price and R. S. Lambert, he is called Mr. Northwood. He had known Irving for 50 years and was still ready to vouch for his absolute honesty. The amazement and wonder over the story of Gef did not dim in his mind with the passing of the years. To quote from his letter dated August 8, 1953:

I certainly regard it as the most amazing thing that has happened in the world.

Mrs. Irving, at the time of Morrison's letter, was still alive, living at Glen Falls, I.M. Voirrey, her daughter, was married and worked in an aeroplane parts factory near Peels. Nobody cared to find her and follow up the story of Gef, her faithful companion and self-appointed guardian during the years of her schooling. Hers is the last word on the miraculous mongoose. It has not been heard.

Had Arthur Conan Doyle heeded the advice that fairies should be seen but not spoken of, he would have saved his reputation from the reflection that the fantastic story of the Cottingley fairies cast upon it. In folklore or in romantic stories fairies cut wonderful figures and the Fairy Godmother—whether considered a Jungian archetype or not—is beloved by all of us, but try to prove that fairies really exist and millions of people will shake their heads in compassion. The author of *Sherlock Holmes* did make such a try in the Christmas number of the *Strand Magazine,* of London, in 1920 and in a subsequent book, *The Coming of the Fairies,* in 1922. He boldly stated that the series of incidents set forth in his book "either represent the most elaborate and ingenious hoax ever played upon the public or else they constitute an event in human history which may in the future appear to have been epoch making in its character."

A heroic declaration, indeed! The background was furnished by two children, 10-year-old Elsie Wright and Frances Griffith, 16, in a small village called Cottingley in the summer of 1917. The two girls consistently claimed that they were seeing fairies and gnomes in the woods. Borrowing their father's camera they took two snapshots in the woods, allegedly for the first time in their life, and got some astonishing photographic support of their stories.

The first photograph showed Frances with a group of four fairies dancing in the air before her. The next showed Elsie, seated on the grass, with a quaint gnome dancing beside her. The fairies appear to be a compound of the human and of the butterfly, while the gnome looks more like a moth. Under magnifying glass, the hands of the fairies seem to be fin-like and the beard of the gnome is an insect-like appendage.

The publication of these photographs created a sensation, promptly followed by the accusation that they were faked. However, expert examination could discover no positive evidence of tampering with the negative. When Edward L.

Gardner, of the Theosophic Society of London (who first called Conan Doyle's attention to the story), presented the girls with a good camera, some more pictures were obtained of leaping, flying fairies and a fairy bower. The latter—something between a cocoon and an open chrysalis lightly suspended amid the grass with several fairy forms about—was declared to be beyond the possibility of faking. But attempts to secure more photographs at a subsequent period resulted in failure. Elsie Wright passed the pubertal age and with that, it was said, she lost the power that may have helped the fairies to "materialize" in her presence.

Conan Doyle thought that the fairies represent a separate line of evolution and noted that children often claim to see them; which was factually established by Dr. Evans-Wentz in *Fairy Faith in Celtic Countries,* in 1912, 10 years before Conan Doyle's book, by a record of 102 first-hand cases in which living individuals claimed to have seen these legendary creatures.

I can subscribe to fairy visions both from my analytic and my parapsychological experience. One of my patients from Boise, Idaho, stated in all earnestness that she had seen fairies in her childhood. They were tiny people, running up her extended palm, dressed like human creatures. She took them for granted and used to tell them all she learned in school that day. Nothing could persuade her in later life that the experience was not real.

In England I used to have a friend who organized a Faery Investigation Society. He was the late Capt. Quentin C. A. Crauford, R.N., a man of considerable scientific acumen combined with a mystic disposition. Lady Molesworth was the President, and the program of the society was to accumulate knowledge and to classify the various orders of nature spirits. According to Crauford, research of this kind was much like making friends with the wild creatures of the woods.

A spiritualistic touch could be added here from a statement of "Feda," the child control (infantile regression?) of Mrs. Osborn Leonard, a famous trance medium:

> Yes, they do exist. They are the nature spirits and there are many classes of fairies. Clairvoyance is needed to see them. They belong to another vibration. They don't have quite the same soul as we do. But they have spirits. All forms of life are used again. Nature spirits don't die like

us. Some are created out of earth or fire or friction. They are all activity and movement.

The honorary secretary of the Faery Investigation Society was herself a trance medium by the name of Mrs. Claire Cantlon. I have interviewed her in my journalistic days for the *Sunday Despatch* and she picked for me out of the amazing letters that the society had received this priceless statement:

> I was staying at an old house in Gloucester, and the garden at the back ended in the forest of Birdlip Beeches which covers part of the Cotswold Hills. It was before the days of the "shingle," and I had washed my hair and was drying it in the sunshine in the forest, out of sight of the house. Suddenly, I felt something tugging at my hair and I turned to look.
>
> A most extraordinary sight met my eyes. He was about nine inches high, and the most dreadfully ugly, dreadfully misshapen, most wrinkled and tiniest mannikin I have ever seen.
>
> He was the color of dead aspen leaves, sort of yellow brown—with a high, squeaky voice. He was caught in the strands of my hair. He was struggling to escape, and he grumbled and complained all the time, telling me I had no right to be there, troubling honest folk, and that I might have strangled him with my hair. Finally, he freed himself and disappeared.
>
> I mentioned my experience afterwards to a professor of Bristol University. He was not surprised and told me that Birdlip Beeches was one of the few places left where there were fairies, and no one could go there because of it.

I enjoyed the story was even more delighted when Mrs. Cantlon added:

> I need not go to strangers for testimony. My house and garden in Putney are overrun by fairies and gnomes. The other day, Robin, my boy of ten, ran to me in great fright. He thought there was a pig in the room. It was a fat gnome, sitting on the chair, looking very cross and grunting. A few days after I heard the noise myself. It was a blend between the growling of a dog and grunting

209

of a pig. I thought it was the dog going at the cat. Last week I saw the gnome. Just as I was putting out the light, I noticed a queer shape trying to climb up the blind cord and fall with a fearful flop. He glared at me, for I had an impulse to laugh, and vanished.

June, my 11-year-old daughter, who is very psychic, saw some little time ago a gnome in a circle of light, sitting on the knob of bedpost and hammering at a ring. He wore a cloak and had a long, white beard.

Needless to say, I was fascinated by this extraordinary story. I thought of Andrew Lang who considered fairy belief "a complex matter from which tradition, with its memory of earth-dwellers, is not wholly absent," though he was more inclined to consider the survival of fairy belief to "old imaginings of a world not yet dispeopled of its dreams."

So let us have more of these dreams.

Mrs. Emma Hardinge Britten, musician, singer, elocutionist, later a well known inspirational speaker and medium, quotes in her *Nineteenth Century Miracles* (New York, 1884) a compatriot of mine, Mr. Kalozdy, a Hungarian author on mineralogy and teacher in the Hungarian School of Mines. He was a kind of folklorist and had collected many narratives of knockings in Hungarian and Bohemian mines. He and his pupils often heard these knockings. The miners take them for signals of the *kobolds,* a warning not to work in a certain direction. The materialized appearance of these *kobolds* was seen by Mme. Kalozdy, an authoress, in the hut of a peasant called Michael Engelbrecht. Lights the size of a cheese plate suddenly emerged; surrounding each one was the dim outline of small human figures, black and grotesque, flitting about in a wavering dance and then vanishing one by one. Such visits were announced to Engelbrecht by knockings in the mine.

A pretty story, with the suggestion of a psychic element. Going back further into the past, we come across increasingly great wonders. The great authority on fairies was Robert Kirk, M.A., whose MSS, *The Secret Commonwealth of Elves, Fauns and Fairies,* is dated 1692. In a 1933 edition we read of women who had been taken away to nurse fairy children. The prize story, however, is that of a midwife from Sweden. Her husband, Peter Rahm, a Swedish clergyman, made a legal declaration on April 12, 1671 that a little man, swarthy of face and clad in grey, begged for help for his wife in labor.

Peter Rahm recognized him as a troll, blessed his wife and begged her in God's name to go with the stranger. "She seemed to be borne along by the wind. After her task was accomplished . . . she was borne home in the same manner as she had gone." [1]

This story takes us back right into the mediaeval lore of fairies that were said to be responsible for teleporting people, kidnapping them and holding them prisoners in a fairy mound and permitting them, finally, to escape after a supernatural lapse of time.

Hartland suspects that the idea of the supernatural lapse of time in Fairy Land was invented by the Catholic Church to frighten people from unhallowed contacts. I have written a chapter, Kidnapped by Fairies, in my book, *Mind Over Space*. In it I developed a totally different idea. It is based on the symbolism of the Fairy Mound or Fairy Ring. I consider it an excellent representation of the pregnant uterus. He who is teleported by the diminutive creatures living in the underground kingdom, is reduced to their size, which is anywhere within the size of the fetus. The enduring feasting, dancing and merry-making in which he joins is also descriptive of the life of the unborn, for whom everything is provided bountifully and without effort on its part. Time does not exist in the womb. It is a postnatal concept. The unborn, at the very best, could feel the rate of its own growth as a form of biological time. Hence, the supernatural lapse of time in Fairy Land is a fetal characteristic, and the motive for fairy fantasies is a psychological one: projection of strength unto the weak (the Little People) whom, in our inadequacy, we wish to dominate, and use thereafter as substitutes for the fulfilment of unattainable dreams of power.

[1] From *The Science of Fairy Tales*, by Edwin Sidney Hartland, London, 1891, p. 39.

Gifts from Heaven[1]

For those who are weak to fight the battle of life on their own, Spiritualism offers a wonderful escape from reality. The

[1] From *Darshana International*, Moradabad, India, Aug. 1962. Reprinted by permission.

spirits of the dead are always willing to guide and succour. A direct contact with them appears to be open to those who can hear voices, see visions, or write automatically with a pencil held in a dreamy hand.

They have probably no idea that they suffer from a dissociation of the personality as the result of a shock. The conscious mind is too monopolistic to allow belief in the existence of a separate mental department. The suggestion that the dissociated person is in contact with another plane of life is almost inescapable. Free help and advice is to be had for the asking. Alas, those who regulate their life accordingly often meet with disaster. A medium whom I knew has died of starvation. The spirits, who painted strange pictures through her hand, had forbidden her to take proper nourishment.

I know of others who, on spirit advice, have broken with family and friends, and do nothing without consulting the "guides." If they want to find a new house they walk, in a trance, until they stop dead in their track. Then they take that house at whatever cost.

There is an instance in old spiritualistic records in which 70 archangels took upon themselves the task of deciding the wallpaper colours for their medium.

In this enchanted atmosphere any perception from the corner of the eye becomes a spirit light or an apparition. Fairies, gnomes and spirits peer at you through the leaves of the trees, in the blades of grass and from discoloured walls. Anything misplaced or lost has been taken by spirits. Any odd objects which you do not expect to find in your house is a gift from Heaven.

A friend of mine for whom I have a good deal of respect has a vast collection of hairpins, bits of stones and similar odds and ends. All these objects were brought by spirits. Sometimes they seemed to come out of his body with a prickly sensation. On other occasions they were just found or were seen to fall. He told me that once an umbrella flew after him in an open car.

People who are in the centre of such strange happenings are called "apport mediums." They are credited with a power by which spirit can transport objects from one part of the earth to another.

Few things could surpass in wonder the apports of Mrs. Maggs, the wife of a Portsmouth editor. According to the late Major General A. W. Drayson, who was Professor of Military

Surveying, Reconnaissance and Practical Astronomy at the Royal Military Academy of Woolwich, her household was supplied with eggs straight from Brooklyn from a spirit circle, and return gifts were sent through similar means to countries as distant as Spain, Australia, India and China.

Apparently, Mrs. Maggs did not believe in keeping all her eggs in one basket.

In more recent days, Lajos Pap, a skilled wood turner of Budapest, had gained the reputation of getting showers of living insects, frogs, snakes and butterflies in his dark séances conducted in strict conditions of control. I went to Budapest to sit with him in 1933.

The laboratory where we sat was almost bare of furniture. I searched the medium and assisted in dressing him in a one-piece robe, on which a number of phosphorescent strips were sewn. Then the sitters were searched.

During the séance, which took place in the dark, the medium was held by the wrists. Under conditions that seemed to be perfect I saw him make snatching movements with that hand which I was holding. After each snatch, he—or rather "Rabbi Isaac," the spirit said to be controlling him—handed to me, and to the others, a big beetle, about an inch in size, very much alive and vigorously protesting against the proceedings.

In less than an hour he caught 30 beetles by this spirit magic.

Then, still held by the wrist, he made scooping movements on the floor, and a handful of scurrying roachlike insects dropped from his hand into a bottle. Several twigs of yellow acacia flowers appeared in the same manner and when the light was turned on two small and crushed butterflies were discovered on the floor. They were not there before.

I was very impressed. I could not explain these extraordinary things, and I liked Lajos Pap's personality. He was tall and slender, with a beard that lend him distinction and with mild blue eyes that radiate gentleness and simplicity.

I had invited him to London for ten sittings. He accepted. But I must have struck a bad patch. The sittings were none too successful, though the second one was very dramatic.

While his arms were controlled by myself and by Mr. Shaw Desmond, a big snake appeared in his hand.

It was dead quite recently. On expert examination, it proved to be a natrix tesselata, a snake which is commonly found in Austria and Hungary but not in England. The medium was

213

in a one-piece luminous robe. Before the séance he was searched by a doctor and by Mr. Will Goldston, the famous magician. During the séance he insisted repeatedly on re-examination. Hands were passed all over his body; his hair, his ears and his mouth were searched.

Nothing was found on him. The room and the sitters were searched before the séance began. Did then the snake come from Hungary by spirit power? Was it a genuine apport? Here was a knotty problem to solve.

The notes of the sitting were dictated by myself from minute to minute through a microphone. These notes told me the precise moment of the snake's arrival and a good deal of activity prior to it. But I was totally unable to find out its real meaning until I discovered that the medium wore a belt next to his skin.

He said that he had dropped kidneys, but the belt was not a kidney belt. Moreover, an X-ray examination gave proof that he had no dropped kidneys. The only justification for wearing a belt was a loose abdominal wall. Then I mused: supposing Lajos Pap had brought the snake from Hungary alive? He could have killed it just before the sitting by holding it under water in the washbasin of his hotel. If he had now placed the snake between two folds of his rolling abdominal flesh, with its extremely soft belly outside, and had drawn the stiff linen belt tightly over it, the hiding place would have defied detection.

I went through the notes of the search and made a startling find. The medium had suffered from a bronchial cold and had managed to find a sympathetic ear in the examining doctor. He was not undressed as he should have been. He stood in shirt sleeves, trousers and shoes. His kidney belt was not in view. The examiners slipped no hand inside it. Even if they had I doubt that they would have discovered the snake.

The medium's waist line was 38½ inches, the length of the snake was 28 inches. As the head was very thin and the body tapering to the thinness of a string, a little over half an inch at the thickest, there was plenty of accommodation for it between two folds of flesh.

Now I understood the meaning of the medium's movements during the sitting. He forced the controlling hands up to his elbow and upper arm. He made rhythmic movements with his arms which allowed him to brush his fingers against his stomach. By drawing in his breath he made the belt loose and prised the snake out. Gradually, he pushed it up to the neck of the robe. Then he twisted the tail around his finger and pulled it out. A photograph taken at the moment of the snake's arrival actually showed a dark ring around the finger of the hand from which the snake hung.

Of the many sittings for apports which I had, one stands out because every apport was coated in a gritty white powder. The medium, a woman, hastened to explain that the powder was condensed ether and ectoplasm. This was something new to me.

The lady was a psychopathic subject with a conspicuous lack of the power of discrimination. In the spiritualistic church which she ran, one could hear the Direct Voice and see materialisations through her mediumship. The phenomena were so childish that they actually argued for her innocence. She made no attempt at stimulating voices or spirit forms. She charged out of the cabinet like a war horse and bellowed through the trumpet, or just walked about in the dark as a spirit without even trying to change her normal voice.

She was very scrupulous that every sitter should have an apport. These objects had to come from a safe place where her husband or her followers, who overran the house, would not have stumbled upon them.

I made a bold guess and sent the scrapes to an analyst. He confirmed my suspicion. The apports came via a pot in the kitchen. The condensed ether and ectoplasm was scouring powder.

Less obvious as to "how it was done" was the case of Hilda Lewis, the Flower Medium, who produced tremendous excitement in Spiritualist circles over 25 years ago.

She was a frail little girl around whom flowers mysteriously appeared. It was said that St. Therese of Lisieux, "the Little Flower," brought them.

Hilda Lewis was taken up by one of the leading Spiritualist societies. The head of this society, since deceased, was the daughter of a famous admiral. She was a novelist, and brought a good deal of imagination to bear on psychic phenomena. For instance, she opposed the ordinary Spiritualist view that the flowers were apports from an earthly source. She thought they were creations and had their corresponding, immaterial shape in Heaven. The medium sat in daylight. At first there was a good deal of secrecy about the sittings, which could only be attended by special invitation.

The late Professor D. Fraser-Harris was very impressed by one experience. He saw a white cloud gather in the medium's lap. When the cloud cleared there was a bunch of flowers in its place. It seemed to be a case of materialisation.

He pursuaded other scientists to come, among them Professor Julian Huxley and his wife. Huxley would not commit himself, but he had an interesting experience on going home. He gave a lift to the medium. As she sat between him and his wife, she was seized with a psychic attack and another bunch of flowers appeared in her lap.

There was a good deal of gossiping over this incident. Had it been so marvelous, Professor Huxley would have shown further interest. But he did not. No doubt, he had his reasons, which Spiritualists would not have liked to hear.

The medium was always seized with "labour pains" before the flowers arrived. She said she gave birth to them. I saw her body contract. As if seized by violent pains, she bent double.

In this position, which conveniently hid her hands from sight, a lump was seen to grow on her back or under her armpit. There was a smell of scent and a rustle of leaves. Suddenly, under the lapel of her coat, a bouquet of flowers appeared.

The value of these demonstrations depended on the search. This, of course, was always left in the hands of lady enthusiasts.

About the flowers themselves there was nothing unearthly. They were seasonal, very tightly packed, sealed with wax at the end and always thornless. The medium said she was thankful for that. The thorns would have torn her inside when the flowers materialised. Sometimes, the flowers were wet. This was dew from the "pastures of Heaven" until the finding of a small rubber tube on the floor after a séance put the damper on the theory.

Besides "Sister Therese" there was another spirit concerned in the phenomena: "Robin," a little boy. He gave us amazing clairvoyant messages which were a hundred per cent accurate. So were the messages of others. There was a good deal of speculation about this until it was discovered that all the facts in these messages had been discussed during the day or before over the telephone.

It was then found that the medium insisted that a list of her would-be sitters should be given to her in advance, and that her job in the city was not as a secretary to a firm but as a telephonist.

A private detective was engaged. He saw her buy flowers before each sitting. The search was tightened. Flowers were found hidden in her suitcase and on the window sill in the room where she retired after the search.

People would not believe the evidence. They sneered at those who doubted. She was now a professional medium and had a great following.

I proposed to make a cinema film of her demonstration. To this she agreed. The film was very successful. It revealed that the bodily contortions served the purpose of bringing the flowers forward from behind the medium's back. She visited me at my flat and in her bag, covered in grease-proof paper, was a bunch of wet flowers ready for apportation.

Then, on August 9th, 1938, at a private house where she was engaged for a demonstration, the flowers were found under her clothes as she was being searched. She broke down and, in a signed statement witnessed by all those present and her own secretary, admitted that she bought the flowers in a shop in Edgeware Road, London.

Though the full story of this exposure was published in the psychical press, many were still unconvinced. They argued that the confession had no value because it was signed under duress.

The finding of the flowers troubled them the least. They said they must have materialized immediately on the medium's arrival.

From flowers to jewels! I saw this form of apport performance at a sitting given by one of London's best trance mediums. The sitting took place at the house of Lady B. and was attended by other titled women.

I had heard remarkable things about this medium's jewel apports. A colonel in the War Office had told me that a stone of the size of a hazelnut gradually grew in his fist as the medium placed her hands over his.

Now I had an excellent opportunity of studying the phenomenon.

From her clenched left I saw the medium pass a stone into her right hand. Then she placed her right fist between the hands of a sitter, opened it, dropped the stone into the sitter's hand and withdrew her own.

At the end of the sitting the sitter swore to me that the

217

stone had grown in her palm without the medium touching it.

In one instance I have seen photographic evidence for the reality of apports. There was a miner medium in Newcastle called T. Lynn. Twelve years before Major Mowbray had a series of sittings with him and took a number of photographs that show strange, smoky spirals between the apport and the medium's body.

I examined the original plates. They were genuine. Major Mowbray was a good photographer. I asked him to give me a copy of his notes.

"Notes?" he said. "Why, I never made any notes. I engraved all the details on my memory."

Perhaps my reader will now understand why psychical research is the most heartbreaking pursuit in the world.

They may, at the same time, want to know: is there any unquestionable proof for the reality of apports?

The nearest is this unique account from the pen of the dean of Italian psychical researchers, Signor Ernesto Bozzano, the facts of which seem to bear out the spiritualistic theory of the modus operandi.

In a sitting in the house of Cavaliere Peretti, in which the medium was an intimate friend of ours, gifted with remarkable psychical mediumship, and with whom apports could be obtained at command, I begged the communicating spirit to bring me a small block of pyrites which was lying on my writing table about two kilometers (over a mile) away. The spirit replied (by the mouth of the entranced medium) that the power is almost exhausted but that all the same he would make the attempt.

Soon after the medium sustained the usual spasmodic twitchings which signified the arrival of an apport, but without hearing the fall of any object on the table, or on the floor. He informed us that although he had managed to disintegrate a portion of the object desired, and had brought it into the room, there was not enough power for him to reintegrate it. He added: "Light the light."

We did so, and found, to our great surprise, that the table, the clothes and the hair of the sitters, as well as the furniture and carpet of the room, were covered with the thinnest layer of brilliant impalpable pyrites.

When I returned home after the sitting I found the

little block of pyrites lying on my writing table; a large fragment, about one third of the whole piece, was missing, this having been scooped out of the block.

I am also tempted to quote an incident from the mediumistic history of Mme. d'Esperance, a British medium. Alexander N. Aksakof, Imperial Councillor to the Czar and Professor Boutleroff, of St. Petersburg University, were the chief witnesses of the sudden appearance in a water carafe of a golden lily, a foot and a half taller than the medium. From root to point it measured seven feet. It bore eleven large blossoms and the flowers were perfect.

The sitters were told that the plant was in the room before they came in and "was ready for being put together" at least an hour before they saw it.

Professor Boutleroff photographed the golden lily, after which "Yolande," one of Mme. d'Esperance's spirit controls, tried to take it back. She was unable to do so and exhibited signs of distress. She said that the plant was borrowed on the condition that she would return it.

Instructions were given to the sitters to keep the plant in darkness until she would come again and take it.

Seven days later in the course of another sitting, the plant vanished as mysteriously as it came. At 9:30 P.M. it stood in the midst of the company, at 9:31 it was gone. Not a vestige remained beyond a couple of flowers which had fallen off. The scent seemed for a moment to fill the room almost overpoweringly and then it was gone.

I have already made clear that no such marvellous experience fell to my share in long years of waiting and hoping. But now and again I have been puzzled by experiences suggestive of apports which had nothing to do with mediums. This is the most peculiar one:

I lost my watch winder and I was annoyed. My wife remarked: Here is an excellent chance for your spirits to bring it back. Three days later the watch winder was still missing. I gave up hoping to find it and went to the watch maker. On my return I told my wife; there goes a perfectly good half a crown, what a nuisance!

I sat down by my writing table. My wife was reading on the sofa. She became restless, laid down the book and said: "I am going to find a ladybird!"

Here I should interpolate that it was midwinter and that

from time to time, to our astonishment, we discovered lady-birds in our living room. The explanation, I think, is that our curtains and furniture covers were green and the ladybirds must have mistaken them for grass and leaves when the window was opened for dusting. But this explanation is too unromantic. Spiritualists whom we met preferred to believe that our ladybirds were brought by spirits as a symbol of good luck.

The odd thing about my wife's hunt for a ladybird was that she did not rise to look at the curtains or at the furniture covers. She rolled off the sofa and, landing on all fours, she cried excitedly: "Look!"

Her finger pointed at the leg of my writing table. There, glittering in the electric light, was my lost watch winder.

Needless to say the writing table and the carpet underneath were the first spots we had searched when the watch winder had vanished. The maid who was instructed to look for it swore that she could not have failed to find it if it had been there. I could not see myself how it could have escaped my attention.

Still, I shrugged my shoulders. The grounds were too slender to think that a spirit had taken my watch winder and had returned it. The fact that my wife looked for a ladybird and that ladybird, in her subconscious mind, was associated with apports, was surely mere coincidence.

And now to the really strange part of this story.

Having succeeded in explaining to my wife how odd coincidences may be, I picked up Mr. Arthur Hill's book, *Letters from Sir Oliver Lodge*, with which I had just come home from a library.

To my amazement, almost immediately I found a passage in which Arthur Hill described how Sir Oliver Lodge, during a visit to his house at Bradford, had lost his watch winder. After he was gone, he (Mr. Hill) had found it and had sent it back to him.

Can any mathematician give me an idea what is the calculus of probabilities regarding such a remarkable series of events occurring by chance?

PART IV.

OF THINGS THAT GO BUMP
IN THE NIGHT

Of ghoulies and ghosties,
Of longleggetie beasties,
Of things that go bump in the night,
Good Lord deliver us.

(SCOTTISH PRAYER)

The Most Haunted House in England

The title is borrowed from a book by Harry Price, England's most intrepid investigator of psychic phenomena for several decades in the recent past; it had been applied by him to Borley Rectory in Essex, built in 1863 by the Rev. Henry D. E. Bull, allegedly on the ruins of a 13th Century monastery.

The book was published in 1940 and was followed by another, *The End of Borley Rectory*, in 1946, both of them best sellers. Harry Price died in 1948. Seven years after his death, three other investigators, notably Eric J. Dingwall, Kathleen M. Goldney (both of them his friends and fellow researchers), and Trevor M. Hall, of the British Society for Psychical Research, published another book, *The Haunting of Borley: A Critical Survey of the Evidence*. This book attempted to expose the Borley mystery and accused Harry Price of having been the ghost who threw stones and who deliberately distorted the account of the Borley affair.

No greater scandal has ever erupted in psychical research than over this preposterous exposure. The haunting of Borley Rectory stretches way back in time, beyond the initial appearance of Harry Price on the scene in 1929. Only in 1937 did Harry Price begin a *systematic* investigation. He rented the Rectory for a year and advertised in the *New York Times* for observers. In 14 months 2,000 paranormal phenomena were reported: voices, footsteps, the ringing of bells, the locking and unlocking of doors, messages on the walls, wine turning into ink, vanishing and sailing of objects through the air, crashes, breaking of window panes, starting of fires, knocks, bumps and thumps, lights in the window, whispering and the sense of invisible presences. The most ghostly part of the haunting was the apparition of a nun on the grounds— asking for Mass and prayers through the written messages— and the vision of a ghost coach and of a headless coachman, bearing on the legend that a monk from Borley Monastery had eloped by coach with a novice nun; on being caught, the man was beheaded and the novice bricked up alive in the Convent.

According to Harry Price, the influences felt in the Rectory were not evil. A child of three who got a black eye, thought otherwise. He said: "A nasty thing by the curtain in my room gave it to me." Nor did the dogs take kindly to the headless ghost. Capt. Gregson, the last owner of Borley before the ghost burnt down the Rectory—as it promised through the planchette—went at night into the courtyard with a black cocker spaniel and this is what happened:

"I distinctly heard footsteps at the far end of the courtyard, as though someone was treading over the wooden trap door leading down to the cellars. I paused, and my dog stopped dead, and went positively mad. He shrieked and tore away still shrieking, and we have not seen nor heard of him since."

Capt. Gregson purchased another dog, also a cocker and it behaved exactly as his predecessor. It began whining and shrieking—and bolted, and has not been seen since.

I will refrain from repeating my fiercely indignant rebuttal of the Harry Price exposure in *Tomorrow* magazine (Winter 1956). All I wish to say that I was not defending Harry Price on the basis of personal feelings. I have never been his friend, nor his enemy. I did not like him, because he was a very difficult man to like. He was intensely selfish, jealous and intent on his own glory at all cost, but these weaknesses of his character do not detract from his reputation as an honest investigator and ruthless exposer of frauds. This was the shining feature of his life. It took considerable courage on the part of the "Terror of Spiritualism" to state in his second Borley book:

> If, six years ago, I came to the conclusion that I could find no better explanation of some of the Borley phenomena than the popular "survival" theory, I unhesitatingly declare that I am still of the same opinion. A further six years of study of the phenomena and of all the new evidence that has accrued during this period, still more strengthens my belief that a more reasonable solution is not yet available. I would even go so far as to state that the Borley case presents a better argument for "survival" than that of any similar case with which I am familiar.

With this statement, Harry Price committed an unpardonable sin: he declared himself for Spiritualism. For this, he had to be destroyed. His enemies found a "more reasonable solution" ready-made: Harry Price was the Borley Ghost.

The only point on which I wish to take issue with Harry Price in his claim that Borley Rectory was the most haunted house in England. Nothing but the "most" could satisfy Harry Price's narcissism. For the sake of truth I want to state that the most haunted house in England (of which Harry Price must have been well aware, from extant literature) was Ballechin House in Perthshire. It was the property of a Scottish Baronial family for centuries. Through the good offices of Lord Bute it was rented and put at the disposal of the Society for Psychical Research. Miss Goodrich-Freer, a well-known and capable investigator, was installed and stayed in the house for 92 days, keeping a daily diary of the haunting— also of an ecclesiastical nature—but surpassing in weirdness the doings at Borley Rectory.

The last owner in the male line of Ballechin House was Major S., an eccentric individual. He had served in the East India Company, was very fond of dogs of which he kept fourteen. He believed that spirits could return to possess the body of both men and animals. He frequently intimated his intention of entering, after his death, the body of his favorite black spaniel. His faith was so firm that his family, when he had died, had all his dogs shot, including the black spaniel, to render, apparently, his return through the body of the dog impossible.

A pack of phantom dogs had haunted the house thereafter. Several witnesses saw the apparition of a black spaniel and there was evidence of other, invisible dogs gambolling in the haunted house.

Here is an entry from Miss Goodrich-Freer's diary:

About 10 A.M. I was writing in the library, face to light, back to fire. Mrs. Walker was in the room, and addressed me once or twice; but I was aware of not being responsive, as I was much occupied. I wrote on, and presently felt a distinct but gentle push against my chair. I thought it was the dog and looked down, but he was not there. I went on writing, and in a few minutes felt a push, firm and decided, against myself which moved me on my chair. I thought it was Mrs. Walker who, having spoken and obtained no answer, was reminding me of her presence. I looked backward with an exclamation—the

224

room was empty. She came in directly and called my attention to the dog, who was gazing intently from the hearthrug at the place where I had expected before to see him.

Four days later:

> Miss Moore and I again this morning heard noises in No. 8, more especially those of the pattering footsteps, just after daylight, and a violent jump and scramble, which we thought was our dog until we found that he was sleeping peacefully as usual on his rug at our feet.

Two weeks later, in the Major's room, Miss Freer saw a black dog which she supposed for a moment to be Spooks, her own Pomeranian, run across the room towards her left. She was adjusting a camera and stopped, fearing that she would shake the table on which the camera stood. Immediately she saw a second dog, really Spooks this time, run towards it from her right with her ears pricked. Another lady in the room also observed and said: "What is Spooks after?" A piece of furniture prevented Miss Freer from seeing the meeting, and Spooks came back directly, wagging her tail. The other dog was larger than Spooks, though it also had long black hair and it might have been a spaniel. Miss Freer, at this time, did not know that the Major's favorite dog was a black spaniel.

Three weeks later:

> Mrs. F. W. slept with me; I was wakened early morning by my dog crying, and saw two black paws resting on the table beside the bed. It gave me a sickening sensation. I longed to wake Mrs. W. to see if she would see them, but I remembered her bad night yesterday, and left her in peace.

Human phantoms were seen on numerous occasions. Twice they were found to be apparitions of living people (at that hour, probably asleep). One of them was a clergyman who had some harrowing experiences in the house and whose thoughts were naturally drawn to it. It was this clergyman, called in the records Father H., who called Lord Bute's attention to Ballechin house. The clergyman thought that Major S. was trying to attract attention in order that prayers might be offered for the repose of his soul. He heard raps, explosive sounds and something like a big dog throwing itself violently against the bottom of his door outside. He threw holy water about and repeated the prayer *Visita quaesumus,* which invokes divine protection for a house and its inhabitants against the snares of the enemy. Between waking and sleeping, there appeared before his eyes, somewhere on the wall, a crucifix, about 18 inches long and of brown wood.

Father H. was cross-examined by Sir William Huggins, the famous astronomer. As a result, Sir William felt absolutely certain that the experiences were not the outcome of morbid hallucination.

The same crucifix was seen later by another clergyman, the Rev. Q. By the open fire, he experienced a curiously cold sensation and shivered to an extent which was quite phenomenal. The fire did not in the least remove the cold shudders which ran from head to foot. In bed, his shuddering sensations were worse than ever. Writing to Lord Bute he said:

> Suddenly I looked up and above the bed apparently on the wall, I got just a glimpse (like a flash) of a brown wooden crucifix; the wall was quite bare, not a picture, nothing to make it explainable by imperfect light refraction. From that time, the sensation of cold and shuddering went away; I don't say immediately, but I was quite conscious of being reassured.

Miss Goodrich-Freer comments:

> On March 4th, Mr. Powles was seized by audible and visible shivers. We did not speak until he uttered some forcible ejaculation of complaint, when, looking towards him, I saw a hand holding a brown [probably wooden] crucifix, as by a person standing at the foot of the bed. He immediately said, "Now I am better," or words to that effect.

The sound of continuous reading, suggesting that of a priest saying his office, was frequently heard. There was a legend that at the time of the Reformation a priest was murdered in the house. Other voices were heard in low talk and fierce argument. No words could be understood, but the timbre of the voices was distinct.

Some time in the past a small house on the grounds was used as a retreat during the summer for nuns. This may offer a clue to the apparition of a nun which was often seen. This is how Miss Goodrich-Freer described it:

Against the snow I saw a slight black figure, a woman moving slowly up the glen. She stopped and turned and looked at me. She was dressed as a nun. Her face looked pale. I saw her hands in the folds of her habit. Then she moved on, as it seemed, on a slope too stiff for walking. When she came under the tree she disappeared, perhaps because there was no snow to show her outline. Beyond the tree she reappeared for a moment, when there was again a white background, close by the burn. Then I saw no more.

The nun was not equally visible to all. Others sometime only heard her voice. Our member of the party sketched her from profile and front. She was given the name Ishbel, to distinguish her from Margot, the phantom of a lay woman. The two were seen arguing in low voices. Through the turning table the experimenters were told that if Mr. Powles were to visit the copse with Miss Freer after 6:30 P.M., he would be touched by the nun on the shoulder. Miss Goodrich-Freer adds:

I was barely able in the dusk to distinguish the figure from my post on the west bank, but the phantasm appeared very near him, as I could distinguish the white pocket handkerchief in his breast pocket. I saw her hand approach this, but could not positively say that it touched him.

They sent for Miss Langton without telling her what happened. Mr. Powles wrote:

I stood again under the sapling. This time I began to shudder almost immediately . . . . Miss Langton said that 30 seconds after I had taken up my position, the figure appeared behind me a little to my left, and seemed to raise its arm. Miss Freer said it was waiting for me, and touched me as before. I felt no touch throughout, only shiverings that seemed to coincide with the appearances.

The noises in the rooms were more upsetting than the phantoms. They were raps, knocks, blows, thuds, crashes, bangs, clanging and detonating sounds, groans, screams and footsteps, both human and animal. The noises occurred in rooms that were locked and were heard both in daytime in the presence of several people and at night. The most effective attempt to imitate the noises was produced by rolling a ball along the stone floor of the hall, and allowing it to strike against the doors or pillars, when the peculiar echoing was fairly well reproduced by the hollow domed roof and surrounding galleries. Here is an uncanny account of the footsteps:

> After dinner, we three sat around the fire and played games: suddenly one of us called out: "Listen to those footsteps," and then we distinctly heard a heavy man walking round the room, coming apparently from the direction of the safe in the wall, adjoining the billiard room, and then walking towards the door, passing between us and the fire place in front of which we were sitting. It was very curious, for the steps came so very close, and yet we saw nothing.

The ghost had the unpleasant habit of pulling people's bedclothes off and lifting up the bed. But it was shy of men of real eminence. Sir Oliver Lodge, after a visit to the house, reported to Lord Bute:

> We have not heard the loud bang as yet. Knocks on the wall, a snoring noise and a droning and wailing are all we have heard.

The noises were so momentary and infrequent that they gave no real scope for a continued examination by a physicist.

Lord Bute twice read aloud the whole of the Office for the Dead in five sections in different places of the house. He was conscious of a sudden impediment of speech and hostile and evil influences. Miss Goodrich-Freer wrote:

> The general tone of things is disquieting and new in our experience. Hitherto, in our first occupation, the phenomena affected one, melancholy, depressing and perplexing but now all, quite independently, say the same thing, that the influence is evil and horrible—even on poor little

Spooks, who was never terrified before as she has been since our return here. The worn faces at breakfast were really a dismal sight.

An extension of the tenancy was applied for in the hope that observations of the sounds could be made with seismic instruments. The proprietor, however, was resentful and feared the further decline of the reputation of the house. Permission was refused and the investigation had to be given up.

The family grew still more resentful when the story of the house was told in a book by Miss Goodrich-Freer, *The Alleged Haunting of B. House*. Some years ago I wrote to the family for information whether the house is peaceful or not, but I received a very curt, non-informative answer.

The importance of the story of this haunted house lies in the fact that the disturbances did not show an automatic, dream-like character. The impression they give is a spiritualistic one. The excessive shivering indicates a drain on the body heat of the living participants of the drama. While Major S. as a surviving personality failed to emerge in the manifestations, the dogs certainly did, and the nun and the clergyman—dead and living—added a remoter and very eery element to the total picture which the passing of time has failed to divest of its upsetting character.

The Ghosts of Raynham Hall

In my younger years it was one of my ambitions that I should be frightened by a ghost. I admit that in some of my later adventures I came near to doubting the wisdom of this desire.

The prospect of meeting the Red Cavalier in the Monmouth Room of historic Raynham Hall was not so inviting as I thought it might be.

I was resting in a huge bed in pitch darkness. A haunted staircase, on which the Brown Lady [another ghost] walks, was right in front of my door. The room was very cold, the silence heavy and oppressive. The press button of my flashlight circuit was my only comfort. I could always smash a ghost to smithereens by blinding light.

In my mind I reviewed the curious history that led me to this haunted room.

Two professional photographers, Mr. Indre Shira and Capt. Provand, of 49 Dover Street, London, "caught" a ghost on the main staircase of Raynham Hall some time earlier. The photograph clearly showed a luminous figure descending the stairs. Mr. Indre Shira saw it coming.

"Quick! Quick!" he shouted to Capt. Provand who was under the black cloth.

Capt. Provand uncapped the camera, the flash went off and the ghost vanished.

I had examined the film. It was as convincing as it could be. Mr. Indre Shira and Capt. Provand had stood my cross-examination extremely well. So I came to Raynham Hall to see the staircase for myself, hoping that good fortune may help me to understand the mystery.

Ghosts are rarely seen in daytime. The chances that a ghost, walking perhaps once in a generation, would descend the stairs just when two professional photographers are ready to take a flashlight picture of the interior of the house, are infinitesimal. But the ways of ghosts are notoriously erratic. The calculus of probabilities cannot be used against them.

Lady Townshend was very sympathetic to my inquiries. She permitted me to photograph the main staircase from the same position where the professional photographers had stood. The result strengthened the presumption that the ghost photograph was genuine. I found that from the position where it was taken an average man, standing on the thirteenth step from the top, shows the same height on the picture as the ghost shows. This effect, by double exposure would be rather difficult to produce. The next question I had to decide was the identity of the ghost.

Was it the Brown Lady that walked into the flashlight trap?

Lady Townshend believes in the Brown Lady. Quite recently two of her guests saw her walking. Family legends say that she was Dorothy Walpole, sister of Sir Robert Walpole. Allegedly she was starved to death at Raynham Hall.

This is, however, not a likely story. As Lady Townshend said:

In the seventeenth century, enforced starvation in surroundings like those of Raynham Hall would have been impossible, unless Lady Townshend had staged a hunger strike of such magnitude that she died from it.

I have accepted the story of starvation as symbolical of Dorothy Walpole's tragedy of starved affections, which always represents such a terrible death-in-life. I would prefer to believe that the ghost as photographed is something else: a symbol of protection.

There is a chapel below the staircase where I pray. The shrine of Our Lady of Walsingham is a few miles away. Holy water from this shrine cured my son when the doctors had given him up. Since then I believe that the Madonna protects my house.

As the Brown Lady failed to oblige me with her appearance on the stairs, Lady Townshend thought that I should try my luck with the Red Cavalier. There were other ghosts, of course, to choose; two ghost children in the stone parlour, a ghostly spaniel in another room and the spectral gamblers of the royal bedroom. It is quite usual, I was told, to find the heavy chairs of this room (which are set overnight against the wall) arranged the next morning round the large card table. The ghosts of the gamblers who had lost a fortune at Raynham in the past are still restlessly trying to recoup their losses!

Lady Townshend thought that the Monmouth Room would give me the best chance. The room is so named because the ill-fated Duke of Monmouth slept in it when he stayed at the Great House with his royal father. He was last seen by a relation of the Townshends, a spinster of uncertain age.

This lady suddenly awoke to see the Red Cavalier standing at the foot of her bed, smiling. She was not in the least frightened, only happily interested "and when, as befitted a courtier, the Duke paid her the homage due to a Princess of the Blood, and bowed himself out into the shadows of the opposite wall, he became the happiest memory of a drab lifetime."

And so I found myself in this odd room in a monster bed, shut off from the moon and the stars by curtains so heavy that the darkness felt thick as slabs of stone. The night wore on with painful slowness. My nerves were tense. The slightest noise traveled down them with the speed and clatter of an express train. They were just noises of the night. I thought my vigil would be in vain when:

Thud . . . thud . . . thud . . .

Muffled sounds came through the ceiling.

A man, I thought, stepping heavily, with boots on.

No, I corrected myself, with one boot.

A club-footed man would make that type of noise.

But it can't be.

Clank . . . clank . . . clank . . . came an answer.

Pots and pans, I told myself.

Then things became livelier.

There was a squeaking, rumbling and screaming as if furniture was being moved on castors.

This was in accordance with the best traditions of ghostland. As a child I was immensely thrilled by a story of a bed moving by its own accord with a terrified boy in it.

The rolls were short but definite. Somebody *was* moving furniture above my head.

I remembered that Lady Townshend's mother was ill. Her bedroom, I thought, might be above me. The night nurse could make the noise by serving food on a serving table.

Should I get up and investigate? The bed was warm and comfortable. I put out my hand as a feeler.

Against my better conscience I argued: it is no use, I cannot find out anything. I shall only make a fool of myself if I stumble into a strange bedroom.

The weird noises from above went on unceasingly. Eventually I fell asleep. But my sleep was very disturbed. The thuds, clanks and rolls from above broke through the protective barrier of unconsciousness. The heavier ones acted like bombshells and brought me back to waking consciousness with a pounding heart.

Towards 5 A.M. they became softer and more remote. I was beginning to wonder, with a sleep-crazed mind, whether I only dreamed them. The doubt was soon settled. Softly but unmistakably, the same sounds came once again.

I decided that I had enough. Somebody *was* making himself a darned nuisance. Something must be done to stop him. I rubbed out of my eyes the little sleep that was left in them and, with a heroic effort, got out of bed. In dressing gown and slippers, with an electric torch held in front of me like a gun, I went on the prowl.

I stopped at the haunted staircase on which the Brown Lady walks. I thought I would first descend. I flashed my torch. From the polished oak the light was reflected harshly. Things of the night seemed to resent my intrusion. There was a cold hostility in the air and I felt an inward chill as I commenced my descent.

I stepped with infinite caution. In haunted houses I never make an unnecessary noise. It is as if, unconsciously, I tried to avoid being discovered by something that may lurk around the corner. The first creak would give me away and everything would become eyes and ears.

My torch cut into the darkness like a dagger. The walls of the ancient hall stared at me in contempt. The antique, priceless furniture seemed to scowl.

I was overcome by a feeling of guilt. I retraced my steps and climbed up to the floor above my bedroom.

The staircase was towards the back. It creaked abominably. But I went on and found myself on a landing on which an electric light burned. Doors opened in all directions. The light was a clear indication that the rooms were inhabited. The linoleum of the floor screamed at me at every step I took. I felt unnerved. A door might open any time; someone would demand to know my business. Supposing this was the maids' quarters!

I knew that I was making excuses to beat a hasty retreat. I did beat it.

With a feeling of distinct relief, I found myself back in my room. The Red Cavalier promised to be a cheerful companion in comparison to the nameless ones. Back to bed. It felt divine. I smiled happily and turned off the light.

No sooner did I do so when three soft thuds came from the opposite end of the room. Then the concert began in full strength. Thuds, thumps, creaks, clangs and screeches. Now they seemed to have a sneering, jeering quality. They laughed at me and hit the ceiling with bangs that gave me a nervous shock. I determined to ignore them, to blot them out of my conscious mind.

I must have been weary because I succeeded extremely well. I fell into a heavy sleep and woke after 8 A.M.

Having got up, I hastened to interview my wife and daughter who were sleeping in an adjoining room: have they heard anything? They did. There was a clatter above, but they did not take much notice.

Then I interviewed Mr. Arthur Kingston, my fellow adventurer who slept a little further away. He did not know what I was talking about. He woke up once in the night and took a flashlight photograph of himself but saw and heard nothing.

233

I called the butler.

"Will you tell me who was sleeping above me?"

"No one," he said. "That room is empty."

I explained that I heard a lot of movement all night above my head. The room I was referring to must be halfway above my bed and the bathroom.

"Oh," said the butler. "That is the old lady. She is always moving in her room at night."

The old lady was another guest. She was 90 years old and came from Scotland. At 1 o'clock we left her still awake in the big room wrestling with her income tax return.

Perhaps she had a bout with the Collector of Spectral Revenues! I laughed until my sides ached.

I wanted to interview her, but I had to get back to town in a hurry. So I wrote to Lady Townshend to find out, if possible, why should a nonagenarian lady spend her nights pushing furniture about, bang and thump and clank pots and pans.

Up to this day I do not know whether Lady Townshend had taken my letter as a complaint. I heard from her, but she ignored my question.

Sometime later, however, in Lady Townshend's own book, I came across a significant paragraph about the same old lady, her name being mentioned:

> She once told me that she was sure some of the servants held secret "revels" in the vicinity of her room. "I think you should speak to them," she said. "Such things ought not to go on; I hear noises coming from the room next to mine quite late at night!"

Lady Townshend assures her readers that no servant could have been responsible for the disturbance of which the old lady complained. It must have been one of the many ghosts of Raynham Hall.

Strange that tables should be so reversed; that the once-maligned servants should now think that the old lady makes noises in her room at night!

People, of course, have strange passions. But somehow I am not fully satisfied that my wretched night was entirely due to the nocturnal habits of an old woman.

The Man Who Bit a Ghost

Everybody knows this about journalism, that if a dog bites a man it is not news, but if a man bites a dog it is news. In fact, bad news—for the dog.

What of the man who bites a ghost?

It is a rather unorthodox behaviour. In Ghostland it may be considered as hitting below the belt. But then, if ghosts wish to avoid being bitten, they should not go in for all-in wrestling. It is bad taste. And in this case, it tasted bad.

So bad that the memory of that bite has haunted Dr. Julius Reiter, the hero of this extraordinary adventure, for many months. He was attacked by a ghost who tried to strangle him. In the fight he caught, with his teeth, the ghost's finger and bit it.

By their taste you shall know them. The finger felt ice-cold and tasted like rubber. There was no blood in it. It was then, and only then, that the ghost-biter, to his horror, realized that his assailant was a dead man.

This is how the first act of the story was played.

A certain Mrs. Harrison had a small basement flat in Manchester Street, behind Selfridges. She was ill with influenza. A young girl, bringing in her breakfast, dropped the tray with a cry of fear. She slammed the door behind her, leaned against it and gasped:

"A man followed me. He was just a shadow. I could see through him."

Mrs. Harrison laughed. The silly girl was seeing things! She herself had never been disturbed in the flat. In fact, she found it extremely peaceful. Though, as she mused, she remembered that a lady visitor, some time before, claimed to see something ghostly in her room: a man with an extreme pallor and marks of suffering in his face, standing behind her and staring into nothingness.

In the evening a friend who came to cook her dinner called to her from the kitchen:

"I did not know you had a visitor. Who is the man who got into your room just now?"

No one came into the room. But the friend insisted that

somebody must have and Mrs. Harrison could not help thinking of the morning adventure.

It would have been odd if after such beginnings the ghost vanished from thee scene. Remember, Mrs. Harrison was ill with 'flu. She may have had fever. Her imagination was stirred. Something was bound to happen to her. The unusual thing is that so little happened.

She tells me that at 2 o'clock that night, as she sat up in bed, she felt that she was not alone. There was the sense of a presence in the room. An ice-cold shiver ran down her spine and she grew very frightened. Then comfort and assurance came to her from an unknown source. She felt three gentle pats on her shoulder as if by an invisible protective hand, and all fear left her. The sense of presence was gone. The room became peaceful again.

Act Two. Enter the ghost-biter.

Mrs. Harrison moved to a bigger apartment. Because her lease was still holding her, she rented the basement apartment in Manchester Street to Dr. Julius Reiter, a German newspaper man. She did not tell him that the flat had a ghost. She hardly believed in it herself. He rang up Mrs. Harrison and asked her if she knew that the apartment was haunted. He had some extraordinary experiences since he moved in. This is how they began. (I am now quoting from a statement which, after I cross-examined him, Dr. Reiter signed for me.):

I was in bed in a state of mind which is difficult to describe. I felt that I was walking along a dark road. Suddenly there was a girl close behind me. For some reason I did not want to turn around and look at her. In the same moment I felt thrown on my bed and shaken vigorously. The shaking lasted for 15-20 seconds and left me numb, unable to move.

Another evening as I went to bed, a luminous figure appeared in the dark. I saw only the upper part of his body. With uplifted hands the apparition bent down twice. I don't know why. He was a swarthy foreigner, with dark hair, cadaverous face and ghostly white hands. I felt paralyzed and could not move a limb. In a few seconds the figure was gone and I fell into a deep sleep.

Next morning my right foot hurt badly. It felt as if somebody had twisted it.

A fortnight later something very terrifying happened. I was in bed, awake. Suddenly, things seemed to change. I was sitting in a chair and somebody was offering me a drink. There was a glass in my hand and I held it out. At that moment somebody upset the bottle and started to fight. He came at me with a rush and tried to strangle me. I defended myself. He caught my finger and bit it savagely. Somehow I got it away. As he was grasping for my throat I caught the small finger of his left hand in my mouth, and with a snap, I closed my jaws on it.

A sickening feeling came over me. The finger was ice-cold. It tasted like rubber. It had no blood circulation. It was the finger of a dead man. The clock struck twelve, and the horror lifted. I was still in bed, quite myself and unable to move.

I realized now that I was not attacked in the body but that something psychical happened to me. That something, however, was so real that I felt sick and faint from fright.

Dr. Reiter was anxious to convince me that he was not telling a story and that he was not dreaming. He could only describe the mental state in which he was as a state of divided consciousness.

It is for you to say whether my attacker was a ghost or not. I have not enough experience of these things. I just told you, very frankly, what happened. The rest I must leave to you.

I was favorably impressed with Dr. Reiter. He stood my questions well. He admitted that he was what we may call psychic. Things occasionally happen to him at which others, less highly strung, laugh.

I told him that the obvious thing to do is to find out the history of the house. Has any strangling drama been enacted in it? If that were the case, he must have contacted the memory of that scene and re-enacted the part of the victim. Violent human passions seem to impregnate the surroundings and a sensitive nervous system periodically may pick up something of the past.

Dr. Reiter then told me that a well-known medium, Miss Lily Thomas, came to see the place and gave him such a story.

She said that the ghost was a Spaniard, Carlos Ferdinando, and that 20 years ago he had committed suicide in that very room. The house was a nursing home at the time and Carlos Ferdinando was a patient. He was in love with a girl and strangled her. Then, afraid of the consequences, he took his own life. Now his ghost is bound to the scene of the crime. It is brooding over it and relives it as in a nightmare again and again. He thinks that the room is still his and that Dr. Reiter has no business to be in it. He tried to throw him out.

Inquiries disclosed that the house was indeed a nursing home in years gone by. The matron had moved out only a few years before, but she left no forwarding address. The rest of the story still awaits verification.

To me the room seemed just like an ordinary room. I would have given much to feel the unaccountable cold drafts of air of which Dr. Reiter complains. He said that they come in the middle of the room in a vortex. I felt very comfortable and the flashlight photograph which I had taken showed nothing more than a huge bed with Dr. Reiter sitting cheerfully at the end.

I have no doubt, however, in my mind that Dr. Reiter had a borderland experience.

Fights between man and ghosts are rare, but strangulation dreams in queer houses are fairly frequent. Such dreams may have a perfectly normal explanation. But if, unknown to the dreamer, death by strangulation had taken place in the house, the coincidence must be considered odd.

In one case which has recently come to my notice from Colchester, a young and very intelligent lady not only dreamed that she was being strangled but awoke choking and gasping for breath. In the morning her throat felt sore, though there were no marks on it. Two other guests, independently, had the same disagreeable experience. The room is now reserved for guests and the lady of the house, the wife of a surgeon in Colchester, never dares to ask them how they slept for fear they would tell the same story.

As I never had the good fortune of such an experience and would not have minded a bit to be strangled, I asked permission to sleep in the haunted bed. It was the best bed I ever slept in. If a ghost came, he moved ever so gently. I woke once, around 2 o'clock, very suddenly. There was no noise in the room and I was rather surprised to find myself awake. I closed my eyes and fired a flash by pressing a button near my bed.

The plate shows me snug and comfortable. Of the strangler there is not a trace.

The Haunter Is a Cat

No haunted house mystery is perfect without a dog. It is supposed to cower, hide in obvious terror, with its hair standing up when a ghostly presence is in the room. It makes an excellent witness that something frightening is abroad because dogs do not hallucinate nor are they affected by suggestions. Cats should make, for the same reason, similar witnesses. It is probably due to population statistics that cats are mentioned less frequently in stories of haunting.

In my investigation of haunted houses in England I came across both cats and dogs. The grin on my face was as wide as that of the Cheshire Cat when, in haunted Dean Manor House near Meopham in Kent, on November 30, 1936, I solved the mystery of a self-opening door by photographing a clever little cat on the sideboard, reaching out a paw and depressing the archaic kitchen latch. It was the delicious smells from the kitchen that impelled a hungry cat to this efficient method of securing breakfast. By the time the door was open, pussy was under the kitchen table, and it just did not occur to the kitchen folk that the cat could be responsible.

The case was important because there was a ghost broadcast arranged from this house by the late Harry Price, and the *Times* of London had severely criticised the B.B.C. for the reckless adventure. Supposing a ghost had actually availed itself of the opportunity to address the nation? What a calamity would have been caused by it! At any rate, luckily enough, nothing dramatic happened during the broadcast hours. The temperature in the cellar dropped to a significant degree but that was all. The ghost lay low.[1]

The case of the Chelsea Poltergeist that I succeeded in laying by psychoanalyzing the ghost-ridden owner of the

[1] From *The Journal of the American Society for Psychical Research*, 1937, pp. 348-349.

house, was somewhat more dramatic. I quote from the signed statement of Miss Jenkins, a journalist:[2]

> I slept well until 5:30 A.M., and was awakened by what I thought to be a scratching upon the front door. It sounded as though a tiger had got loose and was trying to get in. I had a dog and a cat in my room. The dog cowered in a chair shivering, and the cat ran around in panic, hurling itself against the window several times in an effort to get out, then running to the door and clawing at it. I did not have enough nerve to open the door, but I opened the window and the cat flew out into the street, only to return about mid-day. I was severely shaken and decided not to spend another night in the house. I explained matters to a man friend who readily consented to take my place and locked himself in with the animals. At 5:30 the following morning the same thing happened on his door. He flung it open and the cat made a mad rush toward the front door. The dog remained in the chair frightened. No one was in the passage.

There you have it: real terror of both animals. The "tiger" reference recalled to me my previous investigation of Mrs. Forbes, a Poltergeist woman who claimed to have been scratched, again and again, by a "ghost tiger." She also had a cat, of flesh and blood, and reported to me that she found one of its hind paws clearly sliced off as with a knife. She was terribly disturbed. Perhaps she had done it.

The question of the telepathic element is important. Animal lovers will tell you that sometimes they get a message from their pet as clearly as if it were spoken. The occasion usually is that the animal is in peril of life or is actually dying. It is precisely in such eventualities that in human beings telepathy reaches its highest efficiency. We may, therefore, assume that the mysterious mental operation by which an S.O.S. is sent is the same, whether an animal or a human being is in extreme distress.

Before becoming seriously involved in that manifestation, I would like to speak of an odd table turning experiment I participated in, with my family, at the house of Marie Armstrong at Great Neck in 1939. The experiment was suggested in a spirit of fun and soon, all the eight of us, were sitting

---

[2] *Haunted People, op. cit.*, pp. 213-222.

around the dining room table in the dark and waited for something to happen while our hands were laid out on top of the table. Nothing happened until my brother-in-law began to help the spirits. We caught him and banished him from the room.

After we resumed sitting, muffled raps came from below. They sounded quite spooky, until it occurred to us that my brother-in-law was exiled into the room below and he was probably knocking at the ceiling. I was delegated to investigate and, moving cautiously, I saw him standing on a chair and poking at the ceiling with the butt of his pencil.

Just before I left somebody suggested: if it is he let us play a joke on him; let us tie a lady's hat on the Siamese cat and let her downstairs.

In a flash it came to me that the very situation was pictured in my dream the night before. I dreamed of a cat wearing a lady's hat. Did I dream ahead of time? It looked like it, yet the dream could not have been predictive because a cat wearing a lady's hat is obviously a woman. It is a disguise, like a dog wearing a dental plate or a horse in a nightshirt. Nevertheless, the coincidence is very striking. The odds against it are astronomical.

The late Grindell-Matthews (inventor of a death ray, ex-husband of Ganna Walksa) told me a still more extraordinary story. His cat, struggling in the arms of a London veterinary surgeon against suffocation by chloroform, not only sent him an S.O.S. across the Atlantic, but also "televised" the scene of its last moments. In a signed statement Grindell-Matthews says:

In the autumn of 1924 a little black kitten, about six months old, was given to me. She used to play on the roof garden of a block of flats in Hanover Square, where I lived at that time. One night she fell off this roof garden into an area about eight feet below. The caretaker discovered her and brought her up to me in a basket. One of her big teeth was knocked out, and her back was apparently broken.

I telephoned a veterinary surgeon, and asked him to come at once. He examined her carefully and finally said that the only thing to do was to put her to sleep. I held the poor little thing in my arms and she crawled onto my shoulder, and seemed to appeal to me to save her from

241

this fate. I felt I could not lose her, and asked the vet if she were in pain. He said he thought not as the lower part of her body was apparently paralyzed from the middle of the back. He said he would have her X-rayed in the morning to see exactly what the injury was.

He took her away with him, and the next morning I went to his surgery and found that the X-ray plate showed a definite fracture of the spine. I again asked him if she were suffering and he said definitely, "No." So, although he said it would be a long job, and she might never be able to walk again, I decided to see if she could be cured, and left the kitten with him for the time being.

After she had been with the vet for about a fortnight I drove up one night to see the kitten at Highgate, and she seemed so glad to see me that I decided to take her back with me and look after her myself. I fed her on Brand's Essence every two hours, night and day, for three weeks or a month and she gradually got strong and began to run and play about the flat, dragging her hindquarters on the carpet, every now and again making an effort to stand up. After a few months, getting better and stronger, she would sometimes actually walk a few paces with her hind legs. She would always wait for me to come up from my laboratory to my flat, and never left me for a single moment. She slept on my bed and showed an affection that was almost human.

About a year after the accident I was obliged to go to New York, and had to leave the cat behind. I had been there about three weeks, when I woke up one morning about 5 o'clock, in a bath of perspiration. I had had a most awful nightmare of the cat struggling in the hands of a man in a white smock, with a goatee beard, evidently about to destroy her. The bedroom was reeking with chloroform and when my secretary came at 10 o'clock I instructed him to shoot a direct cable to my flat in London, to which I received no reply, asking if the cat were well. All the rooms of the apartment in New York seemed to me to be flooded with the smell of chloroform, though no one else could detect it.

I made arrangements to leave at the earliest possible moment, and ten days later I arrived in London. During those ten days I could not get away from the smell of chloroform. On my arrival at the flat, I was told that the cat had pined and had refused to eat anything from the day I left London, and the housekeeper thought that it would be kindest to have her destroyed. She had been asked to give me this news in reply to my cable.

Two or three days later I checked up on the time and date, and they absolutely tallied with the time I had the nightmare in New York. The veterinary surgeon (whom I had never seen or heard of in my life) had a goatee beard.

By what manner of means did the agony and death struggle of the cat under chloroform reach Grindell-Matthews's mind? The scent was apparently televised. The cat could not have done it. Mr. Grindell-Matthews's awareness must have been instantaneous. The only possible speculation that fits the case is that those whom affection binds together are, like the trees of a forest, always in contact below the level of consciousness. As the uprooting of a single tree is communicated to the other members of the sylvan community by the vibrations of the soil, so may the psychic earthquake of death reach one who loves and unite him, at the greatest crisis of life, with the object of his affection.

The Haunter Is a Dog

In Goethe's *Faust* a black dog coming through the stubble of a field is identified with Mephistopheles. The sinister mental reaction to dogs appears in many old magical tales and ghost stories. It is probably of Eastern origin and its source may be the Turkish creation legend that Ignatz Kunes put in print in the Introduction to his *Turkish Fairy Tales*. According to this:

Allah created the first man and appointed him the Earth for his dwelling place. When the first mortal appeared on the Earth and the peris rejoiced over Allah's wonderful work, the Father of Evil beheld it and envy overcame his soul. Straightaway, he conceived a plan whereby to bring to naught the beneficent work. He would implant the deadly seed of sin in this favorite creature of the Almighty, and soon the First Man, all un-suspecting, received on his pure body the damnable spittle of the Evil One who struck him therewith in the region of the stomach. But Allah, the All Merciful, the Overcomer of All Sins, hastened to tear out the contaminated flesh and flung it to the ground. Thus originated the human navel. A piece of flesh, unclean by reason of the Evil One's spittle having defiled it, obtained new life from the dust, and thus almost simultaneously with man was the dog created, half from the human body and half from the Devil's spittle. Thus it is said that no Mohammedan will harm the dog, though he refuses to tolerate it within his house. The animal's faithfulness is the human inheritance, its wildness and savagery are from the Evil One. In the Orient, the dog thus does not increase, for while the Moslem is its protector, he is at the same time its im-placable enemy.

This charming tale diagnoses the dog as a schizophrenic crea-ture; a split personality, both good and bad. Black has always been associated with evil. The bad dog is a black dog. In a haunted house evil is supposed to reside. Hence, it should be a battle ground for dogs. This specious reasoning lends easy support to many strange canine reactions in the presence of ghostly manifestations. Evil or not, dogs are frightened of the supernatural, more so than men. The terror they display is the best evidence that something out of this world is around.

I quote a typical reaction from a story by Rufus Jarman about the Benton Ghost.[1]

> Once or twice he—a beagle—went over and stood in front of the stairway door, growling way back deep in his throat, as a dog does when he is scared. His hair stood up straight on the scruff of his neck. I couldn't resist slipping up behind him and poking him in the ribs. The dog jumped a foot or so in the air. Then he looked so frightened and pitiful that I was ashamed.

Apparently, it makes no difference whether the ghost is human or not. One would expect a ghost dog to be less frightening.

---

[1] From "The Ghost House Experts Can't Explain," *True* Magazine, Aug. 1960.

Pierre Van Passen's blood chilling story[2] tells us otherwise!

In his house in Bourg-en-Forêt on the Rue Notre Dame de Bonne Nouvelles, one hour from Paris, while ascending the stairway from the basement at 11 o'clock in the night he felt something brush past him and saw a large black dog running down. He searched the house and called his two police dogs in from outside. They showed no signs of agitation. Next night, at the same hour, he again saw the black dog running swiftly down the stairs. As regularly as clockwork, the manifestation was repeated on several ensuing evenings. Then it stopped abruptly. He had to leave France for five weeks. When he returned the maid gave notice: the house was haunted, she would not stay. A neighbor came with his son, a boy of 19, armed with heavy sticks and a revolver. Van Passen wrote:

> We sat in my room, with the door wide open and all lights in the house on full blast. And sure enough, at the stroke of 11, we heard the patter of dog's feet coming down from the second story. . . . A big black dog stood at the foot of the stairs in the vestibule downstairs. The dog looked up at us. My neighbor whistled and the animal wagged its tail. We started down the stairs, keeping our eyes on the apparition. We had not gone three steps when the outline of the dog grew fainter and fainter and presently vanished altogether. Then we searched high and low once more, but no trace of a dog.

So far the story is just remarkable: the dog showed signs of recognizing humans and vanished, like the Cheshire cat, in front of the eyes of three people. They tried to joke about it, calling it "Fido, the phantom poodle." Then Pierre Van Passen decided to have his two police dogs watch the apparition.

> This led to a horrible scene. The dogs pricked up their ears at the first noise on the floor above and leaped for the door. The sound of pattering feet was coming downstairs as usual, but I saw nothing. What my dogs saw I do not know, but their hair stood on edge and they retreated growling back into my room, baring their fangs and snarling. Presently they howled as if they were in excruciating pain and were snapping and biting in all directions,

[2] *The Days of Our Years,* Dial Press, N.Y., 1946, pp. 248-251.

as if they were fighting some fierce enemy. I had never seen them in such mortal panic. I could not come to their aid, for I saw nothing to strike with the cudgel I held in my hand. The battle with the invisible foe lasted less than two minutes. Then one of my dogs yelled as if he were in the death throes, fell on the floor and died.

An invisible dog, fighting and killing a police dog—surely this is material for a thriller. Only one story rivals it in horror: haunted Ballechin House in Perthshire, England, which Lord Bute had leased for an investigation by the Society for Psychical Research. (Refer back to "The Most Haunted House in England," beginning Part IV of this book.)

Can a dog return from the dead? I have a personal contribution even though I do not know that my dog was dead or alive somewhere dreaming himself back to my house so vividly that we heard the patter of his feet and something much more incredible.

I gave away the dog because it chewed up valuable things during the night. It was a bad day for us. My daughter sobbed and we were all very upset as the dog was very affectionate and we loved him. I thought that the society to which the dog was returned would give him away to somebody else. It never occurred to me that the dog might be destroyed, and—subsequently—I was afraid to inquire.

The dog used to sleep in a small passage in front of my bedroom. At night I suddenly woke up. Something was scratching my bedroom door as if seeking admission or trying to waken us (which my dog never did). Then both myself and my wife (who was now also awake) heard the pattering of footsteps dying away in the direction of my drawing room. Then, suddenly, two bangs sounded on the piano in the manner my daughter taught the dog to play it. He used to jump up on the piano stool and hit the bass and treble end of the piano with each extended paw. My daughter was asleep and outside myself and my wife there was no one in the apartment. There was no dog. Was it my guilty conscience that produced a hallucination, shared by my wife? Was it the dream of the living dog or the ghost of the dead dog that came to haunt us? No fear assailed us, only wonderment, and the experience was never again repeated.

I have heard many similar stories. It stands out in all of them that loving animals never come back to hurt or scare. It seems as if they would only appear to give a message of continued existence. Here is a story by Mrs. Henry Wipperman, of Howard Beach, L.I., telling a simple anecdote:

Seven years ago I had two dogs: Skippy and Teddy. Skippy died from asthma. We buried him in the yard. I became sick with grief. I loved him as much as any person could love a dog. That evening I heard him, that certain wheeze of his. My mother also heard it and Teddy, the other dog, lifted his ears and looked all around for him.

This year Teddy had to be put to sleep because he was ill for almost three years. We carried him up and down stairs, did everything to make life easier for him. I prayed for him to die a natural death, but after he had been helpless for a week I had to take him to a vet. We brought him home to die. I broke down crying and patted his head. He let out a long sigh. The next day he was dead and we buried him. That evening I heard the special pant he had since he became sick. I was embarrassed to mention it, but when I heard it again I asked mother: did you hear him? She said, yes, she had heard him, but did not want to tell me lest it upset me.

A very straight and candid story. No doubt, many animal lovers have similar experiences. Hallucination is not an answer. Teddy could not have hallucinated when Skippy died and "returned" to wheeze. We do not know whether this "return" is not a phenomena limited in time. The life substance or the personality that makes up a devoted animal may persist for a while. Whether it endures, that is the great question which concerns human beings and animals alike.

Haunted Rings and Pearls

Rings that get sick when their owner is ill, rings that split as an omen of death, rings that sting like a snake, pearls that tie themselves into an evil knot and try to strangle the wearer, necklaces that burn the encircled neck—might be accepted without question in a thriller but prove to be very disturbing problems when presented in parapsychology.

The belief that rings change color and pearls get sick if the wearer is ill, is very old. Descriptions were published in the British *Medical Journal* during my stay in England by Dr. J. P. Jones, of Birmingham. The gold wedding ring of a patient, and that of her mother, mysteriously changed color when the owners experienced nervous headaches and prostrations. If either of the rings was taken off the finger and placed overnight on the mantel piece, its golden color returned in the morning; but after being replaced on the hand for a few hours the ring became the color of platinum. Dramatically enough, if the ring was not worn during the attack, the illness was far more severe, and the patient felt deprived of the power to do the simplest things.

Another extraordinary case brought to my knowledge concerned the gold wedding ring of Mrs. V. Roe, of North Finchley. She was stricken with paralysis from the waist downward, and at the beginning of her illness her ring turned black. For six months she was confined to her bed, and the ring regained its color when she became well again.

It is not necessary to look for magic in cases of this type. The rings probably reacted to some vital radiation of the human body. No such explanation fits the ring of Major S., which opens up the whole vast problem of omens of death and premonitory haunting in ancient British families. It was a tradition in the Major's family that the first-born son was always warned of the impending death of his father by the strange behavior of the ring. Suddenly, and unaccountably, the ring will split. It was a very old tradition that was handed down from father to son, but no one knew exactly how and when it arose.

I have seen the actual ring of the present head of the family. There was a thin cut in it right through as if it had been split by a razor blade. The story was that his father became seriously ill and he was called home. He arrived in good time; in fact, it seemed as if he had been summoned rashly, as his father's condition began to improve.

Then one morning the uncanny happened. He washed his hand and placed the ring in the soap dish. As he dried his hand, he heard a sharp metallic click. He looked at the ring and, to his horror, he found that it was split right across. He rushed to his father's room, but arrived too late. His father had breathed his last.

I have tried to explain this form of ancestral haunting[1] by postulating the existence of a Family *Gestalt,* a kind of mental entity created by hundreds of years of family history, pride and possessions. I suggested that the death of the head of the family acts as a shock for the *Gestalt* and the warning for the successor is effectuated by the use of dynamic energies that become liberated at the moment of death, as if to say: fathers may come, fathers may go, but the family must go on forever.

The story of the ring that acted like a snake originates from Sir Arthur Conan Doyle. It was communicated by an enthusiast of his Sherlock Holmes stories. It was a secondhand ring, snake shaped and of dull gold. The correspondent, whom Conan Doyle calls Mrs. Seagrave, usually took the ring off for the night. One night she forgot to do it and had an awful nightmare in which she was pushing off a furious creature that fastened its teeth into her arm. On awakening she felt pain in the arm, and the next day the imprint of a double set of teeth appeared upon the arm, with one tooth of the lower jaw missing. The marks were in the shape of blue-black bruises which had not broken the skin. Quoting the lady in *Memories and Advantures,* Conan Doyle proceeds:

> "I do not know," says my correspondent, "what made me think that the ring had anything to do with the matter, but I took a dislike to the thing and did not wear it for some months, when, being on a visit, I took to wearing it again."

To make a long story short, the same thing happened, and the lady settled the matter forever by dropping her ring into the hottest corner of the kitchen range.

Conan Doyle believed the story. He knew well as a medical man that in some subjects a strong mental impression does produce a physical effect. Thus a very vivid nightmare with the impression of a bite might conceivably produce the mark of a bite.

So far so good. If we had known the mental conflicts that ranged in the psyche of the lady, we might presumably ascribe the dream to the bites of her conscience. The serpentine shape

---

[1] *The Haunted Mind, op. cit.,* pp. 47-54.

of the ring provided her with an excellent symbolic representation. The marks would fall into the stigmatic category, an unusual but not impossible somatic phenomenon.

As to the healing of sick pearls, let us remember Kipling's great story in *Kim* of Lurgan Sahib. In actual life he was Jacob of Simla, a diamond merchant of fabulous reputation. He revealed himself to Kim as the Healer of Pearls in these words:

> There is no one but me can doctor a sick pearl and re-blue turquoises. I grant you opals—any fool can cure an opal—but for a sick pearl there is only me. Suppose I were to die! Then there would be no one!

I was fortunate enough to meet intimate friends of Mr. Jacob in my early years in London. He may have been wonderful with pearls, but his occult reputation—to be very charitable—was pure make-believe.

The remarkable string of pearls which figures in my next story originally also came from India and it has been in the possession of the family of Baroness von Dalwigk, of Germany, since 1701. There was a mystery attached to these pearls but no one suspected their gruesome power.

At the time of the story, the necklace was the property of Countess Ellinor, the sister of the Baroness. On paying her a visit one day, the Baroness inquired after the pearls. She found them faded, "ill," and persuaded the Countess to wear them. The lustre of the pearls slowly returned. Two weeks later the Countess had a shock; the pearls were moving and twisting on her neck of their own accord. Baroness von Dalwigk was frankly skeptical.

During the night Countess Ellinor fancied that she saw masked Indians who threatened her. The next morning a double fisher knot was discovered on the string. The clasp was untouched.

Pale as the pearls themselves, the Countess refused to wear them. Baroness von Dalwigk, still skeptical, put them on. She was walking in the garden with the Countess who screamed all of a sudden and flung her hands to her own throat as if she were choking. Her gaze was fixed in horror on the pearl string around her sister's neck. The Baroness looked down and found a double knot in the middle of the necklace. The clasp was undisturbed. Physically, it was an impossibility for the necklace to knot.

At this stage the Countess' husband became alarmed. He took the pearls, untied the knot and locked the necklace in a box, the key of which he retained. Next morning he looked into the box and—to his intense astonishment—found the string knotted. From that time the knotting became a daily occurrence.

Not long after this the Countess decided to wear the mysterious pearls at a reception she was giving. While the string lay unclasped on her sister's dressing table, Baroness von Dalwigk saw a strange sight. The pearls moved, twisted, and the string stood up, straight as a candle.

Seized with terror, but collecting every ounce of courage, she stepped to the table and pressed her hand over the top end of the string. It resisted, but collapsed in a few seconds.

Nothing further happened until dinner time. Then panic broke out. There was a sudden scream, the face of the Countess became livid, and her eyes almost started from her head. With a groan, she fell senseless into her chair. Her dress was opened, and a blood red mark, the width of two fingers, was found round her neck. The string of pearls was broken. The Countess lost her hearing. Two days later her deafness disappeared, but the marks did not vanish from her neck for some time.

When the pearls were taken to an old jeweller, he examined the thread carefully and said that a violent effort would have been needed to break it.

"I have read of strange things in old chronicles," he allegedly said. "Is not the Countess one of those people, born once in a thousand years, on whom pearls knot?"

A beautiful mystical finish to a story fantastic enough. There is a stigmatic touch in it, together with strangulation, which again raises the question of a conjunction of guilt with paranormal talent. It is noteworthy that no previous wearers had left a record of similar occult adventures in the history of the family. The malignant behavior of the pearls could only have been an objectification of some deep, dark secret in the personal history of the Countess or the Baroness.

While I have never seen a necklace knot and strangle, I know of one that had left burn marks around the throat of the wearer. It was an "apport" necklace, arriving—allegedly— from nowhere and nestling on Mrs. Forbes' neck "red hot." No one saw the necklace arrive, and no one found out its history.

But the event was part of a Poltergeist story (see *On the Trail of the Poltergeist*), and I was skeptical enough to conclude that hair curlers were more likely to cause self-inflicted burns than a hot journey through another dimension. The explanation was not romantic, but the lady was beautiful and so was her story.

Who Rings the Bell?

This is a sixty-five dollar question. You cannot answer it by saying: I will go to the door and find out. You may not find anybody there. Would then the ring be an auditory hallucination? Would you be trying to rouse yourself to a message from your unconscious? You almost admit the possibility when you use the phrase, that rings a bell, in your mind.

An old friend of mine told me that when she met her present husband for the first time she heard, through the open windows, church bells ring. She understood the message: it was wedding bells.

I used to wake up myself at 8 A.M. every morning by hearing the door bell ring. The ringing broke my sleep. I went to the door and found no one there. The alarm was so real that I would never accept it as a dream. Each time it made me jump out of bed and go to the door, though I now knew that it was only a dream bell. Some time later I moved to a hotel where there was a knocker on the door. It took me only a few days to adjust to it. Instead of the bell, now I heard the knocker sound off and wake me without fail.

This has led me to develop, for my friends and patients, the psychic alarm clock technique. It is very simple: you use an imaginary alarm clock, go through every movement of winding it up, setting the hand and the alarm bell and put it on your night table, still in your imagination, next to your head. After a few days of doing it, the alarm will ring, in your sleep, at the appointed time and wake you up without a shock.

Clearly then, the bell you hear may be a mental bell. Yet, when you are awake, you cannot believe it. It is just as well because there is a mystery about ringing bells that we have not yet been able to solve.

To take first a case where the unconscious of the percipient merges in action with the invisible ringer of bells, I will refer to the Chelsea Poltergeist that I have succeeded in laying by psychoanalysis.[1] The Poltergeist is an invisible racketeer. Footsteps, belonging to an invisible man, were heard to approach the door of Miss Whalen's cottage in Chelsea, London, then the knocker of the door "lifted itself" and banged again and again. Between 1-2 A.M. this has been going on for eight months prior to my entrance on the case. Mrs. Whalen had a thyroid operation that left her in a very depleted state. Each time she had a shock from the knockings. Presently, however, she had a brain wave. She put a sign on the door. "Please ring the bell." From then on the ghost never knocked again but—as if the sign on the door had been taken for an invitation —an invisible man entered the house with a shuffling gait and made bottles of whiskey, tins of biscuits, coffee cups, saucers and plates of hot food disappear.

I believe that the sign on the door worked like a posthypnotic suggestion. Mrs. Whalen's unconscious was unable to disobey a wish which, through the written and then forgotten request, was placed on the same level on which the ghostly manifestations originated in her own mind. It proved to me that it was her own ghost that had walked out on her and that the control of the phenomena lay in her own hunger for things she was denied by life.

A different variety of mental legerdemain appeared in a trance session with Naomi Bacon in London in which messages came through from a communicator who claimed to be the spirit of Edgar Wallace.[2]

"Something about a peal of bells," said the medium. "Something about a disappointment." Was he playing bells? "Something he was doing. I don't know what it means. He says you don't know either." Who would be an agent with some work he was doing? Was there anything done in a theatre with bells? "He does show me bells and says: 'Something to do with a play.' He was disappointed over that. It did not take well over *there*."

Where? I asked.

"In Nueva York."

[1] *Haunted People, op. cit.*, pp. 213-222.
[2] *The Haunted Mind, op. cit.*, pp. 295-308.

Up to this day I do not know why New York was pronounced in such an odd manner, but the reference to the bells was a bull's eye. *The Ringer*, one of Edgar Wallace's most successful mystery stories, was made into a play. In England the play was very successful, but in New York it was a failure.

Here is another variety of bell mysteries. It comes from a correspondent in Long Island, and it is quite recent:

> About 5 years ago my door bell rang at 6 A.M. I ran to open the door, thinking that my husband, who had already left the house, had forgotten something and was returning for it. No one was there. I looked up and down the driveway and then went back into the house. At 6:15 the bell rang again. This time I ran to the front of the house and looked out. Not a soul was in sight. My mother heard the bell, so did my dog. It barked. Later in the morning we heard that my aunt's (mother's sister) husband died in Chicago at 5 A.M. (which is 6 A.M. in New York). The bell never rang after—or before—when there was no reason for it.

The bell ringing in this case seems to have served the purpose of announcing the death of a close relative. It was objective because the dog heard it too. To fall back on coincidence is convenient but not too convincing.

Whether haunting it to be tied up with the dead or not, the ringing of bells in haunted houses is not uncommon. Here is a statement from Beatrice Jamieson, an intimate friend of mine in England:

> In our home at 19 Ulsterville Ave., Belfast, the door bell rang at 9 o'clock every evening for about a week. The maid went to open, but found no one outside. We thought that naughty children were playing pranks. One evening, I was about 16 years old at the time, I stood in the hall, waiting for the bell, determined to catch the ringer. The bell, an ordinary electric one, rang. I threw the door open. To my surprise there was no one there. This was very puzzling. Many evenings afterwards, at the same time that the bell rung we heard footsteps on the stairs. I thought here was a ghost in the house as if, having opened the door promptly when the bell rang, I let it in. The bell never rang again.

On one occasion we were sitting around the fire with Mr. Michael Black, a visitor (who, at the time, could have been about 40 years old). He knew nothing of the bell ringing or of the footsteps. The maid was out. My parents, my sister and myself were sitting in the drawing room with our guest. No one else was in the house. Suddenly, the footsteps were heard running upstairs. Mr. Black, thinking that a burglar got in, jumped up, ran out of the room and dashed upstairs. He found the gas burning in my mother's bedroom (which was on the third floor on the front with a sheer drop). No one was there and no one acknowledged having lit the gas.

Both the bell ringing and the footsteps, while they lasted, were heard by several people at the same time. There was never any explanation. The only other manifestation occurred one evening when my sister and myself were alone in the house. I was playing the piano. The room was lit by gas. Outside it was dark. The door suddenly opened wide and touched the piano. Then it began to close slowly. My sister, Mrs. James Fitzsimon, of Stratherm, St. Souci Park, Belfast, screamed. We were both frightened and got hold of each other's hand. Nothing else happened, so we persuaded ourselves that a sudden draft opened the door, though we never had a similar occurrence.

We got so used to the footsteps that we paid later on no attention to them. We never told the maid and she never complained. The dog in the house, a spaniel, was always quiet, except on the occasion of the opening of the door. Then he seemed frightened.

This is a case of a well-behaving ghost who was fond of the piano, considered the house his own home and tolerated the inhabitants who, for all we know, might have appeared as ghosts to him.

All these bells were ordinary electric bells. Possibly such a bell could ring through an accidental short circuit, but that is not likely to occur at regular times and then to repair itself. Old-fashioned wire bells present a more difficult proposition; they require strength to pull. They still exist in ancient houses in England and I had an occasion to investigate the system at Aldborough Manor, near Leeds. The house was owned by Lady Lawson-Tancred. The bells rang for five days without visible or normal agency. On the third day two maids saw—independently—a phantom woman leaning over an ancient cradle. Both girls had a shock. The nerves of one were so shattered that she had to be sent home. The other recovered and carried on. The phantom woman was seen again. Doors opened mysteriously and Lady Lawson-Tancred was considering the disagreeable possibility of leaving the house.

Unfortunately, when I arrived on the scene, the bells had already stopped ringing. The maid who fled with a nervous breakdown might have been involved in the mystery. The bells rang angrily during the night following her departure and in the morning after. Then the power seemed exhausted and the house grew quiet. The maids were above the age of puberty (at which time Poltergeist manifestations usually break out), no crockery was broken and no objects stirred mysteriously. The hand-bell in the house never rang, but the wire bells did when both the bell pulls and the clappers were watched. Jean, the remaining servant girl, presented a mystery, but a different one. She was a beautiful girl of 16 who had some curious affinity with nature. I was told that birds would alight on her shoulder and stay there when she walked into the house. Also that mice would not run from her; she could catch them with bare hands. Inasmuch as the bells rang during the night and in the morning when she was around, Lady Lawson-Tancred—on suspicion that she may have had a psychic share in the disturbances—discharged her. Possibly it was a wise decision. The disturbances never recurred.

To conclude the mystery in a light vein, I had a friend who, much to his surprise, saw a notice of his own demise in a morning paper in London. As the announcement, to use the words of Mark Twain, was slightly premature, he rang up a friend on the telephone and asked: "Say, did you see the notice of my death in the morning press?" "Yes," answered the friend, "where are you speaking from?"

Since the days of the *Flying Dutchman*, the vision of phantom boats over seas and rivers has been an omen of disaster. Why ships that went down with a load of iniquity into Davy Jones' locker should ride the waves in ghostly shape, or why the sight of phantom boats should be a warning of impending tragedy or danger, no one can tell. Facts should come first, questions after. Here is a story from a British evening newspaper in which the facts loom large.

My brother and I—writes Mr. F. W. Clarke, of 6 Trinity Road, Southend-on-Sea—had been fishing from our boat about three miles from Southend pier, towards the Nore lightship. It was evening and as the light was failing, we were making all possible speed towards Southend to pick up our moorings; my brother was at the engine and I had the tiller. Suddenly, across our bows, but a few feet ahead, there loomed a racing yacht under full sail. Hull, sails, mast and flag—all were pure white. I shouted to my brother and, putting the tiller hard over to port, nerved myself for what seeemd an inevitable collision. It never came. It seemed that we cut right through her amidships, and as we did so, we felt a cold, damp mist that chilled us to the bone and filled us with awe. When I related the incident at the club the following evening, the story was received with a "grain of salt." And then three weeks later, whilst we were acting as mark boat for the yacht racing, the bow of our boat was crushed in a collision with the racing yacht "White Swallow," and my brother sustained a fractured collar bone.

When the appearance of a phantom yacht so strangely coincides with an actual collision, it follows one may be forgiven for seeking a casual link between the two events and for classifying it as a premonition in a visual shape.

Was it due to a presentiment of a similar type that the picture of a sinking boat with all its attendant horrors so often returned to W. T. Stead's writings? His earliest "foreboding" took the form of a narrative by a survivor of an ocean liner struck by an iceberg. It was published in 1892 in the *Pall Mall Gazette*. The ship in the illustration of the story was *The Majestic,* but the tragedy was purely fictitious. It was, however, further illustrated by the picture of the *Majestic's* real captain and the following editorial note was appended:

> This is exactly what might take place if liners are sent to sea short of boats.

Twenty-six years afterwards 1,600 lives were lost on the *Titanic,* owing to a shortage of boats; Stead went down among them and the captain of the ill-fated liner, who also lost his life, was the same Captain Smith, whose picture was published in Stead's fictitious story in 1892.

Three years before the sinking of the *Titanic,* in criticising the standard of evidence demanded by the Society for Psychical Research as regards communications from the dead, Stead, before the members of the Cosmos Club, drew a graphic, imaginary picture of himself shipwrecked and drowning in the sea and calling frantically for help.

> Suppose that instead of throwing me a rope the rescuers would shout back "Who are you? What is your name?" "I am Stead! W. T. Stead! I am drowning here in the sea. Throw me the rope. Be quick!" But instead of throwing me the rope, they continue to shout back: "How do we know you are Stead? Where were you born? Tell us the name of your grandmother."

Before he sailed, the presentiment of a great change came to him again. He wrote in a letter:

> Something is awaiting me, some important work the nature of which will be disclosed to me in good time. But what it is, whether journalistic, spiritual, social or political, I know not. I await my marching orders, being assured that He who has called me will make clear His good will and pleasure in good season.

However extraordinary this story is, it does not follow that ideas of sea-disasters or the vision of phantom boats should always have a personal application. The phenomenon may be of the haunting order, linked up with a particular locality and not with the percipient. My experience with the Phantom Boatmen of Maidenhead appears to be of the latter type. No accident has befallen me. The peculiar atmospheric conditions which prevailed may have been, in some mysterious manner, responsible for the strange event.

I was spending the summer in a cottage on the Thames at Maidenhead. The day was August 21, 1932. For some time before the night fell, a storm was gathering. People scuttled home like rabbits. By nine o'clock a heavy mantle of darkness covered the visible world and thunder hung in menace over the subdued countryside. Ominous growls came from the distance. Rumbling and rolling, the storm was slowly but relentlessly approaching.

I was asleep before it broke in fury. The first clap of thunder shook me back to wakefulness. My nerves tingled with the shock of the crash. The artillery of the heavens opened with a fearful cannonade. Like a barrage fire, one lightning stroke followed another. They rent the sky, they shook the earth. It was a storm the like of which I have never seen in England. To sleep was an impossibility. I felt my nerves stick out of my body and curl. My daughter cried in fear, crept into our bed and hid her head under the cover. My wife was hard put to banish her fears and stop her tears. After the fireworks came the rain, a veritable cloudburst, walls of water stretching from heaven to earth, swishing and beating with merciless monotony.

I am annoyed and irritated if I am kept from sleeping at my own time. I was helpless against *Jupiter Tonans* but, inwardly I was smoldering. My daughter remained in our bed and was very restless. I called out harshly. My wife spoke to her in a whisper. Then the rain stopped and the world was plunged into the stillness of a bottomless well. Silence as awe-inspiring as the celestial cannonade reigned supreme. To my nerves it was a balm. I was sliding and slipping into a happy sleep when, half-awake, I heard the sound of splashing waves and dipping oars. My brain noted the sound and interpreted it as an approaching boat. I might have cursed, but I was not sufficiently awake for that. I wanted to sleep and keep off everything that would prevent me. The sound persisted. At first it was far away, now it came near and, in the stillness of the night, it became a positive nuisance.

With the increase of annoyance, my brain functions became clearer. For the first time, it struck me as puzzling that after the dreadful storm and cloudburst (which swamped and filled every boat on the river) at so late an hour (it was after one o'clock) and in Stygian darkness anyone should be out rowing. For some time I digested this. Then, finding the occurrence stranger and stranger, I jumped out of bed to investigate.

Our bedroom opened on a glass-covered porch which overlooked the river. The glass door giving on the porch, and the middle windows of the porch were open. From the bed the river could not be seen. To reach the porch window I had to take five or six steps. As I jumped out of the bed, the oars grew silent and the water stopped splashing. The sky was covered with black masses of clouds. There was no moon but a sheen over the river permitted me to see.

Near or far, there was no boat. The water was still. There was not a ripple on its surface. I listened intently. No noise dying away in the distance as of a boat reached my ears. No footsteps crunched on the gravel or thudded in the grass as of the oarsmen landing from the mysterious craft.

Boat, oarsmen and swishing oars vanished as a dream. Only I knew it was no dream; nor was it hallucination. The idea that I heard the approach of a ghost boat never entered my head. My hair did not stand on end. I felt no chill in my bones. There was no eerie feeling in the atmosphere. I just felt puzzled because the boat should have been there somewhere, and it was not. It left no trace of its passage. Its occupants vanished without a sound. I went back to bed wondering. I thought that my wife and child were asleep, and I crept in quietly so as not to awaken them. A second or two later, however, my wife asked me in a whisper: "What was it?" I said, "I heard something like a boat." She said: "I have seen two boats, one had eight or ten people in it, sitting in pairs; one man had his head bandaged in white. In the other boat there was a single man in a drooping position. I shall tell you more in the morning."

My natural conclusion was that my wife heard the sound of the approaching boat as I did, and wove it into a dream. Here was then confirmation that the sound was objective; which I did not doubt for a second. Still another confirmation came in the morning from my daughter. She also had heard the boat.

I asked my wife, recalling the incident to her, what else she had to say. She repeated what she said during the night and added something intensely curious. The first boat with the wounded man was closely followed by the second, and was "half-way through." Her prow was no more visible.

As I remarked before, from our bed it was impossible to see the Thames. Standing up and moving outward a step or two, a section of the river would have come into view. Looking out from that position one might have seen the middle and the stern of a boat while the front passed out of sight. What had this spatial relationship to do with my wife's dream? To find it at all in the dream was most unusual. We liked the river and always took in the full view afforded by the porch. It seemed as if, asleep, she had been standing at a certain point in the room and looking out, she had dreamed within the limitation of her physical sight. That a dream-image should conform to sensory limitation is in itself a very odd phenomenon.

Hunting the Table-Tilting Ghosts[1]

Table turning became a tea-party craze when the first wave of modern Spiritualism broke over the shores of England from America. Under the light touch of persons sitting in a circle the table trembled, answered questions by tipping with one leg, and moved across the room as if a spirit had possessed it.

Causes suggested for the tables' movements included unconscious muscular pressure, discovered by the famous scientist Faraday. Another well-known scientist, Dr. Carpenter, put forward the theory of "unconscious cerebration"—unconscious mental processes. The clergy suspected the Devil was responsible. London was flooded with warning pamphlets and as a result of this splendid propaganda the tide of Spiritualism began to rise.

The truth is, both Faraday and Carpenter were too dogmatic; neither unconscious muscular pressure nor unconscious

[1] From *Fate Magazine*, April 1963. Reprinted by permission.

cerebration completely explains table turning. For a table may move without being touched!

Spiritualists constantly claim this as the best argument against a materialistic explanation. I do not agree with them.

I share the views of F. W. H. Myers, Cambridge scholar and pioneer in psychical research. He stated, "If a table moves when no one is touching it, this is not obviously more likely to have been effected by my deceased grandfather than by myself. We cannot tell how I could move it; but then we cannot tell how he could move it either."

But, of course, the primary question is: *does* a table move when no one is touching it?

It was in a Welsh mining village that I first saw a table moved without being touched. The religious fervor of those participating ruled out the question of practical joking. The end of a large and extremely heavy dining room table rose in the air. Bent knees simply could not have raised it to stand, stork-like, on one leg. I was favorably impressed, but it was not a scientific experiment. Table levitation cannot be regarded as proved unless the sitters are well removed from the table and there is sufficient light to see.

In such conditions I have seen a heavy oak table moved on a carpeted floor. This happened when I was the guest of the composer, Clive Richardson, and his wife, in London, in April, 1938. There were only the three of us and the table around which we held hands weighed at least 80 pounds.

I stood far back from the table where I had a good view of the bottom cross bars of the table and of the feet of my host and hostess. There was no contact between Mr. and Mrs. Richardson and the table. The hostess addressed a request to "Douglas," her spirit-guide, to produce his usual manifestations. "Douglas," her fiance before her marriage to her present husband, had died in a motor car smash at the age of 30. They had been very much in love and "Douglas," I was told, now expressed his devotion by means of the heavy oak table. The table began to creak and groan. Slowly and jerkily it shifted on the carpet in this and in that direction.

I asked "Douglas" whether he could hold down the table so that I could not lift it. He promised to try. With great effort I succeeded in just wrenching it off the ground. I asked "Douglas" to desist and then I could lift the table easily.

Next I put my whole weight on top of the table, and then on the cross bars below. Straining and groaning under my

262

weight of 170 pounds, the table moved with me across the carpeted floor. No one else was touching it. This part of the demonstration took place in darkness, yet it was convincing for I could not have failed to notice any approach on the part of my host or hostess.

I arranged to take photographs believing that a power able to shift the heavy dining room table could easily lift a light table into the air. In this expectation I was disappointed. The table skipped, but the people around it moved so much also that it was not possible to secure a satisfactory photograph. However, something very odd was recorded on plates exposed from a quartz lens camera on two occasions. The plates showed what appeared to be a "silent" electric discharge.

Plates simultaneously exposed in other cameras did not show anything unusual. As the quartz lens is sensitive to light rays invisible to the human eye and not to be seen in the visible spectrum it seemed possible that the photographs indicated a discharge of energy which would not pass through an ordinary camera lens.

This might have led to an important discovery. But in psychical research something always goes wrong before you get to the end of the road. This time one of my co-workers blundered. He explained to Mrs. Richardson, who apparently provided the psychic force, that "Douglas" was not a spirit but her own "biological force." In other words, she herself was unconsciously moving the table.

I was willing to subscribe to this explanation, but it was fatal to further research. The lady lost faith in "Douglas." There were no more queer photographs. The table no longer moved by itself.

* * *

Spiritualists often are asked why the spirits are partial to tables? Why don't spirits move other pieces of furniture? They answer that a table is more convenient for spelling out messages, but other furniture can be moved equally well. To this I can bear startling witness.

A man who had been acquitted of a charge of espionage and murder during the First Great War, came to see me in 1936 with an incredible story. He had a spirit-guide, "Barbara," who in life had been an old family servant and practically a mother to him. She was now attached to him from the "other side" and could produce the most startling manifestations through a suitable medium.

I asked Mr. Coyne if he knew of such a medium and, as a result of advertising in the psychic press, one was found. She was Mrs. S. L. Dickson, of North London, a charming woman who knew nothing of Coyne's past and was quite unprepared for the methods by which he "got the power up."

Mr. Coyne arrived at Mrs. Dickson's flat with an armful of beer bottles. Already he must have emptied a few. He continued alternately gulping beer and jeering and swearing at the spirits. When the last drop was gone he declared he was in a sufficiently deep trance for the demonstration to begin.

There was a big wardrobe in the room, resting on a low bottom piece. Mrs. Dickson placed her fingertips against its side and Mr. Coyne put a shaking finger on the ledge of the bottom part. Then he adjured "Barbara" to get busy.

In the light of a 100-watt electric lamp, I witnessed an incredible sight.

The wardrobe began to show signs of animation. It creaked and groaned. The strain increased. Then, with a jerk, the end of the heavy piece of furniture near the medium shifted out two inches. The jerks continued until the top piece stood five inches out. Mr. Coyne, in a croaky voice, commanded the wardrobe to move back. The wardrobe rocked and tilted, and, before my staring eyes, began to back away.

This tilting soon assumed such dangerous proportions that Mrs. Dickson and her husband became very nervous. The wardrobe, containing two mirror panels, did not belong to them and if it fell over they would be responsible for any damage.

Mr. Coyne, however, had complete faith in "Barbara." He sat down with his back to the wardrobe, bent his head, extended his arms and defied the wardrobe to fall over on him.

I felt so uneasy that I stepped in front and braced myself to catch it. Slowly, it leaned over. I could feel the weight coming down on my palms. The point of balance was passed, the angle of the tilt increased, but the weight on my palms remained very light, just as if an invisible hand was checking the wardrobe's downward movement.

Mr. Coyne gave a sharp command. The animated furniture gently leaned back and, without the slightest noise, stood on its base once again!

264

I placed myself in Mrs. Dickson's position to see what effect I could make on the wardrobe by my 10 finger tips. I could make none, unless I pressed against it with the palm of my hand and so caused the wardrobe to lift upward.

By this time I had a good deal of respect for "Barbara" but none at all for Mr. Coyne. He became so unruly that I had to threaten him with an empty beer bottle. He flew into a vile temper and swore that he would withdraw "Barbara" from Mrs. Dickson. Then he departed in a rage.

I don't know what he did. But he did it well. Only once more was Mrs. Dickson able to produce the same phenomenon.

This time I made a curious discovery. When the wardrobe was moved away from the wall no manifestation took place. Apparently the relative darkness between wall and wardrobe was an essential condition for the mysterious "power" to operate.

I suggested Mrs. Dickson attempt to see whether the base on which the wardrobe rested would move at the same time as the upper part. It was obvious that no pressure by Mrs. Dickson's fingers on the top of the wardrobe could affect the whole bottom piece. Nevertheless, with creaking and groaning the whole wardrobe, base and top, tilted forward. The lifting force seemed to be applied right underneath. The tilt was about three inches.

My assistant tried to duplicate the feat. He bent down, slipped and fell.

I tried it myself and, after repeated efforts, just managed to budge the furniture. Mrs. Dickson was standing all the time with only her 10 finger tips on the wardrobe.

For a month I tried various experiments with Mrs. Dickson but had to give up. the "power" became less and less. Whoever "Barbara" was she had gone after the mysterious Mr. Coyne.

Another experience I had with table tilting concerned Anna Rasmussen, Denmark's star medium whom I invited to London in 1938. Her record was a remarkable one. It included moving pendulums suspended in distant glass cases and producing spirit raps from within her body.

The "spirit-rapping" was amazing. At a distance of two yards one could hear dull thumps coming from Mrs. Rasmussen's body. With these knocks "Dr. Lazurus," her spirit-guide, answered questions. Professor Charles Winther, of Copenhagen, failed to localize these sounds with a stethoscope and found he heard them better without a stethoscope. Mr.

Harry Price reported in one of his books that he, too, was impressed. However, I am sure if he had an opportunity to study them as I did in London, he would have solved their mystery very soon.

I found the raps were under Mrs. Rasmussen's conscious control. If she failed to understand a question or did not know its answer there were no raps. No rapping occurred when she was speaking. The rapping ceased if the stethoscope was placed on her neck. It was this last observation which gave the doctors associated with me in this investigation the clue to the mystery. They unanimously concluded that the raps were produced when Mrs. Rasmussen compressed air on her larynx.

It requires no abnormality to do this but it takes constant practice to make the sounds loud enough to be heard. One of the ladies who attended the sittings with Mrs. Rasmussen could do a tolerable imitation at a moment's notice. The late Shaw Desmond learned to do it, too, and became quite proficient.

The wonder was that for 20 years no one had solved this mystery.

The knocks which "Dr. Lazurus" produced in the table at which the medium sat stood very little investigation. As soon as Mrs. Rasmussen was placed so that she could not kick the leg of the table the knocks stopped. When she was allowed to sit nearer the table the knocks started again.

Of course, I tried the experiment with the pendulums too.

They were suspended in a specially built glass case which was placed on a very heavy mahogany table. The pendulums moved only if the medium was allowed to place her hands on the table leaf and make rhythmic pulls at the wood.

Here again, was the lesson: no phenomena should be accepted on authority. The "Danish Wonder" was reputed to be one of the last great mediums!

Miracle-mongering produces queer perversions of the mind. Daughters cheat their fathers and wives their husbands. Neither friendship nor social standing can guarantee authenticity.

Occasionally, without having the gift of second sight, people are seized by the feeling that the man they are talking to is about to die. As a rule, they cannot account for the sensation.

Medical foresight is ruled out in cases in which the death that is foreseen results from an accident. Such instances present a problem in precognition. Other cases may be explained by strong antipathy, amounting to an unconscious death wish or by coincidence; but the emotional reaction that follows the "presentiment" suggests a deeper problem. The sense of sight or smell may be involved. Impending death may be inferred from a shadow in the eyes or, in rare cases, it may be an olfactory perception.

This smell of death is a very curious phenomenon. Here is an illustration from a correspondent:

> We certainly have most strange things happening in our sitting room. Even a cat we had often used to spit and get its back up for nothing at all that we could see, and if anyone dies, there is an ice-cold blast of air. Some years ago my daughter, then aged 12, flew out of the room, saying that there was a smell of death in it. The following morning we had a letter to say that my brother-in-law died at the very hour.

In this case we find an olfactory premonition of death amidst phenomena of the haunting class. Cats do react to things of a ghostly character and the ice-cold blast appears to be a thermal objectification of the idea of the coldness of the grave. The smell of death is an interpretation of the sensation on a more acceptable level.

In other cases, the purely subjective character of the sensation is self-evident. I knew a lady whose nostrils were assailed by a smell of chrysanthemums whenever she entered a house where someone was about to die. A curious childhood passion of roaming in the cemetery where the graves were covered with chrysanthemums explained the association. Plainly, her unconscious coupled the smell of chrysanthemums with death; but the awareness that mobilized the perception still remained a mystery.

The smell of a corpse is due to the commencement of decomposition. It is because most of us know this smell that a premonition of impending death might be clothed in a super-acuity of olgactory perception. The death-howl of dogs is, no doubt, due to the smell of decomposition that starts in the human body hours before actual death.

The same key might apply to some gruesome cases of haunting in which unbearable stench rises from the ground where, in the grim past, bodies were left to putrefy. Infinitesimal olfactory particles or their "psychometric" residue, may become magnified by terror and revulsion. For the smell of death also stands for corruption and evil. The strange earthy smells, for instance, of which we read in ancient chronicles of evocation of the devil, were probably real in the sense of an unconscious protest against an evil practice. This was the explanation I favored in the case of a woman who, through a hypnotized young man, tried to evoke the Devil. Being well-versed in demonology, she expected the "earthy smell" together with the weird perceptions she described; but the olfactory hallucination may have also been due to the psychic self-defense of the young man involved.

Foreboding of an impending calamity may find expression through the same olfactory mechanism. I knew a teacher who was suffering from attacks of horrible odors. If she rushed to the open window, she soon recovered. If she did not, she fainted. I found out that she had a very troubled life and the attacks were of a premonitory character; they always preceded some unpleasant happening.

As some people are assailed by bad smells, others are surrounded by clouds of delicious odors of a mysterious origin. This is the other side of the picture: the great spirit perfume mystery. However, before being carried away into the spheres, it would be well to consider an orthodox approach.

It is a medical fact that in certain illnesses the skin gives out a scent of violet, pineapple, musk, etc. The phenomenon is due to the presence of buthyric ether in the human system.

Psychological states, for reasons as yet unknown, may provoke physiological symptoms similar to those we find in abnormal somatic conditions. The odor of sanctity, as claimed in the life of the saints, should be approached from this angle. To mention some instances: St. Cajetan emitted the scent of orange blossoms, St. Francis the smell of musk. When the body of St. Casimir, Patron of Poland was exhumed in 1603, 120 years after his death, it was found entire and it exhaled a sweet smell.

The mystery is how a psychological state can perpetuate a somatic reaction long after death. The reaction necessarily suggests a continued interaction between the body and the departed spirit, hence the phenomenon appears to be an indirect evidence of survival after death.

In certain psychic phenomena we have definite indication of an unknown physiological process behind the odor mysteries.

To William Stainton Moses (1839-92), an Anglican clergyman, M.A., of University College School, London—whom Spiritualism claims as one of the greatest mediums of the last century—we owe the best records of olfactory mysteries.

Scents issued from his head, and the more the scent was wiped away, the stronger and more plentiful it became. The most common scents were: musk, verbena, new-mown hay and one unfamiliar odor which was said to be "spirit scent." During his séances, the scents usually came down in showers. Stainton Moses was fully aware that the clue to the production of these scents was in his organism. In his notebook under the date of July 4, 1874, we find this entry:

> While in the garden, before we began to sit, I was conscious of scent all around me, especially on my hair. When I rubbed my hair, my hand was scented strongly. I tried the experiment many times. When the peppermint came I was conscious of its presence first near my head and it seems, as it were, to be evolved out of the hair. I have before noticed the same thing but not so markedly as on this occasion.

He suspected that the process was remedial, because the effusion of scent from his scalp was most marked when he was suffering pain. Something very peculiar was observed about these scents.

> The odor was circumscribed in space, confined to a belt or band, beyond which it did not penetrate. It surrounded the circle to a few feet, and outside of that belt was not perceptible; or it was drawn across the room as a cordon, so that it was possible to walk into it and out of it again—

269

the presence and absence of the odor and the temperature of the air which accompanied it being most marked.

I have known the same phenomenon to occur in the open air. I have been walking with a friend, for instance, and we walked into air laden with scent, and through it again into the natural atmosphere . . . . I have even known cases where wet scent has been produced and showered down in the open air. On one special occasion, on the Isle of Wight, my attention was attracted by the patter of some fine spray on a lady's silk dress, as we were walking along the road. One side of the dress was plentifully besprinkled with fine spray, which gave forth a delicious odor, very clearly perceptible from some distance round.

Another curious fact recorded by Stainton Moses was that the illness of one of the sitters would cause the scent to be coarse and pungent. A bad mental influence had a still worse effect. This is how the appearance of an unwelcome "spirit" is described by Dr. Speer, Stainton Moses' recorder at one of the sittings:

> The other evening a newcomer slipped in, and stank us out of the room by throwing down from the ceiling a large quantity of *Sp. Pulegii*. Everything that it touched was impregnated for 24 hours. The dining room cloth and my own nether habiliments had to be exposed to view in the back garden; and on the following morning our dining room floor and passage had to be freely fumigated with pastilles. That spirit has not been invited to join us again.

One wonders whether fumigation by incense may not have originated as a banishing rite against unwelcome spirits in an age when the belief in spirits was more universal than it is now.

However, it may be, I can confirm some of the findings of Stainton Moses from personal experience. In the case of Mrs. Forbes,[1] violet smells came and went in clouds in various parts of our séance room. We could walk into this cloud and almost draw the boundaries by sniffing around. Sometimes these smells were followed by the "apport" of real violets, sometimes—at her home—they were followed by a smell of decomposition. Once I even found it hanging as an invisible

---

[1] *On the Trail of the Poltergeist, op. cit.*, pp. 151-156.

curtain at the bottom of the steps that led up to an evil smelling bathroom. The two odors, we were told, appeared in strong succession on her wedding night, together with showers of violet flowers falling down on the nuptial bed. The suggestion of some moral horror was clear. It was not just of sexual origin. Memories of a girl called Violet, who died of cancer of the throat at the age of 28, appeared as a motive for unconscious catharsis. Then there was a state of trance before the fireplace (long before our investigation) in which a bleeding cross was traced over one of her breasts. Under this cross, carcinoma was found and had to be excised. To these pictures of horror the fetid odor of a "ghost tiger" should be added. The clawing of her body could well have been due to her own nails and an urticarious condition of her skin, but the stench of the tiger, smelt by several of our lady assistants in the investigation, may have been part of a past traumatization, even though a physiological explanation was easy to postulate.

It is well-known from Poltergeist cases that vomiting, gases and excrements may rise to a torrent under the dominating idea of evil. In the case of the five devils of Anna Ecklund, exorcised by Father Theophilus at the Franciscan convent at Earling, Iowa,[2] an incestuous father was one of the original evil possessors. When Father Theophilus came in the ritual of exorcism to *A Spiritu Fornicationis Libera Nos, Domine,* the possessed woman's body squirmed desperately. The exorcistic ritual, relentlessly pursued for 72 hours, came to a culmination on September 23, 1928 and it finally liberated Anna from the obsessing spirits. As their parting shot, "an unearthly, unbearable stench" filled the room.

By whatever means the stench was produced, for Anna Ecklund it was a symptom of spiritual death. The exorcistic ritual was effective because it shifted the burden of guilt to the possessing devils. This was catharsis, deliverance from the demons of her own conscience that, without priestly intervention, she was unable to lay.

---

[2] Reported in *Fate Magazine*, June 1959.

Discussing the problem of remarriage on the analytic couch, the beautiful widow of a publisher confessed that she had turned down the proposal of an old and faithful friend because her husband, before he had died, uttered the threat: I will come back and strangle you if you get married again. A year later, the friend had died and left over a million dollars that would have been all hers and would have solved the problem of financial insecurity for the rest of her life. The reason why she refused him was solely due to her superstitious fear of the power of the dead.

This tragic story affords an opportunity to make inquiries in several directions:

1. If we survive the change called death, will love and jealousy survive as an enduring obsession with the affairs of the living?

2. Does the survival of love include an unabated interest in sex?

3. Can this sexual interest affect the living?

All three questions threaten to carry the inquiry into the nebulous realm of spiritualistic teachings and philosophy. The threat, however, can be ignored. The example of the publisher's widow proves that the love and jealousy of the dead can be a tremendous psychological problem for the living independently of the problem of survival. At the same time, and contradictorily, the superstitious dread of the widow of her deceased husband is a clear echo of the fundamental claim of spiritualistic philosophy: that we do not change by virtue of dying, and that we shall be ruled, at least for some time, by the same emotions that had ruled us before death. Hence, a consuming passion may not end with death. This is what Coventry Patmore must have had in mind in his poem, *Love a Virtue:*

> Ice-cold seems heaven's noble glow
> To spirits whose vital heat is hell;
> And to corrupt hearts even so
> The songs I sing, the tale I tell.

The truth or untruth of the survival of passion need not be challenged at this point as the problem re-appears in the second and third question: is there sexual activity in the Great Beyond and can the living be involved in it?

In occult schools of thought the answer to the first question is yes. Marriage as an institution does not survive. Human relationship is governed by mutual attraction. Those in love will continue to love, but the marital bond ceases to exist. Sexual interest continues but only so far as spiritual development permits carnal desires.

All this, however, rests on teaching and the value of it is for anyone to take it or leave it. It is a problem that need not concern the living as long as our days are not run. The second question: can the living be involved in the sexual desires of the dead, is of our close concern. It is an absurd, terrifying and obscene issue, apt to evoke frightful spectres of the Middle Ages that we have believed laid for ever.

I am referring, primarily to the demon lovers: the incubus and the succubus, a male and female demon that in mediaeval lore were supposed to rank with the minions of Hell. No one was more surprised than I on finding out that these nightmare creatures still haunt the living whether as purely psychological entities within the mind of the afflicted or something bewilderingly more.[1] The refusal to be involved in an intellectual consideration of these vestigial horrors is eminently sane. It has too much historical association with witchcraft that we now consider an indictment of human mentality, and with the ruthlessness with which the Church has made a holocaust of all sorcerers. Once, however, we discard the notion of demoniality and replace the servants of the devil with the spirits of the dead who are still obsessed with carnal passions, an approach opens up, however spiritualistic it may seem, to the psychological and psychoanalytical appreciation of the problem involved, and we can breathe easier.

I will not, at this point, give a summary of any of the incubus visitations that I have placed on record in previous books; but I shall quote, for rare flavor, the Franciscan Father Sinistrari of Ameno, a Professor of Philosophy, then of Sacred Theology at Pavia, in the 17th Century, who, in his posthumous *Demoniality* or *Incubi and Succubi*, published in 1779 in Paris,

[1] *The Haunted Mind, op. cit.*, pp. 270-286; *see also* "Lo, The Incubus," beginning Part III of this volume.

tells a first-hand story of the terrible persecution by an incubus of Hieronyma, a married woman of "unimpeachable morality." She had herself exorcised but it did not help. Father Sinistrari relates:

> The good lady kept persevering in her admirable constancy till, at last, after some months of courting, the Incubus—incensed at her disdain—had recourse to a new kind of persecution . . . . he began to strike her cruelly, and after each beating bruises and marks were to be seen on her face, her arms and other parts of her body, which lasted a day or two, then suddenly disappeared . . . . Sometimes while she was nursing her little girl, he would snatch the child away from on her breast and lay it upon the roof, on the edge of the gutter, or hide it, but without ever harming it. Sometimes he would upset all the furniture or smash to pieces saucepans, plates and other earthenware which, in the twinkling of an eye, he restored to their former state. One night that she was lying with her husband, the Incubus—appearing in customary shape—vehemently urged his demand which she resisted as usual. The Incubus withdrew in a rage and shortly came back with a large load of those flagstones which the Genoese, and the inhabitants of Liguria in general, use for roofing their houses. With these stones he built around the bed a wall so high that it reached the tester, and that the couple could not leave their bed without using a ladder. This wall, however, was built without lime; when pulled down, the flags were laid in a corner, where during two days they were seen by many who came to look at them; then they disappeared.

Hieronyma finally vowed that she would assume and wear a monk's habit for 12 months if she were freed of the demon's attention. She was being led in solemn procession into the church of St. Michael, according to Father Sinistrari:

> She had no sooner set foot on the threshold of the church, than her clothes and ornaments fell off to the ground, and disappeared in a gust of wind, leaving her stark naked. There happened fortunately to be among the crowd two cavaliers of mature age, who seeing what had taken place, hastened to divest themselves of their cloaks

274

with which they concealed as well as they could the woman's nudity, and having put her in a vehicle, accompanied her home. The clothes and trinkets taken by the Incubus were not restored by him before six months had elapsed.

. . . I might relate many other most surprising tricks, which that Incubus played on her, were it not wearisome. Suffice it to say that for a number of years he persevered in his temptation of her, but that finding at last that he was losing his pains, he desisted from his vexatious importunities.

The priestcraft of Pavia had taken enormous trouble to lay the Incubus. The simple recipe recommended by Pliny had no apparent appeal to them. It is a decoction in wine and oil of the tongue, eyes, liver and bowels of a dragon, wherewith, after it has been left to cool all night in the open air, the sufferer should be anointed every morning and evening. Dragons must have been scarce in Pavia!

From the parapsychological point of view, the first observation is the Poltergeist-like character of the manifestations. We have destruction, mysterious vanishing and reappearing of objects called apports and teleportation of a child. The only evil that strikes the modern observer is the consuming sexual passion of the Incubus. Walling in husband and wife because of marital intimacy is a unique feature in all ghostly manifestations. Even there a limit seems to have been placed on the activities of the Incubus. He could go only so far and no further. He could not commit rape—which raises the suspicion that cooperation may be a necessity. What is rather unusual is that this sexual persecution should have lasted for years. Had Hieronyma been able to find a spirit of someone dead behind the wooing, the story may have had an earlier and happier ending. In the age of Catholic bias and the absolute dominion of the Church over the soul of the faithful, this construction of the visitation was a manifest impossibility.

Cooperation with an Incubus is a form of necrophilia, that is, if you accept the Incubus as an apparition of the dead. In a number of cases that came to my knowledge, the Incubus was much less: a cover for the psycho-sexual mechanism of self-abuse. Ascribing the sexual fantasy to a ghost, helps to eliminate personal responsibility and guilt for erotic activity. It also satisfies a wish-fantasy for the fulfilment of a love lost by death. On the mediumistic level, however, we meet with a different situation.

In describing how clairvoyant and prophetic vision had suddenly flashed upon her mind, Eileen Garret says in her autobiography:[2]

> Waves of nausea often accompanied such visions and sometimes left me exhausted and ill as though I had spent my strength in living through the experience I had just seen. I began to observe also, that when such sensibilities were active, I felt an intense drawing upon the sex centres.

With materialization mediums and generally with those that produce physical phenomena, the drain on the sex centers is much more pronounced. Prof. Enrico Morselli observed Eusapia Paladino passing into a state of voluptuous ecstasy "throwing about her arms, squeezing us with her tense thighs and trembling feet, resting her head and abandoning her whole body on my or Barsini's shoulder while we fearlessly resist this innocent attack against our masculine emotions."

This observation is far from being unique. "Ectoplasm" may emanate from any orifice of the body of a materialization medium, including—in most cases—the genitalia. Labor pains and voluptuous ecstasies seem to go hand in hand in this process. Anyone with an obscene mind may call this erotic manifestation a form of ectoplasmic self-abuse. At least this is what the composer of this verse had in mind:

> A man from Exham made love to a ghost.
> In the midst of a spasm
> The pure ectoplasm
> Said I could feel it almost.

Making love to a ghost recalls, from the annals of Spiritualism, the rape of Yolande, a spirit control of Mme. d'Esperance. She was a beautiful girl who was seen apart from the medium in the cabinet and apparently liked to flirt. One of the sitters took advantage of the situation, with the result that—due to ectoplasmic "repercussion"—Mme. d'Esperance was rendered critically ill.

[2] *My Life as a Search for the Meaning of Mediumship*, Oquaga Press, N.Y., 1935, p. 105.

I am also reminded of a statement made to me by Alex Dribell, a friend of Harry Price, who had some remarkable experiences with Guy L'Estrange, a young materialisation medium in his prime. In a séance held in his own house a naked African dancer materialized and hobnobbed with the sitters. I asked Dribell: how did you know it was really a woman? He answered: I smelt it.

These revelations should not give the reader the impression that I want to make them take a flippant view of séance room phenomena or the morality of mediums. The darkness of the séance room may offer excellent opportunities for a play for young people who are so minded, but I would not recommend it. Events may take an unpleasant turn. Such was the case of Adalbert Evian who pleaded guilty to petting. In his biography of Maria Silbert, he describes what happened as follows.

The medium did not come out of trance after the séance was over. Evian lived in the same house on the third floor. Before he could get into his bedroom he relates:

> The door opened of itself. Maria Silbert stood behind it, quite changed, and stared with green-gleaming eyes at me. She was taller than usual, a head taller than me. Her features had stiffened into a lifeless gray, menacing, fearful mask. Lightning flashed from her body here and there. I was now really distressed, and the more that my conscience reproached me . . . . I drew back into the sitting room and she tramped behind me with machine-like steps. She made her way slowly towards the switch. With a leap I was there, and set myself in front of it. It should not be dark. I was determined not to yield . . . . Unfortunately, I was not strong enough . . . . She switched the light off, and it was pitch dark in the room. That was the end of my courage . . . . I sprang to the door, went out and double-locked it on the outside. Now I was calmer, and looked about for my hat. I heard heavy steps in the locked room, that stopped before the door. I chuckled to myself a little, when I thought that Maria Silbert had not been able to stop me locking the door and was locked in. I was just about to go out when the double-locked door slowly and silently opened and Maria Silbert stood in the doorway, her head nearly touching the lintel.

Now I was mad with fear. I leapt up the hall door of the flat, got outside, shut it and retreated about ten paces, keeping my eye upon it. I tried to persuade myself that she would not leave the flat and I got a little calmer. Unfortunately, I was mistaken.

Now for the first time I saw the medium penetrate matter, a thing that was fearful to look upon, because it was so unnatural and set all physical laws at nought. Later on, it often happened.

As I looked at the entrance door, which was varnished in light color, it seemed to become transparent in the middle. At the same time I saw dull flashes of light through it. I sprang up a couple of stairs to the upper flat and sat down on a stair.

The transparent looking part of the door was somewhat darker, and the dark form of a body was visible, and a half-formed head, about two metres from the floor. There were flashes of lightning, which became ever brighter and more distinct as if the door, which was my defense against the lightning, was more and more easily penetrated by it. Then the lightning stopped and I stared at the door.

Yet again a powerful flash, and the medium stood in the door, not emerging from it, two-dimensional as it were, as though her body had been projected, life size, upon the surface of the door like an X-ray picture. With bulging eyes I gazed at this phenomenon, which was new to me, and I rose, to be ready to run to the upper story. There was a flash, and Maria Silbert came out of the door surface and moved towards me. The stairs resounded to her heavy steps. The expression on her face was, if possible, more distorted than before, and it was looking up. And now I lost my self-control: I took four steps together and ran up to the second story.

The account, however colored it may be by Evian's excitement and guilt feeling, is unique; Maria Silbert appears to have reduced herself to a two-dimensional plane instead of passing into the fourth dimension which is supposed to be the operational medium for penetration of matter by matter. The only thing that approaches this in the history of Spiritualism is that in some materialization séances (notably those of Baron Schrenck-Notzing, Gelei and Mme. Bisson with Eva Carrière) two-dimensional pictures were seen built up and photographed. They looked like cut-outs and caricatures, and some times they were traced to newspapers for identity, yet the experimenters were satisfied that they were mental images super-normally produced. Reduction of a body to two dimensions in order to pass through another dimensional object is a new angle for the phenomenon called penetration of matter by matter. It would be much easier to pass a two-dimensional object through molecular openings in a solid body than a three-dimensional one. The danger is that unless we stop this type of discussion, we shall soon find ourselves at the Mad Hatter's tea party.

Finally, I must place on record a story that is even more incredible than Evian's adventure with the puritanical spirit of Maria Silbert. I can vouch for it though, because the dramatis persona has been a friend of mine for over 30 years. She is an internationally known person who makes no secret of her emotional life. It is an open secret to all her friends that she is a lesbian.

The story begins with the death of her girl friend to whom she was passionately devoted. Let us call her Fidelia. In total despair over an irreparable loss, she had the body embalmed and carried her along in a beautiful coffin on all her travels for many months. She visited Holland, Fidelia's native country, then tried to enter England. The coffin was refused entrance, and she returned to Holland where the authorities, alerted, seized Fidelia, coffin and all, and buried her lest corpse-poisoning develop.

Renata—the name I shall give to my friend—was in a towering rage and frustration, but there was nothing she could do. Fidelia was lost, or so it appeared. There was more to her than a stiff body in a coffin. Renata told me the story of her adventure with a trumpet medium in Detroit and New York. Her name was Mrs. Stewart, a chronic alcoholic but a wonderful medium. Through a trumpet floating in the air voices issued that claimed to be voices of the dead. Renata told me that she took every possible measure of control to prove that these voices were not issuing from Mrs. Stewart's throat. She had locked her in clothes closets and the toilet, and yet she heard the voices outside. Moreover, she spoke to Fidelia and though intensely pessimistic over all spiritualistic claims she could not deny the prima facie case of established communication.

Time took its toll and as the years passed, Renata found herself in a New York hotel alone in the early morning hours with a girl who promised to be another Fidelia. They reached an interesting point of intimacy when the telephone shrilled.

Renata was struck by the crazy idea that it could be Fidelia and dared not pick up the telephone. After a while, the ringing stopped and proceedings were resumed. Then the telephone shrilled again and again. This was too upsetting. The spell of love was broken and the girl left.

In the morning, Renata made a scene with the manager. How dare they ring her in the middle of the night. The manager made an investigation and apologized profusely. It appeared that a telephone call came from Detroit and pleaded an urgency of life and death. Hence the night operator tried to put the telephone call through.

Renata was non-plussed—but not for long. The following day a letter arrived from Mrs. Stewart saying: Fidelia came to me in the night and insisted that I should ring you and give you a message. She said it was very urgent. The message was: "I am so disappointed!"

Was my friend Renata a ghoul? By no means. She was a very sophisticated worldly woman, without shame and guilt in the matter of sex, with a tremendous sense of humor and a great deal of worldly wisdom. I don't know what happened during those months that the coffin was trailing after her in her travels. The warmth of life was very important to her. I assume that she needed the body to carry on conversations with the dead Fidelia, and that she may even have imagined that she was alive and responding. Perhaps this is necrophilia. After all, there was Tudor Mary whose decapitated body was raped by the soldier who sat on guard over it for the night. He was beheaded for his crime. The parallel between the two cases is very weak. If there is anything to learn from Renata's story and of the stories that precede it it is that human passion is a tremendous power that transcends the line that separates the living from the dead.

PART V.

Of ghoulies and ghosties,
Of longleggetie beasties,
Of things that go bump in the night,
Good Lord deliver us.

(SCOTTISH PRAYER)

Against the inroads of parapsychology into religious mysticism the Catholic Church used to defend itself by ascribing mediumistic phenomena to the agency of the Devil while those of the saints and religious ecstatics were claimed to be due to divine grace. Most of the phenomena were the same, only the interpretation differed.

The Catholic evaluation always had the recommendation of simplicity. A miracle needs no explanation, it is self-sufficient; but it requires a religious setting and a certain magnitude of the phenomena claimed before scrutiny is granted to it. However, once accepted nothing can change the commitment. Miracles permit no compromise or alternatives. Divine grace is not subject to argument. Hence no parapsychological approach could be expected to make an impression on the Church. The gulf between the ecclesiastic and parapsychological discipline has not been bridged. Each discipline has had to go its own way. Attempts at reconciliation have been unthinkable.

It was, therefore, a notable event that such an attempt was made in the October 1960 issue of *Information*, a monthly magazine with the sub-title: *The Catholic Church in American Life*. It published a long illustrated article on "What Makes the Madonna Weep," by T. F. James, and quoted, in interviews, statements from me and from Dr. Piere Cassoli, a noted Italian parapsychologist of Bologna.

The occasion for the interviews was the weeping of a tinted picture of the Blessed Virgin in the attic of Mrs. Pagona Catsounis at 41 Norfolk Street, Island Park, New York, on the evening of March 16, 1960, and on subsequent days. The Rev. George Papadeas, the pastor of 22-year-old Pagona and her husband, Pagionitis Catsounis, at St. Paul Greek Orthodox Church in Hempstead, N.Y., was promptly called in, and was convinced that he was facing a miracle. The lithograph framed in a glass, a wedding gift of Mrs. Catsounis's, was shedding tears. Rev. Papadeas said:

When I arrived, a tear was drying beneath the left eye.

Then just before the devotions ended, I saw another tear well in her left eye. It started as a small, round globule of moisture in the corner of her left eye, and it slowly trickled down her face.

The news of the Weeping Madonna spread fast. In the first week more than 4,000 people poured through the Catsounis apartment to pray before the picture and see the tears flow. Reporters came and went, and the picture continued to weep through the whole week. The tears gently flowed to the bottom of the frame and then vanished.

Father Papadeas blessed the house and the tears stopped flowing. On March 23 the lithograph was taken to St. Paul's, enshrined on the altar and surrounded by lilies and ferns. Over 3,500 people streamed into the church daily to pray before the picture.

Before Father Papadeas had a chance to recover from the overwhelming effect of the miracle he had to face the wonder a second time. The call came from the house of Antonia Koulis, at 41 Oceanside Park, Oceanside, N.Y. It appeared to keep the mystery of the Weeping Madonnas in the family, for this 40-year-old woman happened to be the aunt of Mrs. Catsounis. There was an improvement as far as tears were concerned; they flowed more copiously from the eyes of the Koulis Madonna. The weeping was witnessed by Archbishop Iakovos, head of the Greek Orthodox Church in North and South America, and was promptly declared a miracle. Father Papadeas took off the glass frame in the presence of reporters so they could examine the back of the picture. The bottom was found soaked with liquid but the tears, on chemical analysis, were found *not* to be human tears. However, no evidence of fraud was found and when the Archbishop exchanged Mrs. Koulis's picture with another Madonna, on May 7 this, too, began to weep, and continued to do so intermittently for three weeks in the church where it was enshrined.

Dr. Cassoli who made a special study of weeping Madonnas in Italy (occurring on the average of two a year in that country) called special attention to a case in the house of Antonietta Janusso of Syracuse. It concerned a plaster statuette of the Immaculate Heart of Mary which, on August 29, 1953, began to weep and continued weeping for four days. This time, however, chemical analysis proved the liquid to be human tears. Antonietta was 20 years old, pregnant, with symptoms of toxemia, convulsions, attack of blindness, mutism, and total nervous exhaustion. Her statuette wept while it was shut in a drawer in horizontal position, in the hands of observers that included the Commissioner of Police, and while it was hanging outside on the wall of her house in Via degli Orti in a district which was known as the "Devil's Quarters" because of its evil smells and low moral condition. Under the tremendous excitement known as the Day of Lacrimazione, she returned to radiant health.

The Syracuse miracle caused a minor epidemic. As Dr. Cassoli reported, on December 15 of the same year, Concette Mesiano of Calabre saw tears of blood fall from some postcard size pictures of the Madonna. On April 3, 1954, Inez Bottazzi of Mezzolombardo noticed tears streaking the cheeks of a picture of the Madonna, which had been cut out of a newspaper and pasted on a piece of cardboard. Both times the tears were seen by numerous witnesses. In Angi, on May 12, 1954, a picture of the Virgin Mary of Syracuse, which lay flat on a dresser, wept for eight days and eight nights. The picture was at first dried in the sun, but the tears soaked it again and again. On March 15, 1955, Anna Carnerale of Casapulla saw a porcelain picture weep. In Rocca Corneta on April 27, 1957, a papier-mâché statue of the Madonna poured tears for several days. Dr. Cassoli found a yellowish, translucent substance along the lower rim of the eyes. He suspected the presence of some chemical that drew moisture out of the air and condensed it on the statue.

Barring this instance no suspicion of fraud was attached to the weeping miracles. T. F. James quotes Cassoli and myself in favor of a mediumistic explanation. I am supposed to have spoken of projection and a materialization of the tears:

The identity of the praying person with the picture of statue is so complete and the emotions are so intense that the tears are actually materialized on the object.

The quotation is not quite accurate. The phenomenon, as a mediumistic manifestation, is almost unknown. I did not try to explain it by projection and materialization. I considered it a phenomenon in a class of its own, a phenomenon of "atoneness" or mystic union, if religious terminology is preferred. Through religious ecstasy the Madonna and the worshipping housewife merged and became one. Form and space that kept them apart vanished. The Madonna was shedding Mrs. Catsounis's and Mrs. Janusso's tears of self-pity. Nothing has been mentioned of Mrs. Catsounis's psychological condition at the time of her prayers when the first tears appeared, but Mrs. Janusso's pitiable state of health is all too apparent. She was blind and felt one of her epileptic attacks approaching when her religious fervor reached a peak she had not known before. Like the Yogi practitioner who fixes his gaze at a point until he becomes one with it, Antonietta and the Suffering Mother merged. She was Mary and Mary was Antonietta. Her suffering brought her own tears into the statue's eyes. The case of Mrs. Koulis, I assume, was similar to telepathy-à-trois, a third party tuning into a circuit of emotions. Intense identification with her niece may have precipitated her into the whirlpool of ecstasy that Mrs. Catsounis was experiencing. The tears had stopped when the reasons for self-pity were removed by blessing and return of health. At-oneness could no longer be maintained and each woman regained her insulated identity.

Intense religious emotion as the *sine qua non* of such phenomena is suggested by an instance in the research history of Mrs. Linczegh-Ignath. "Nona," her spirit-guide who claimed to be a pure spirit, never incarnated, asked seven sitters to step in front of the picture of the Madonna of Sixtin and fervently pray there. They did so, and lo! tears appeared in the eyes of the picture and ran down the face. As Mrs. Ignath did produce miniature materializations, the mediumistic element definitely enters into this case. And so it does into some Poltergeist disturbances, not necessarily in the form of tears but in the form of the production of water or other liquids.

In an old book, *A Faithful Record of the Miraculous Case of Mary Jobson* (1841), Dr. Reid Clanny reported that water from nowhere was sprinkled in the sick room where 13-year-old Mary lay confined to bed by convulsions that lasted for 11 weeks. Like Mrs. Janusso, she became alternately blind, deaf and dumb. When she was in her senses she claimed to hear voices that claimed to come from the Virgin Mary, from apostles and martyrs. After eight months of unaccountable illness, she was mysteriously cured.

On August 30, 1919, oil was reported spurting from the walls and ceiling of Swanton Novers Rectory, near Melton Constable, Norfolk, England. Paraffin and petrol "rained" first, then showers of water, to be followed by methylated spirits and sandalwood oil. About 50 gallons of oil were caught in receptacles. Of 13 showers on September 1, two were of water. The Rev. Hugh Guy, the Rector, was forced to move out. A 15-year-old servant girl was duly accused because the first of the showers appeared in her room. Magician N. Maskelyne investigated, but could not explain the mystery. He was quoted in the *Daily Mail* of September 10 saying that barrels of fluid appeared during the time of his observations.

The Poltergeist appeared to act in a more religious mood in an Irish case. As summed up by Charles Fort:[1]

> On Saturday [Aug. 21, 1920] all statues and holy pictures in the home of Thomas Dwan of Templemore, Tipperary, Ireland, began to bleed.

A devout 16-year-old youngster called James Walsh was said to be responsible. In the earthen floor of his room a hollow, about the size of a teacup, kept filling with water. No matter how it was drained—and thousands of persons took away quantities—water from an unknown source always reappeared. The fact that objects were also moved by invisible forces in his presence gives a definite Poltergeist touch to the case.

It follows that from a study of Poltergeist cases in which the pubertal victim has intense religious feelings we may learn a good deal more about the weeping and bleeding religious statues than from religious ecstatics. At-oneness apparently is not the only mental mechanism by which the miracle can be produced. But the Poltergeist does no good and invariably produces accusations of fraud. The purely religious manifestation not only does not hurt but it is often followed by a return to health and miraculous cures in a worshiping crowd. Hence, religious ecstasy of the Weeping Madonna type is of social and ethical value. It restores, whereas the Poltergeist senselessly frightens and destroys.

---

[1] *The Books of Charles Fort*, Henry Holt, New York, 1941, p. 585.

In olden days people used to pray for miracles. Now they receive them with misgivings. If it is in Church that something looking like a miracle happens, even clergymen grow uneasy. They want to hush it up. It is too upsetting to have a miracle staring in one's face. The ecclesiastical authorities are certain to start a gruelling examination. It is good policy to keep such things from the public. Hence, ecclesiastics scowl at parapsychologists because they have the nasty habit of putting these things on record.

During the years that I lived in England I have investigated two such unwanted miracles. One took place in Christ Church Cathedral at Oxford, the other in Llandaff Cathedral at Cardiff. Both were in the same class: the miraculous appearances of the portraits of the late deans on a plaster wall. The Oxford case was widely publicized; the other one was dug up by my own labors.

Dean John Liddell, a famous Oxford cleric, died in 1898. Twenty-six years later, in 1923, it was reported in the London press that on the plaster wall under the Burn-Jones window in Christ Church Cathedral near the tablet erected to the memory of Dean Liddell and his family, a remarkable likeness of the late Dean began to form. It appeared as if the mineral salts of the plaster were slowly undergoing the same type of chemical change as the salts of silver on a photographic plate. The other essentials of a photographic process—lens, focussing, subject —were missing. But the fact was that a remarkable portrait of the late Dean was gradually seen to form on the wall.

The face was too striking to be taken for a damp mark. Moreover, it *was* the portrait of the Dean. There was no question about the identification. As if to remove the last doubts on the matter, as the years went by, the face of Mrs. Liddell also began to take shape on the wall.

It was bad enough to have one miracle. To have a second one was too much. People took notice of the Liddell head and rendered things uncomfortable by asking questions. So did the press. *Cassell's Weekly* described the portrait in its issue of Sept. 11, 1926:

A faithful and unmistakeable likeness of the late Dean.
. . . One does not need to call in play any imaginative
faculty to reconstruct the head. It is set perfectly straight
upon the wall, as it might have been drawn by the hand
of a master artist. Yet it is not etched; neither is it
sketched, nor sculptured, but it is there plain for all eyes
to see.

In 1931 the ghost portraits were yet visible to all. Mrs. Hewat
McKenzie, President of the British College of Psychic Science,
reported that "the Dean's face is beautifully clear and there
certainly seems an emergence of other outlines close by, which
bear a resemblance to two human heads."

In 1932 when I looked for them, I found a new altar built
in front of the wall.

No normal explanation was ever put forward. But I happened to find out something about the intimate history of this
phenomenon. This is that the face of John Liddell began to
form after a significant family event: a reunion and reconciliation in the Church after 25 years of hostility between the two
branches of the Dean's family, the Liddells and the Raven-
worths, the occasion for which was a marriage celebration.

It is a poetic thought that in this newly born atmosphere
of love the spirit of Dean Liddell found power to stamp on
the wall his smiling face as a seal of approval.

The case of the Dean of Llandaff is very similar to Dean
Liddell's. Dean Charles John Vaughan died in 1897. Two
weeks after his death the Dean's portrait appeared, as if produced by supernormal agency, on the West wall of Llandaff
Cathedral. Crowds came to see it and "so great was the
nuisance that the Chapter ordered an investigation, and it
was found that damp working through the stone had caused
the phenomenon."

This finding, however, did not explain the most baffling part
of the phenomenon. This was the initials D. V. which appeared
within the "texture" of the portrait.

I succeeded in obtaining the only original photograph of this
ghost portrait. It was taken by a Mr. W. Sharp of Cardiff. The
letters D. V. were in it, not only plainly but forming an integral
part of the portrait. There was no sign of superimposition. As
if in order to leave no doubt about the meaning of the face
on the wall, they had been formed at the same time as the
portrait itself.

Mr. Sharp exposed and preserved the plate out of curiosity. He wrote to me that he was in no way interested in psychic phenomena, and he obliged me with the following particulars:

Dean Vaughan was attached to Llandaff Cathedral for a great number of years. Shortly after his death, which occurred in October 1897, a damp stain started to appear on the left-hand side of the main entrance of Llandaff Cathedral. The stain just seemed to grow steadily until at last it had produced a striking likeness to the late Dean, even the letters D. V. forming on the side of the face. It naturally caused a host of speculation, but the Cathedral authorities themselves had to come to the only conclusion that it had not been worked by any individual, and it was simply a damp stain. After a while, the stain dried back, and a notice board was placed over the spot in question, and the same is there to this day and no one knows whether the phenomenon occurs or not in the damp season, as the board is there and the authorities say there it has to stay.

I inquired for particulars about the taking of the photograph. Mr. Sharp wrote:

I took the photograph with an ordinary single lens stopped down to F. 16, and it was taken in the afternoon with good light. I also developed the plate with ordinary pyrosoda developer. You have the one and only plate I took of same. I question whether anyone else has a negative besides the one in your possession. I also definitely state that I neither faked the damp stain nor in any way retouched the plate.

I have had the plate examined at the International Institute for Psychical Research by our Mr. Leon M. Issacs, a professional photographer of 20 years' experience. He confirmed that the plate has not been tampered with and that the photograph was genuine.

In this case the motive that I uncovered in the Liddell case remained missing. The story was too old for an effective investigation. For the incredulous, reports of similar miracles are accessible on this continent.

The New York *Sun* reported on Jan. 16, 1929 that on the

dark oak door of St. Ann's Roman Catholic Church in Keansburg, N. J., hundreds of people saw the figure of a woman in trailing white robes emitting a glow. The pastor of the church, the Rev. Thomas A. Kearney, stated in an interview:

> I don't believe that it is a miracle or that it has anything to do with the supernatural. As I see it, it is unquestionably in the outline of a human figure, white robed, and emitting light. It is rather like a very thin motion picture negative that was under-exposed, and in which human outlines and detail are extremely thin. Yet it seems to be there.

More impressive was the story reported by New York newspapers on Feb. 23, 1932, of the apparition of a clearly discernible figure of Christ in the variegations of the sepia-toned marble of the sanctuary wall of St. Bartholomew's Church on Park Avenue and 50th St., New York. Dr. Robert Norwood, the rector of the Church, gave this statement to *The New York Times:*

> One day, at the conclusion of my talk, I happened to glance at the sanctuary wall and was amazed to see this lovely figure of Christ in the marble. I had never noticed it before. As it seemed to me to be an actual expression on the face of the marble of what I was preaching, "His Glorious Body," I consider it a curious and beautiful happening. I have a weird theory that the force of thought, a dominant thought, may be strong enough to be somehow transferred to stone in its receptive state.

I know of no photographs to prove the objectivity of these two visual perceptions, but Dr. Norwood at least had a theory to account for what he saw. When I published the Llandaff photograph in evidence of a recognized face on the wall, I received a letter from a Mr. William Prangnell, of Fulham, London. He stated that he found markings working through the wall of his bathroom; they gradually assumed "the distinct outline" of his deceased wife's face. On my request he took a photograph and sent it to me. It was not a very good photograph. But the outline of a woman's face was there. Being an outline only, it was impossible for me to make an identification with the photograph which Mr. Prangnell placed at my disposal. I felt that with an ability to visualize the face of the deceased, Prangnell was in a far better position to judge the issue than a stranger could be.

There I had to leave the case. But I had a chance at another one a few years later. There was a house at Chelmsford from which the tenants, a Mr. and Mrs. Kear, had to move because a strange face kept on appearing in the mirrors of various rooms. Mrs. Kear was kept busy "rubbing him off," but the face always came back and finally appeared in the form of a wet mark, in the plaster of the kitchen wall. They scratched it off, but it stayed there just the same.

On a visit to Chelmsford, I was disappointed in the face on the kitchen wall. It was no more a face, just a discoloration. It could not even be photographed. But as far as the mirror apparitions were concerned, both Mr. and Mrs. Kear stood the cross-examination to which I had subjected them through Eric Cudden, a barrister and a member of the Council of the International Institute for Psychical Research, exceedingly well. We could not shake off the impression that the experience was not of a hallucinatory character. As we were told by Mrs. Kear, a bluish mist appeared over the mirror, leaving a greasy mark. In the mist, looking from a certain angle, the face of a man was clearly visible. The face was always turned to the left and showed the same features on every occasion. Now and then, the whole figure of the man appeared. On the first occasion he was lying in bed, on another he was in a business suit, apparently going out.

The vision had a purpose that Mrs. Kear seemed to grasp. The man who had built the house died in it. His widow left it. The message which the apparition conveyed mentally was that the widow should return to the house and continue living in it.

The vision in the mirror was seen simultaneously by several people. On one occasion it appeared doubled in the right and left hand side of the mirror of the same wardrobe. It could never be wiped off completely, though Mrs. Kear tried it hard. Mrs. Kear declared that she was not a Spiritualist and knew nothing of psychic phenomena. But on inquiry it was found that the widow of the owner had seen the face too, and was so upset by it that she had the mirrors turned back to the wall, and moved out as soon as she could do so.

Looking for chronicles of similar events I chanced upon a testimony by Anna Blackwell before the Dialectical Committee that had been set up to investigate the phenomena of Spiritualism. She stated that the face of a beloved relative appeared on a window pane in the house opposite to her window. It faded away several times, and appeared again. There seemed to be a sort of dark iridescence upon the pane out of which the face evolved; each appearance lasted about eight seconds, and each was darker and fainter that the preceding one.

Anna Blackwell also quoted the case of Mrs. M. G. who in the tortoise shell handle of a new parasol saw the face of Charles Dickens soon after his death. The face was small but with every feature perfectly distinct; and as she gazed upon it in utter amazement, the eyes moved and the mouth smiled.

These images usually appear on polished surfaces. They may be seen by several people and they disappear after awhile. In Volume II of *Phantasm of the Living,* published by the London Society for Psychical Research, an apparition of this kind is recorded of a Capt. Towns. It was witnessed by eight people who saw the captain's face, six weeks after his death, on the polished surface of a wardrobe.

A shiny surface lends itself far better for such visions as a hypnotic element may enter into the perception. Alone, however, that is not sufficient to explain these happenings. Some versions of it are so weird that you would only expect to encounter them in a thriller.

Wonders in the Sky

Then spake Joshua to the Lord in the day when the Lord delivered up the Amorites before the children of Israel, and he said in the sight of Israel, Sun, stand thou still upon Gideon; and thou, Moon, in the valley of Ajalon.

And the Sun stood still, and the Moon stayed, until the people had avenged themselves upon their enemies. Is not this written in the book of Jasher? So the Sun stood still in the midst of heaven and hasted not to go down about a whole day.

And there was no day like that before it or after it, that the Lord harkened unto the voice of a man; for the Lord fought for Israel.

(*Joshua,* 10:12-14)

No miracle on such astronomical scale has been recorded in ecclesiastic history until October 13, 1917, at Fatima in Portugal. It was the culmination of a series of apparitions of the Blessed Virgin to three children of a small hamlet situated 62 miles north of Lisbon. A total of 70,000 people were waiting for the apparition—that did not come—but to quote from Zsolt Aradi's *The Book of Miracles:*[1]

> After the Rosary had been recited by the multitude, the dark sky opened, and the sun, appearing in a clear blue sky, suddenly began to tremble and shake, and turn about swiftly like a great wheel of fire, casting off long shafts of light which colored the sky and earth. This spectacle continued for ten minutes and was observed at a distance of 25 miles. Then the sun broke loose from the sky and plunged downwards through space directly over the people, who fell at once to their knees, crying for forgiveness for their sins.

We are told that the editor of the Lisbon daily *O Seculo* described the event at great length under the headline: "AMAZING PHENOMENON: *How the Sun Danced at Fatima at Midday.*"

What should a psychologist say in face of miracles of this magnitude? Ignoring it will not help, accepting it is contrary to everything scientific. Is there a meeting ground between these two extreme attitudes? There is. The hypnotic demonstration of time distortion is the possible clue to the miracle that Joshua wrought. Time can be stretched out under hypnotic suggestion to such an extent that one hour may become the equivalent of a day. Practicing for one hour at the piano can be lengthened in mental acceptance to many hours with the corresponding benefit.

Another way of experiencing time distortion is by taking hallucinogenic drugs. I experienced it myself under the effect of mescalin. Time slowed down perceptibly and the corridor in which I walked stretched out to a great distance. Both time and space were distorted. Lysergic acid (L.S.D.) produces the same type of hallucination. So do the miraculous mushrooms. *Amanita muscaria,* the sacred mushroom was known in ancient Egypt as a means of foretelling the future. This knowledge may have been part of the secret tradition of the

[1] Monarch Books, 1961, pp. 237-238.

Jews. But even if Joshua had no knowledge of time distortion, an accidental abundance of mushrooms in the mess of the Army could well have distorted an hour into a day. In his time, it was the sun that moved around the earth. So it was the sun and the moon that appeared to stop and the credit for the miracle would have naturally been given to Joshua.

One thing is obvious. The sun or the earth could not have been stopped or the whole solar system would have been destroyed. The Lord surely had more economical means at his disposal for smiting the enemies of Israel. Hence, whether we have evidence for it or not, we have to fall back on time distortion as the only sensible explanation of Joshua's apparent miracle.

Does this help to understand the event in Fatima? It does. Time distortion, as pointed out, is accompanied by space distortion. The sun could not have moved out of its orbit at Fatima. It could not have come crushing down to earth. Hence, the perception had to be a spatial hallucination. Aradi is wrong in claiming that 70,000 people could not have been the victim of a mass hallucination. If such a thing is not recorded by psychiatry, it is because psychiatry does not deal with such vast numbers. Crowd psychology does. The greater the number, the greater is the contagion of the ideas. A single member of the crowd can start an avalanche of mass hallucination. It is much easier to hypnotize somebody in a great audience than privately. The safety factor for the individual appears to be greater. So it is in any crowd, which is on a much lower functional level than the individual. Moreover, the 70,000 were waiting for a miracle. They were conditioned by their religious frenzy or fervor to experience something out of this world. They did. It was space distortion.

Solar phenomena of lesser magnitude than the stopping of the sun or moving it out of its orbit are reported in Exodus and in the Gospels of Mark, Matthew and Luke. It is the blotting out of the light of the sun. In Exodus, it is the ninth plague and it is described as a thick darkness in all the land of Egypt that lasted for three days. "They saw not one another, neither rose any from his place for three days; but all the children of Israel had light in their dwelling." *A New Commentary of the Holy Scriptures* by Bishop Gore suggests that the darkness could well have been caused by a sandstorm of unusual magnitude, but it fails to query whether the light in the dwelling of the children of Israel was the light of the sun or an artificial light. The second instance in which the light of the sun was blotted out from noon until 3 P.M. is reported from the time of the Crucifixion. Luke and Mark report it as darkness over all the earth, Mark as over all the land (that may mean Judea only). Luke, alone of the three, adds that the veil of the Temple (the double curtain between the Holy Place and the Holy of Holies) was rent in the midst. The commentators agree that an eclipse of the sun could not have been responsible because that was impossible at the time of the Paschal full moon. They fail to notice the correspondence between three hours at the time of the Crucifixion and three days of darkness in Egypt. Was the former a legendary echo of the latter? Or was there an earthquake as a momentous accompaniment to the drama of Crucifixion? Darkness is a phenomenon that is known to accompany upheavals of the Earth. Why is John silent regarding these events? As he is farthest removed in time, one would have expect the wonder to grow.

A different type of wonder is the sight of a cross in the sky. The best known historical example is Constantine's vision of a luminous cross in the sky with the lettering: *In Hoc Signo Vinces.* (In this sign you will conquer.) The vision took place on the eve of Constantine's battle with Maxentius in 312 A.D. Eusebius, who was a friend of Constantine, writes in his book on the life of Constantine that the Emperor himself told him of the experience. It not only converted him to Christianity but induced him to proclaim Christianity as the official religion of the Empire. The vision was a divine order to him. He obeyed it and from then on his life was a series of triumphs. He was firmly convinced that God was with him. The explanation, as suggested by Dr. Sylvano Ariety,[2] is that the Roman Empire was in a state of advanced decadence and Constantine was strongly predisposed to become a Christian on account of the influence of his mother who was a Christian. Also, there were many Christians in Maxentius's Army. They could be expected to rally to him if he was converted. The Christians were well organized and disciplined. The pagan majority was disorganized and divided. But the Imperial tradition would not permit Constantine to take such a momentous step. He needed the mystical experience of a miracle or hallucination. He could

[2] "The Loss of Reality," *Psychoanalysis* and *Psychoanalytic Review,* Fall 1961.

place the responsibility of whatever might happen on the Christian God.

The motives that produced a miracle at Ipswich, England, was a slightly different but also a very powerful one.

On May 6, 1944, the New York *Sun* published a report according to which hundreds of residents in the East Anglian town of Ipswich had seen a vision of Jesus on the cross in the sky for 15 minutes during the time of an air raid alert. At first, a large white cross appeared, then the form of Jesus. According to the Rev. Harold Godfree Green, Vicar of St. Nicholas Church and chaplain to the British forces:

> His head was bowed and his feet were crossed—all who saw agreed on these details. . . . When it disappeared, it did not drift way like clouds but vanished instantly and entirely.

Having interviewed a great number of people of the town, the Rev. Green stated further:

> There was scarcely any variation—if any—in these accounts . . . . I have satisfied myself beyond any doubt of the authenticity of the vision. I regard the sign as a good omen . . . . I did not myself see the sign and for this I am sorry.

The significant element on which the Vicar fails to dwell is that the vision occurred during the air raid alert on April 27. Instead of an omen, the search for a wish-fulfilling mechanism would have been more appropriate. Deliverance from evil is centered by devout Christians in the sign of the cross and Jesus. A desperate need for help during the air raid alert—a threat of destruction coming from the sky—may well have focused the hope of salvation of a crowd on the strange cloud formation and, by a contagion of perception, replace the fear of death with the promise of life.

Clouds can assume strange shapes. The Vicar himself was wary of this objection when he spoke of the instantaneous vanishing of the vision. He himself saw nothing and in the professional practice of his faith he may have needed no succour. Some people see visions in clouds like in a crystal ball. Such visions can easily be shared by others in abnormal conditions. Given abnormal conditions like an air raid, a mass illusion is almost inevitable. After the first perception, it would grow like a snowball.

As an alternate, a metaphysical explanation could be advanced: that the combined mentality of the masses, focused on the single idea of deliverance from evil, could affect the vapor—a kind of "ectoplasm," just one step from solidity—and shape it in accordance with Christian devotions. This would make the vision a parapsychological phenomenon instead of a religio-mystical one. However, in its essence, this is an alternate name for a miracle. Nevertheless, the personal interference of Divinity being left out, science might find this theory easier to deal with.

To sum it all up: there are wonders in the sky. But a wonder is not yet a divine miracle. It is only a miracle of the human mind.

Phantom Priests of Joan of Arc

Was Joan of Arc's role in history foreseen by King Arthur's bard and magician, the great Merlin, centuries before? It is stated in the *Encyclopaedia Britannica*, Vol. XV., that she (Joan) "was almost certainly ignorant of Merlin's prophecy, that a Maid should come from Bois Chénû to do great deeds." (Les Prophecies de Merlin, ed. J. A. Paton, 1927.)

There is a monument to her great deeds: the Basilica of Domremy, in the chapel of which flags of many nations pay respect to the memory of the Maid of Orleans. The English flag was, for many years, conspicuously absent. In 1925, the omission was rectified by Lady Palmer, wife of Lord Palmer (1858-1948), the first man raised to the peerage for his services to music.

Something strange happened on this occasion. The story is told by a photograph that the Salvation Army was selling for the modest charge of 2 shillings, as proof of divine intercession. It shows Lady Palmer and two priests, who were *not* there, both wearing Joan of Arc's insignia, the fleur-de-lys. Lady Palmer did not know that she had company when she posed for the photograph all alone, and this is how the story is told on the back of the picture postcard the Church Army circulated:

On a visit to the Basilica of Domremy, dedicated to St. Joan of Arc, the Lady Palmer noticed that the Chapel had no Union Jack in it, whereas the Americans had their flag.

Feeling it was but England's duty to be represented, she collected, in very small sums, enough to send a silk Union Jack "with England's homage" round the staff, and the flag bearing the signatures of Field Marshal Haig and of Marshal Foch. It was taken and placed by Prebendary Carlile on June the 9th, 1925.

In October of the same year, Lady Palmer went to see it. Miss Townsend, who accompanied her, then took this photograph, none but the two being in the Chapel. When developed, the visibility of the two priests was found and they wore surplices spotted with fleur-de-lys, the badge of the heroine.

The King's photographer said it could not possibly have been faked.

I had a lantern slide made of this remarkable photograph, showed it at a meeting of the International Institute for Psychical Research in London and read out a letter I have received from Lady Palmer, giving her own version:

The picture is of myself standing under my Union Jack in the Military Chapel of the Basilica at Tomremy. I was standing being photographed with it for a friend who, through illness, could not come. A friend stood with her little old camera taking me (she was a non-believer really in the nearness of the spirit world). When I returned to London I wrote to her to know why my photographs had not been sent. Whereupon she did so. I wrote back: "But who are the priests? No one was there." She replied: "That is why I did not send them."

I took the photograph to Conan Doyle, who told me it was one of the finest spirit-photographs he had ever seen. Might he have a slide made of it? I went and saw it at Queens Hall when he was giving a display of spirit-photos on the screen. It got the ovation of the evening.

A Roman Catholic lady called on me to ask for a print.

I said: "Your Church will not approve of me having taken it." "Oh yes, they do," she answered. "It is a miracle. The priests represent St. Joan's period. They are wearing her robes."

I gave Cardinal Bourne an enlarged copy. He was charmed with it.

Prebendary Carlile took my Union Jack out there and always carries in his notebook the picture of the priests. He once put me up before about 150 people and said: "Now tell us, Lady Palmer, what you feel about these priests."

"Well," I replied. "I consider it was six of one and half dozen of the other. The French sold St. Joan to us for 10,000 pounds. Imagine what that was in those days. We burnt her. The Flag has round its staff 'With England's homage.' Foch, the head of the French army signed it. Haig, the head of the English Army, also. You, Prebendary Carlile, the head of the Church Army, signed it. And I feel our Lord allowed these priests to come in acceptance of our Union Jack."

I did not find the mark of the fleur-de-lys as clear for evidential purposes as it should be. But phantoms do not have much consideration for would-be critics. The suggestion that was conveyed by the apparitions alone was remarkable. However, my job was to criticize and I found two points of objection:

1. There was a time gap between the taking of the photographs and the arrival of the prints into the possession of Lady Palmer.

2. There was no guarantee that the film had not been tampered with.

Lady Palmer was satisfied on both scores. She saw the point of weakness and had the film examined by the King's photographer. Nevertheless, what was evidence to her may not satisfy others. It is easy to fake a ghost by double exposure. It is not easy to do it without tell-tale signs. A very clever photographer would have been needed to fake this particular photograph—and no monetary or other inducement was discoverable. Miss Townsend was not a photographer, only a friend of Lady Palmer, and she was satisfied of her good faith. An accidental double exposure still could have taken place if Miss Townsend had exposed a film on pictures of priests of Joan of Arc's period. But such an accidental double exposure would have been discovered by expert investigation. As it was not, the case stands as a genuine mystery.

To Cross the Abyss[1]

In the space that we cover in our journey through life, two main discontinuities of the plane can be counted upon. One is the mountain, the other is the abyss. The spiritual significance of the mountain is too well known. The Tables of Stone were delivered on a mountain, and churches were originally built on a high elevation because "the . . . mountain, and all that surround thereof, shall be most holy." (Ezekiel) The abyss is more or less associated with evil, Hell and falling from Grace. However, this orthodox concept is not maintained in magical literature.

Here is a wonderful dream of an attempt at rebirth and of reaching to God from a magician who was a disciple of Aleister Crowley, a man of strange talents and terrible reputation in the 1920s and 1930s:

> I was in an Egyptian camel corps. We wore green jackets and rode small, young camels. A group of us started out on an assignment. I was the last. As I passed, I threw two newspapers, the *Sun* and the *Post*, to a friend to look after them for me.
>
> Then we came to a fork in the road. The others went to the right, I went to the left. Soon I came to a big building. There was a woman and a man there. I asked if the building had a path leading through to the other road. I trotted through a hallway or passage on the camel. I came to an area fenced in by wire at the back of the building or hotel. I saw a boy there. I asked him a question, and he eagerly opened the wire door and let me in. The camel was now gone and I seemed to be a prisoner of two boys.

[1] From *Darshana International*, Moradabad, India, October 1961. Reprinted by permission.

The dreamer had never ridden a camel. As he started off in the dream the camel felt like a pair of stilts—which children would use. Speaking of a "young" camel was an additional reference to childhood. Concerning Egypt he recalled:

> . . . a number of semi-mystical passages in some of Crowley's more mature writings . . . . One of the sentences which made an abnormal impression on me was: "I, too, am the Soul of the Desert. Thou shalt seek me yet again in that Wilderness of Sand." The person "I, too" is supposed to be Crowley's own higher genius or inner self, and the wilderness was the Egyptian desert. I also recall something else from Crowley's "Book of the Lies," which is a series of paradoxical utterances. They are numbered from 1-91. Crowley reformed the Golden Dawn system of magic. He would have a number of grades going up to SEVEN EQUALS FOUR. Seven is the cabalistic Shepirah of Hessed. All the grades are supposed to be in the world of mind, but the grade above them, EIGHT EQUALS THREE, is in another, spiritual world, altogether separated by the great gulf called the Abyss. In order to cross the Abyss, it is as though one would be broken up into component parts. In Binah, the Great Mother, one is reassembled to form an entirely new being, the being whom Crowley calls the Babe of the Abyss. The "Book of the Lies" was written for the Babes of the Abyss. Every page is black margined as though to show the idea of death. There is something in there about aspiring to this very high grade and crossing this great great gulf of death which is the Desert. Then he says: look at the five footprints of the camel: VVVVV. The five V's were his own magical motto for that grade. The camel ride in my dream may stand for the five footprints of the camel, for my own crossing, leaving a trace that anybody after me could see.

Divested of the bewildering verbal trappings, the associations clearly reveal the dreamer as following in Aleister Crowley's footsteps in order to overcome death and become a Babe of the Abyss. About the green jacket, he said:

> Green means youth, hope and aspiration. Green is also the color of Venus, the Goddess of Love, therefore Venus

is related to Binah, the Shepirah one has to cross to reach the City of the Pyramids. In this city of Pyramids, where the grade EIGHT EQUALS THREE, live the Babes of the Abyss. Eight equals three because eight is counted from the bottom of the Tree of Life. Counted from above, we find it equal to three.

As Binah is the Great Mother and he relates Venus to it, a baby's incestuous emotions seem to be behind the dreamer's mystic quest. He failed to mention that green—in Mohammedan countries—is the color of the Prophet. I made a mental note that his "assignment" stands for a power-drive, which is a frequent motive behind fantasies of returning into the womb. He was not far from understanding this as his next statement linked him up with his family:

> I was the last in my family of seven children. On waking from the dream, I had the impression that the other members of the group were members of my family which I associate with "the last will be first, and the first will be the last." I determined to be the first in the family.

Here then is the chief determinant of this patient's magical obsession. I asked him about the *Sun* and the *Post*. He said:

> The Sun is the Golden Dawn, the magical system that Crowley reformed. I left it but always felt that I would have to return to it. Post is the idea of communication, actual crossing, going into the Abyss. Egypt is the Land of the Sun. Heliopolis is the City of the Sun. The Egyptian priests were called Sons of the Sun. I am an Adeptus Minor which is the FIVE EQUALS SIX grade to which the sun is attributed. In this ritual, the candidate is bound on a wooden cross and takes an obligation to remain always devoted to magic and to strive finding one's higher self. Therefore the Cross and Resurrection are equal to the Sun.

Did the dreamer feel entitled to wear the green of the Prophet because, in his initiation, he was symbolically crucified? Why did he go left on parting from his family?

> The Abyss is on the left of the Tree of Life. When I

was a boy, there was a wire cage in our backyard. Mother kept hens in it.

It is fairly clear now that the abyss represents the maternal womb. Prodding the dreamer for more associations about the camel, confirmation was coming fast:

> I heard Scots pronounce Campbell as camel. In my High School the teacher was a Miss Campbell who pronounced her name as "Camel."
> "The Campbells Are Coming" is an old Scots song. I recall also this:
>> My young man is a jockey
>> A jockey is he,
>> All day he rides horses
>> At night he rides me.
> Miss Campbell, since she was a teacher, suggests my mother, and the hallway or tunnel in the big building through which I rode would have a uterine implication.

Nevertheless, the dominating motive in the dream is not an incestuous one. In pagan ideology immortality was gained by rebirth through the maternal body. The hotel where all the needs of a guest are attended to is an excellent representation of the body of the mother. The wire cage is the womb, and here he is caught at a crucial stage of his journey. The abyss is another symbol for the womb.

> In the symbolic rites of the Golden Dawn the seven-sided chamber is the uterus, the two pillars on the outside are the thighs, and one goes in through the Venus door. The two boys who kept me prisoner could possibly represent the two adept officers of the ceremony.

Or also, by the plural: unless you become like little children you cannot attain to the Kingdom of Heaven.

The patient then recalled Crowley's adventure in the desert with a disciple.

> Crowley was having a series of visions using the Enochian magical invocations. Suddenly, there was a break, and he was given instructions to try a different technique as he was about to cross the Abyss. He then

303

performed a magical ceremony for invoking the Demon of the Abyss, which is really the mind itself, disconnected, chaotic and loose. All of that had to be passed through, broken up. He sat within a triangle drawn in the sand. At each point of the triangle he placed a pigeon he had caught and killed, sprinkling its blood on the sand to emit sufficient, shall be say, "ectoplasm," to enable the Demon of the Abyss to materialize. This reminds me of the chickens in my mother's hen house which we used to catch and kill. The name of the Demon of the Abyss was Choronzon, and its number was supposed to be 333, half of the Number of the Beast.

I am sorry to say that my notes contain no information whether the Demon of the Abyss had appeared to Crowley or not. All I know is that the dreamer's own symbolic journey for immortal life was not completed. Eight months later he was still trying to cross the Abyss, and revealed new symbolic meanings of the attempt. He dreamed:

I was with a large crowd of people, walking in a park. We came to a small house which was a place where monks lived and worked. It was very still and quiet. People spoke with hushed voices. A man inside was trying to call my attention to the fact that I was not making the sign of the cross right. I made the upper bar only, at the same time saying a blessing in Hebrew.

Later we left, and continued on our way, but before we did so we had to clean our shoes, three or four of us doing it at a time. I was in the last group. By the time I finished, all the others had gone forward and apparently crossed the river in the park by descending into a gully to the right. I walked on by the path, past the gully. It was only after I walked some distance that I realized I was alone or lost. I could hear and see occasionally the people on the other side of the river. So I turned around and retraced my footsteps to the gully.

As before, the dreamer was again full of wonderful associations. A monk, to him, was a holiness ideal. The hushed conversation recalled Mme. Blavatsky's The Voice of the Silence, and an invocation from the Golden Dawn: "Hail unto you,

Men of Myalba, another pilgrim has crossed to the other shore."

A real monk with a very tranquil mind and some degree of spirituality should be able to talk to the birds. I accept literally some of the old legends of holy men going into a forest and none of the animals harming them, or birds clustering around them as they did around St. Francis of Assisi. I feel it must be a mark of a wonderful personality if the birds perch themselves on a man's shoulder. A real monk is that sort of a person.

We see a merging of monk and magician, of the religious and of the magical quest. The sign of the cross, though imperfectly drawn, receives a Hebrew blessing. The Adeptus Minor can now descend from the cross on which he was tied at the time of receiving his degree. The upper bar calls attention to the lower: intellectual versus genital, the problem of how to use lower sexual forces for creativity. The task is not yet accomplished. He is still lost. The gully, as a split of the land, is a symbol of the split in his personality. But his isolation is about to end, the schism between Judaism and Christianity is being healed, and his family (represented by the groups that stood for siblings in the previous dream) is to be reaccepted on a higher level.

Jesus washed the feet of his disciples. To me feet represent understanding. My understanding, which must be purified before I can approach the spiritual mysteries, before I can see God.

In the light of this statement, the groups of three may also stand for the Trinity: Father, Son and the Holy Ghost, integration, and the approaching end of the magical quest.

I was always conscious that I had lagged spiritually. I have never been able to express practically the things which others, with less understanding, were able to do.

A magician, so humble, was clearly on his way to greatness.

The Wounds of Christ

"Ego enim stigmata Domini Jesus in corpore meo porto!" (I myself carry the stigmata of Lord Jesus in my body!)

This statement appears in one of the epistles of St. Paul. It would make him the first stigmatic in the history of the Catholic Church, but as such phenomena were unknown for the first twelve centuries, his words were taken figuratively. The devil had left teeth and claw marks on the body of many escetics before, but the history of divine wounds dates from St. Francis of Assisi who received them on Mt. Alvernia in 1224, two years before his death. After fasting through the 40 days of St. Michael, his obsession with the Passion of Christ reached the height of somatic at-oneness with the body on the cross and as a result "his hands and feet appeared to be pierced through the middle with nails, the heads of which were in the palm of his hands and the soles of his feet; and the points came out again in the back of his hands and the feet, and were turned back and clinched in such a manner, that within the bend formed by the reversal of the points a finger could be placed as in a ring, and the heads of the nails were round and black."

He could no longer walk, was in constant pain and the suffering, together with the loss of blood, hastened his premature decease. The nails appeared to be of horny material and were tested by a doubting cavalier, named Jéronime, who touched them and moved them in the presence of the breathren and many seculars. The reality of the strange growth and wounds was no longer questioned—and so the first impetus was given to the *crucifixion complex* that developed through later centuries. The physical conformity to the sufferings of Christ became the foundation of a union with the Divine as a form of religious obsession, creating for psychiatry one of the most baffling demonstrations of unknown powers of the human mind and furnishing, for religion, an example of divine intervention.

Not that in our own days ecclesiastic powers too easily accept the miraculous. They make a distinction between stigmata that are deeply imbedded in the flesh and between the smaller wound marks and bleedings of hysterical origin. They make allowance for nervous disorder and morbid psychology before the stigmatic development and they distinguish between the real stigmatists and the compatients whose phenomena are in the incipient stage. Not even in the full stage is acceptance too readily forthcoming while the stigmatists are among the living, as the cases of Therese Neumann, of Konnersreuth, and of Padre Pio, of the monastery of San Giovanni Rotondo, near Foggia, Italy, reveal. The first case is treated with extreme reserve because of Therese Neumann's abnormal life, the second is attributed to suggestion neurosis because of the life of Padre Pio is exceedingly normal.

Therese Neumann received the stigmata during the Lenten season in 1926 while reliving, from Thursday to Friday on March 4 and 5, the Passion of Chirst. Against her stands the traumatic injury she suffered eight years before during a fire-fighting accident that resulted in coughing blood, failing eyesight and convulsions; also the fact that since 1923 she has refused to take any solid food and is now said to have been living for 33 years without eating. Padre Pio's stigmata appeared on September 20, 1918, during his prayers in the Church. He collapsed and the wounds that appeared on his body (two in his palms, two in his feet and one in his side) have never disappeared and bleed copiously while he celebrates the Mass. No hysteria was proved against him and the constructive nature of his life is best proven by the huge hospital, costing more than a billion liras (two million dollars) that he was instrumental in building, literally out of nothing, in the neighborhood of his monastery. He has never fainted, never had convulsions, horrible dreams or showed any signs of nervous disorder. On the other hand he has given evidence of a gift of clairvoyance, of bilocation (having been seen in places hundreds of miles distant while remaining in the monastery), and of the gift of healing that include the miraculous restoration of the sight of the blind. Oddly enough, all this seems to count against him. The decision of the Holy Office, issued on July 5, 1923, was that his phenomena had not been proven to be supernormal and the faithful should maintain an attitude in accordance with this decision.

With the growth of scientific knowledge the Church is bent rather on discouraging than encouraging stigmatic phenomena. No notice was taken of the case of Anastasia Woloszyn, a 24-year-old Polish peasant girl who developed stigmatic phenomena in ecstatic states in 1936 even though a committee appointed by the Archbishop of Lemberg concluded that there was no normal explanation of the case. Her stigmatic wounds failed to yield to medical treatment, though they were apt to disappear by themselves after a period. The most recent case was the stigmatisation of Francis Santoni, a 21-year-old Italian on the island of Sardinia in 1956. In a state of trance he sweats blood from several parts of his body; blood appears on his forehead and sometimes on his hands and feet. When the trance is over, the bleeding stops and the blood disappears. Aradi concludes that this "at first sight . . . seems to be a strictly medical case." [1]

The disappearance of the blood of the stigmatics has been noted in several cases. The skin remains clean and the bed clothes are unsoiled. Sometimes, the wounds are luminous and exhale a scent. They never produce pus and after death frequently the entire body remains exempt from putrefaction. It is stated, for instance, of La Bienhereuse Lucie de Narni (1476-1544) that her body was found intact four years after her burial, the stigmatic wounds were open and blood flowed from it from time to time. In 1710 she was again exhumed and the body was still found intact.

This is a phenomenon that neither medical science, psychiatry, psychoanalysis or parapsychology can solve. But a study of initial phenomena that may lead up to stigmatisation, yields a rich harvest.

It is known from hypnotic experiments that if a hypnotized subject is given the suggestion, on being touched by a pencil, that a burning cigarette was placed against her skin, a burn mark will develop. This is hypnotic stigmatisation. Charcot was the first to demonstrate its experimental reality. It is also known that auto-suggestion can produce similar results. Hereward Carrington cited, from an original signed document,[2] the remarkable case of a woman who was frightened to death by a burglar. The man, on seeing her, ran down the stairs and out of the door. But "during the moment he was standing in the door, although he did not actually move, I had the distinct impression that he had run up the hall and grasped me firmly by the arm, and I was for the moment petrified with fear. The next day my arm was black and blue in the exact

[1] *The Book of Miracles, op. cit.*
[2] Cited in *Psychic Research,* September 1931.

spot where I thought he pinched me; and this mark continued for several days until it finally wore off. I told Dr. Carrington about this two days later when he called, and showed him the mark."

A vivid nightmare may produce a similar impression. It is well known that the pain of a dream-wound can be positively felt for a few minutes on awakening. The mark may appear from a greater intensity of emotion. A patient of mine used to menstruate under her armpit by exuding oedima, and the bleeding eyes of stigmatics, like Therese Neumann, may well repay study from the angle of their menses. As a matter of fact the sweating of blood alone is no longer accepted as a miraculous phenomenon by the Church. It is recognised as belonging to the realm of psychopathology. Prof. Richet mentions (in a footnote to his *Thirty Years of Psychical Research*) the case of Count Baschieri who placed a handkerchief to his eyes and withdrew it stained with blood. His eyes were sweating blood, without conjunctional ecchimosis. In the September 1930 issue of the *Zeitschrift fur Parapsychologie*, Hans Schubert writes of the tears of blood of Edwig S. during deep emotional states induced by a certain piece of music. Cold light is thrown on such phenomena by a note in *Fate Magazine*, May 1962, of the case of a 2-year-old boy at the Mayo Clinic in Rochester, Minn. He cried tears of blood until the doctors discovered that his eyelids were infested with blood-feeding lice, a phenomenon previously unheard of. After two weeks of treatment with a special ointment, the weeping of blood completely stopped.

The noose marks that I and my fellow researchers observed in plain daylight on the neck of Mrs. Forbes as, in trance, she produced amnestic memories of rape, belonged to the stigmatic class on a lesser scale. The cross on her chest that led to the discovery of breast cancer was probably also of stigmatic origin. On the other hand, the later appearance of a similar cross on her forehead, the claw marks of a "ghost tiger" and the punctures of a "vampire" on the back of her neck, together with her aerophagia (blowing up of her stomach to simulate pregnancy with "apports," internally hidden) were of semi-conscious and conscious origin, as reported in my *On the Trail of the Poltergeist*.

Genuine, fully developed stigmatic marks in cases of mediums are exceedingly rare for the simple reason that they do not cultivate states of religious ecstasy. The only exception on record that I know occurred in the case of Mrs. Lujza

Linczegh-Ignath in Oslo, on her forehead, while "Nona," her spirit-guide, delivered deeply moving addresses on the subject of religion.

Stigmatic marks, or the equivalents, may occur without religious obsession. The case of Eleonore Zügun is much to the point. She was bitten by unseen teeth, her face became scarred and disfigured and all this was ascribed to Dracú, the devil in Rumania, an idea that this young Rumanian peasant girl accepted. The phenomena were of a Poltergeist character and first appeared in 1925 when Eleonore Zügun was 11 years old. The bite of Dracú was seen to arise in full daylight at the National Laboratory of Psychical Research in London and the report of Harry Price concluded that a stigmatic markings appeared spontaneously in various parts of Eleonore's body, but that Eleonore was not consciously responsible for the production of the marks. Toward the end of her fourteenth year, at the approach of her menses, Eleonore Zügun lost her psychic powers and Dracú, the devil departed from her life.

Similar case was reported by Malcolm Bird in *Psychic Adventures:*

> Frau Vollhardt suddenly gave a very realistic shriek of pain and held out her hand for all to see. On the back of her hand was a quantity of red marks, some actually bleeding . . . . A handful of forks could have been held in such a manner as to inflict these wounds, but no single instrument that I ever saw would have done the trick—unless it be a nutmeg grater. The holes were small and round, and quite deep; after ten or fifteen minutes they were still plainly to be seen.

Maria Vollhardt was the wife of an official of the Berlin Postal Ministry. The mystery of how her wounds were produced, deepened when some sitters saw on her hand a small object, the shape of a bird's beak or claw. They put a potful of farina on the table and asked for an imprint. They got it—in the shape of a chicken's foot. When the marks appeared, Frau Vollhardt felt as if an electric current had entered the surface of her skin and passed through her body. Dr. F. Schwab who experimented with her for two years *(Teleplasma und Telekinese)* observed the phenomenon 50 times outside the séance room in good light. When he made photographs with a stereoscopic camera, he got a picture of a sort of a claw of several branches, poised upon the perfectly controlled hand of the medium. He believed it was a materialised symbol of the medium's unconscious notion of oppression and torture, which is a very similar conclusion to that of the investigators of Eleonore Zügun.

There is a twilight zone between the Devil and the obsessive *crucifixion complex*. It is inhabited by ghosts that leave a burn mark on the body which they touch. The first such stigma may have originated from the conscience of Cain after he killed his brother Abel. "And the Lord set a mark upon Cain, lest any finding him should kill him." His conscience demanded enduring suffering, so he made the Lord the agency. What kind of a mark was it? It had to be on his forehead to be visible by all and the possibility is strong that it was a burn mark of somatic origin or by the Holy Ghost if you prefer to call conscience by that name.

Ghosts less holy but with the fiery touch have been placed on record in many ancient chronicles. The exhibits in Father V. Joeuet's Other World Museum at Rome comprise photographic records of such marks left—apparently—by earthbound spirits who appear to be dominated by the Catholic idea of Hell. One of the outstanding stories of burning by a ghostly hand concerns Lady Beresford who made a death-compact with Lord Tyrone. According to T. M. Jarvis (*Accredited Ghost Stories*), Lord Tyrone appeared to her after his death and on being asked to leave a mark of his presence, the apparition seized Lady Beresford's hand and burned her wrist by his touch. Throughout her life, thereafter, Lady Beresford wore a dark ribbon to conceal the mark. After her death, Lady Netry Cobb, an intimate friend, took off the ribbon and found the burn.

Similar records are to be found in more modern days. Frank Podmore reported a case [3] in which an icy hand pressed against the face of a sleeping woman. She cried out and complained of a burning sensation. "The gas having been turned up higher, we saw on one side of her face, a very vivid red mark, which rapidly took the form of a hand, with fingers open."

Stainton Moses, a minister of the Church of England and one of the most remarkable private mediums of his day, lost

[3] Proceedings of the *Journal of the American Society for Psychical Research*, Vol. X, p. 204.

a friend by suicide. In the night he woke up and saw a spirit trying to reach him, and struggling with two other spirits. He was inspired with horror and repulsion. The spirit got nearer and stretched out his hand. In the morning, he found on his forehead an oblong dull red mark in the exact place where his friend had wounded himself. The mark was a red discoloration and faded in two or three days.

To the same class of records belongs the case of dermography: writing on the skin as a message from the dead. The skin writing disappears in a few minutes, which, of course, opens the door wide open for fraud. An urticarious skin will swell up in welts a few minutes after a blunt pencil traced letters on it. The medium who chose this form of communication as his forte was Charles H. Foster, the Salem Seer. His biographer, George C. Bartlett, speaks of an amusing incident after a visit to Foster by a certain Mr. Adams. The medium saw the room filled with spirits. At 2 o'clock in the night he woke up Bartlett, complaining that he could not sleep because the room was still filled with the Adams family. They were writing their names all over him. Bartlett, to his astonishment, counted eleven distinct names, one written across Foster's forehead, others on his arms, and several on his back.

Lest this be considered a cheap mediumistic trick, the case of Mme. Olga Kahl should be quoted who, in 1933 at the Institute Metapsychique in Paris, produced on her skin a mentally communicated word or image. A hysterical patient produced the same phenomenon for Krafft-Ebing and, to return to religious chronicles, Thomas Killigrew testified to the appearance of the names of St. Joseph and Virgin upon the hands of the Prioress of the Ursuline Nuns at Loudon in France about the year 1635.

We know little of the mechanism of skin writing—much less of the burn marks we discussed. But if the latter were produced by suggestion or vivid imagination, the question arises, would not the same mechanism in reverse—a strong belief that fire cannot hurt—account for fire-walking and other demonstrations of immunity to fire?

Is There an Authentic Portrait of Christ?

In a strong safe built inside a thick wall behind the altar of the St. John the Baptist Cathedral of Turin lies deposited, for over 250 years, the greatest relic of Christendom: the Shroud of Christ.

It is a length of linen, 14 by 3 feet, and it bears the imprint, front and dorsal, of a crucified man.

It is believed that the imprint was made by the body of Jesus as, tortured, sweat-laden, and covered with blood, it was wound "in linen clothes with the spices, as the manner of the Jews is to bury," and placed temporarily, by Joseph of Arimathaea and Nicodemus, in the sepulchre in the Garden of Gethsemane because it was "the Jews' preparation day" and "the sepulchre was nigh at hand."

Tradition holds that the Shroud of Turin is the very grave clothes which the two Marys saw lying on the floor of the empty Tomb. Peter "kept it, but we know not if it has been discovered," wrote St. Ninon in the fourth century.

Three hundred years later the Shroud came to light in Jerusalem. Bishop Arculfus saw it. It was kept in the Holy City for 400 hundred years. At the end of the 11th Century we find it in Constantinople. After the sack of the city by the Crusaders, the Shroud disappeared and passed into France.

It is only from this date on that we have a reasonably authentic history of the Shroud and can trace its identity through the succeeding centuries. It was owned by the Dukes of Savoy, the ancestors of King Victor Emmanuel of Italy. We know that in the 14th Century there was a fierce ecclesiastical controversy over it and that the Shroud was not recognized by the Church. In 1532 a fire destroyed the chapel in which the Shroud was kept. Though damaged, the Shroud was saved.

Of its great antiquity, there was never any doubt. The attention of the world of science, however, might never have been attracted to it but for a remarkable discovery in 1898. In that year, the Chevalier Pia, a wealthy amateur photographer, obtained permission from King Victor Emmanuel to photograph the Shroud.

313

When his plates were developed, the astonishing fact came to light that the image on the Shroud was reversed. It was a negative and, as a result, the photographic plates showed a positive picture, a noble human face with an expression of deep sorrow and with a minute fidelity to nature even in minor details.

By a miracle, or by some unknown natural process, the Shroud had acted as a photographic plate to reveal the portrait of Christ. The Shroud bears the imprint of the full length of the body, showing that Jesus was over medium stature, 5 feet 8 inches in height. It also adds some curious particulars to our knowledge of the Crucifixion and of the events that followed. One may well understand that claims of this nature were considered highly sensational. A heated controversy developed over the authenticity of the Shroud and over the conclusions to be based thereon.

Dr. Paul Vignon, Professor of Biology at the Institute Catholique, Paris, assisted by Lieutenant-Colonel Colson, then Professor of Physics at the École Polytechnique, undertook a series of experiments and laid the results before the French Academy of Science.

In the early 1930's there was a public exhibition of the Shroud in Turin. A set of new photographs was taken and two commissions of investigation were formed, one in Turin, the other in Paris. They now claimed to possess convincing proofs that the winding sheet of Turin is the actual grave cloth of Jesus the Christ.

Dr. Vignon who served as Secretary-General on the commissions was positive that the impressions on the Shroud are not paintings. The idea of a negative image is only known since the invention of photography. The painting of a negative involves many principles of science and of art which were totally unknown or poorly grasped until comparatively recent times.

It is hard enough [he says] to carry out these principles in an ordinary positive painting in which the light and shade have their normal values. On the Shroud, they are perfectly illustrated with the lights and shades reversed, though it takes a photograph to reveal the fact. Even today no artist can paint so exact a negative. No artist, in fact, has yet succeeded in making an exact copy of the negative figures on the Shroud, though competent artists have made the attempt.

Apart from this consideration, the linen is soft, fine, and thin. Before it could have been painted in oil or in water colour, it would have had to be prepared (sized) and such preparation would have rendered it stiff.

How then did the negative image of a crucified man appear on the Shroud?

Dr. Vignon's researchers give a very interesting answer to this question. In the sweat which physical torture or fever produces, there is an abundance of urea. In fermentation, urea gives off ammoniac vapours. The Shroud in which the body of Jesus was wrapped, was treated, as we are told in the Gospels, with aloes and myrrh. Ammoniac vapours react chemically with aloes. The Shroud thus became sensitized like a primitive photographic plate. The events of the Crucifixion were favorable to this extraordinary condition. We know that the body of Jesus was not washed. It was covered with dried perspiration and clots of blood from the crown of thorns, the nails, the scourging and the wounds inflicted by the soldiers. Because of the approaching Sabbath, the body was laid in a closed cave where no motion of air interfered with the radiation of ammonia vapors from the urea in the sweat. In consequence, with the linen pulled flat and straight, both theoretically and practically it was possible for an image to form on the sheet. This image would be denser where the body touches the sheet and vaguer where it does not.

Dr. Vignon proved the point by placing cloths prepared with aloes over plaster figures soaked in ammonia. He had obtained images similar to those on the Shroud.

Thus the core of the mystery has been cleared up. But many points required yet further understanding.

The image on the Shroud is perfect. It stands out with the harmony and contrasts of a living face. It is impossible to say how vapours reacting with aloes could produce so startling an effect. Another difficulty is that the clots of blood which dried on the body were transferred to the Shroud. The transfer itself is no mystery as ammonia dissolves the fibrin in coagulated blood. But the clots transferred to the sheets are so complete and so minutely exact that they may be called "portraits of blood." Dr. Vignon could not experimentally produce such perfect transfers. Neither could he understand why these clots of blood did not scale off the cloth in the course of centuries, and why their colour is a dull carmine whereas very old blood is brown.

Another puzzle is that the Shroud reveals traces of small drops of serum on the brow and at the back of the head. The flow of serum from a wound indicates the first stage of decomposition. But from a decomposing body ammonia emanates rather extensively and in hot climates decomposition sets in very fast. The Shroud, therefore, should have been "fogged." The impression of the soft action of the vapours from the perspiration and bloodstains should have been wiped out while the body lay in the rock-hewn tomb.

There is, however, a permissible answer to this; and it is a very strange one. The body of Jesus was laid in the sepulchre Friday night. Sunday morning, it was found gone. There is no intimation in the Bible as to how the body disappeared. If Dr. Vignon's conclusions are correct, it must be assumed that the body disappeared almost immediately after the sepulchre had been closed by a stone. Otherwise increasing decomposition would have wiped the picture off the Shroud.

On the story of the Crucifixion as told in the Bible, the Shroud permits interesting verification. The wound in the hand is clearly shown in the photographs of the Shroud. But it is not in the centre of the palm as it has been represented by artists for centuries. It is in the wrist, which is anatomically strictly logical as a heavy body could not have been held up by a nail in the palm.

This startling feature alone disposes of the objection that the impressions on the Shroud were painted. No painter in the Middle Ages or after would have dared to deviate from the general belief. Nor would he have dared to paint the body of Jesus without swathing. He would have run the risk of being proclaimed a heretic and suffering punishment of death.

The markings of the crown of thorns and of the scourging are well visible. It is even possible to reconstruct the whip which was used. It must have been a *flagellum*, having two or three thongs, each provided with a metal ball at the end.

In the right side of the body there is a wound such as would have been caused by a lance thrust. According to the Bible, Jesus was dead when his side was pierced. Medical examination of the Shroud confirms this. Serum flowed from the wound and left its trace on the Shroud. The flowing of serum is a certain sign that when the wound was inflicted death had already ensued.

It was not customary at the time to give the lance stroke to the crucified. As a rule, the executioner broke the shin bones to ascertain that the condemned man was dead. The deviation from the customary procedure had brought about a fulfillment of an Old Testament prophecy that "not a bone shall be broken."

Dr. Vignon performed an immense amount of labour to elucidate the baffling mystery of the Turin Shroud. This was his final conclusion:

> The date of the Shroud, with the Gospels as a key, are a means of identification as sure as a photograph or a set of fingerprints. It was Christ who left His imprints on this cloth with a vivid record of the drama of Calvary, and with His true likeness hidden in the stains till photography revealed it again to the world.

EXPLORE THE WORLD OF THE OCCULT

VENTURE INWARD by Hugh Lynn Cayce

The son of Edgar Cayce, the most amazing psychic of modern times, takes you into the unexplored world of the unconscious to reveal the mysteries behind:

*What mediums tell us of life after death
*What dreams tell us about the future, past and present lives
*Secrets of "automatic writing" and the Ouija board
*How to achieve the physical and mental state to VENTURE INWARD

(54-792, 75¢)

EDGAR CAYCE ON REINCARNATION
by Noel Langley

Explore the many startling facets of the concept of man having more than one life. This book, composed largely of Cayce's own words, treats reincarnation not as an occult fantasy but as a feasible effect of Christianity, and shows how modern man may achieve immortality. It is an invaluable aid for everyone fascinated by metaphysics and parapsychology.

(54-559, 75¢)

EDGAR CAYCE ON ATLANTIS by Edgar Evans Cayce

America's "sleeping clairvoyant" reveals the mysteries of the strange lost continent of Atlantis—and predicts where and when it will rise again!

(54-656, 75¢)

EDGAR CAYCE ON PROPHECY by Mary Ellen Carter

Includes hundreds of predictions on domestic, international, psychological and scientific affairs from the celebrated Life Readings of Edgar Cayce. EDGAR CAYCE ON PROPHECY is an illuminating guide to the basic readings of America's most authenticated seer.

(54-699, 75¢)

**EDGAR CAYCE ON DREAMS
by Harmon Hartzell Bro, Ph.D.**

Understand your dreams, and make them work for you. Learn how your dreams can be used to achieve self-understanding, happiness, success, and to relieve nervous tensions.

(54-776, 75¢)

THE EDGAR CAYCE READER
under the editorship of Hugh Lynn Cayce

For the first time in one book, Edgar Cayce's insights are offered on a number of consistently fascinating topics: Karma, psychoanalysis, telepathy, out-of-body travel and reincarnation.

(64-037, 75¢)

EDGAR CAYCE ON DIET AND HEALTH
by Anne Read, Margaret Gammon and Carol Ilstrup

Edgar Cayce's most practical suggestions for proper diet and achieving glowing mental and physical health through eating the right foods in the right combinations at the right time. Includes provocative questions and answers on vitamins, minerals, drinking water, tobacco, exercise, and the correct psychological approach to eating.

(64-095, 75¢)

If you are unable to obtain these books from your local dealer, they may be ordered directly from the publisher.

PAPERBACK LIBRARY
Department B.
315 Park Avenue South
New York, N.Y. 10010

Please send me the books I have checked.
I am enclosing payment plus 10¢ per copy to cover postage and handling.

Name ....

Address ....

City .... State .... Zip Code ....

_____ Please send me your free mail order catalog